A MANSION IN THE MOUNTAINS

THE STORY OF MOSES
AND BERTHA CONE
AND THEIR BLOWING ROCK MANOR

A MANSION IN THE MOUNTAINS

THE STORY OF MOSES
AND BERTHA CONE
AND THEIR BLOWING ROCK MANOR

by
PHILIP T. NOBLITT

1996

Parkway Publishers, Inc.
BOONE, NORTH CAROLINA

Library of Congress Cataloging-in-Publication Data
Noblitt, Philip T.
    A mansion in the mountains : the story of Moses and Bertha Cone
and their Blowing Rock manor / by Philip T. Noblitt.
       p. cm.
    Includes bibliographical references and index.
    ISBN 978-1-887905-02-2
    1. Flat Top Manor (Blowing Rock, NC.) 2. Blowing Rock (N.C.)-
-Buildings, structures, etc. 3. Cone, Moses. 4. Cone, Bertha.
5. Blowing Rock (N.C.)—Biography. I. Title.
F264.B59N63 1996   96-6277
975.6'843—dc20   CIP

For Iris

TABLE OF CONTENTS

List of Illustrations

ACKNOWLEDGEMENTS

I would like to acknowledge the many people who assisted me in my research and writing. Without them, this work would have been greatly diminished and so would my pleasure in preparing it. Since this book began as a thesis when I was a graduate student at Appalachian State University, it is only appropriate that I thank my thesis readers, Dr. Michael Wade and Dr. Janet Hutchison. Throughout my study of the Cones, they offered constructive comments and suggestions. I am especially indebted to my thesis director, Dr. Charles Alan Watkins, who encouraged me to explore the Cone estate as a thesis topic, gently nudged me on when I needed it, and encouraged me to publish the finished product. My study of the Cones, and hence, this book, would not have begun and would not have been completed without him. In addition, Dr. Watkins honored me by nominating my thesis for the University's Cratis D. Williams Thesis Award. I am deeply appreciative of Dr. Joyce Lawrence, Dean of the Graduate School, and her review committee for bestowing that award on me in May 1995.

I must also acknowledge a number of institutions and individuals for helping me locate source materials and for being so courteous and accommodating. These include Sara Nixon and Dianna M. Moody of the Belk Library, Appalachian State University; Stanley Gorski, Philadelphia College of Textiles and Science; J. Stephen Catlett, Greensboro Historical Museum; the staff of the reference section and the North Carolina Collection of the Pack Memorial Library, Asheville, North Carolina; William R. Erwin, Jr., and the Manuscripts Department at the Perkins Library, Duke University; Diane Clark, Special Collections Department, State University of New York at Oneonta; the staff of the Washington County-Jonesborough, Tennessee, Library; Caroline Stelljes of the Caldwell County Library, Lenoir, North Carolina; the reference department of the Greensboro, North Carolina, Public Library; the Beinecke Rare Book and Manuscript Library, Yale University; Jean Haskell Speer, Center for Appalachian Studies and Services, East Tennessee State University; and Catherine Bishir, Ron Holland, Stephen Massengill, and George Stevenson of the North Carolina Division of Archives and History. I also wish to thank Gary Everhardt and Al Hess of the Blue Ridge Parkway, and Jim Nicholl, Western Carolina University, for reading portions of the manuscript and suggesting improvements.

The following people willingly shared their personal collections, insights, and memories of the Cones and their estate with me: Wade E. Brown, Omer Coffey, Edward Cone, Dorothy Teague Koontz, James Robert (Bob) Moody, Mrs. Ruby M. Walters, and Barbara Lentz Wright. Charles F. Craig and Hank Bixby were also most accommodating in giving me access to the Sandy Flat Baptist Church one chilly, rainy Saturday morning, while my friend and first-rate photographer, Mike Booher, cheerfully lent his expertise in making photographs for this book.

A special note of thanks is due several people, among them, E. Frank Fary, Jr., and Carolyn R. Hines of the Public Relations Department of Cone Mills Corporation. They not only made available the invaluable materials in the Cone Mills Corporation Archives, but they were ever-courteous and professional and showed a genuine interest in my research.

Ellen C.B. Hirschland and Nancy Hirschland Ramage volunteered their time to meet with me in Asheville and to visit the Asheville Cotton Mill, the first textile mill the Cone brothers owned. Descendants of Moses' sister Carrie, whose husband worked at the mill, and accomplished scholars, these women shared recollections, family letters, and other source materials, and provided useful information about the decorative details of Flat Top Manor and the art that hung there during the estate's historic period. Mrs. Hirschland also read and suggested improvements to my manuscript. I only hope that they enjoyed as much as I did the Sunday morning that we spent tramping about the old mill.

I am at a loss to thank adequately Mrs. Isham (Judith) McConnell and Mrs. Richard W. B. (Nancy) Lewis. These women spent their childhood summers living at Flat Top Manor with their great-aunts, who included Bertha. Their vivid memories of life on the estate and the furnishings inside the manor inform large sections of this book. In addition to interviewing Mrs. McConnell and Mrs. Lewis at Flat Top Manor on several occasions, I visited them at their homes, where they allowed me to photograph a number of objects that had belonged to the Cones and that had been in the manor during the 1930s. They also made available a family history, photographs, and genealogical notes that proved extraordinarily enlightening and helpful. I must also acknowledge the wonderful hospitality that they and their families extended to me when I was a guest in their homes. During those visits,

Dr. Richard Lewis graciously took me to the Beinecke Rare Book and Manuscript Library at Yale University and helped me locate very useful materials in the Gertrude Stein Collection. On my own, I would not have found these materials so quickly or enjoyed my research at Yale so thoroughly. Altogether, the help and hospitality of both families were more than any researcher could have asked.

Finally, I have to thank those people who are closest to me. My long-time friend and writer-historian Roy Morris, Jr., helped me clarify many thoughts by patiently listening to my long discourses about the Cones and by asking insightful questions. Both he and Patty Wheeler, of Appalachian State University, read my manuscript, finding more mistakes than I would care to admit and suggesting changes that universally made good sense. My parents, Doris Noblitt and the late John P. Noblitt, and my brother John, and sisters Alisa Nichols and Carolyn Howard have always encouraged my education and shown an on-going and genuine interest in my occasional writing. My immediate family—Iris, Patrick, Wayne, and Jennie—variously helped with computer glitches (which more often than not turned out to be operator errors, not equipment or program malfunctions) and allowed me to escape such mundane chores as mowing the lawn and washing the family cars. They patiently endured the blank stares that I often gave them when thinking and daydreaming about the people and places of the past, and they never begrudged the time and family resources that I spent on research trips. This brief acknowledgement hardly does justice to the understanding, encouragement, and support that they gave.

PROLOGUE

This is a story about people and place, specifically, Moses and Bertha Cone and their Flat Top Manor estate at Blowing Rock, North Carolina. It is also a story about acceptance and belonging, about how two children of German immigrants prospered and, in the largest sense, established themselves as true and substantial Americans. It is also the outgrowth of an admittedly personal inquiry. Flat Top Manor (today the Moses H. Cone Memorial Park) was always a curiosity to me. I first visited it in 1987, shortly after becoming a district ranger on the Blue Ridge Parkway. I was simultaneously struck by how large the estate was, and how little was said about Moses and Bertha Cone and their reasons for building such an elaborate place at Blowing Rock. The craft shop that was in the manor house sold fine, handmade items, and the book shop offered a number of publications about the Parkway and the surrounding region. Yet except for framed portraits of Moses and Bertha, which hung in the manor's entrance hall, a small pamphlet, and two outdoor signs, nothing more was said about the Cones.

Although sparse, this information supplied a thumbnail history of the estate. Through it I learned that Flat Top Manor encompassed more than 3,500 acres, contained some 25 miles of carriage roads, and was built about 1900. Moses Cone was one of North Carolina's leading textile manufacturers. His mammoth cotton mills in Greensboro made him one of the largest producers of denim in America. Cone had come to the mountains, according to the literature, to escape the stress of his textile business, and also because, like Thoreau, he loved the outdoors. For his own amusement and profit, he raised apples, planting and tending thousands of trees and winning awards for the quality of his fruit. Cone was also a philanthropist, and to help the children of his employees who lived on the estate, he built a school nearby. After Moses died in 1908 at the relatively young age of fifty-one, his widow continued to operate the estate until her death in 1947. The couple had no children. Upon Bertha's death, Flat Top Manor and the grounds were donated to the National Park Service, which soon reached an agreement authorizing the Southern Highland Handicraft Guild to open and operate a craft center in the manor house.

This information was enlightening but seemed inadequate, considering that Flat Top Manor was one of North Carolina's finest turn-of-the-century estates. As I learned later, one reason so little was said was because no one knew very much about the Cones or their mountain retreat. A Park Service-commissioned *Historic Resource Study*, completed in 1987, synthesized oral histories, student papers, and Park Service archival materials that were readily available. As helpful as this study was, it did not tell how Cone got started and prospered in textiles, or why he chose Blowing Rock as the location for his sumptuous estate. This study also gave relatively little background about the manor house, a physically imposing structure with twenty-three rooms and more than 13,000 square feet. The manor's architect remained unidentified, and there was no indication of where the materials that went into the house were bought or made. This seemed especially intriguing since Blowing Rock was in the mountains of Appalachia and, according to popular wisdom, far removed from the luxuries of modern living. Furthermore, the *Historic Resource Study* said nothing about how the house was furnished or how Bertha Cone managed the estate for nearly thirty-nine years after her husband's death. Similarly, the circumstances and rationale for putting a craft shop in a country estate remained unexamined.

This book is my attempt to answer all these questions and to place the Cones and their country estate into a valid historical context. It is also an effort to provide a clearer portrait of the place and the people who built it and lived there, to put, if you will, a human face on a most imposing edifice.

A MANSION IN THE MOUNTAINS

CHAPTER 1
FROM PEDDLERS TO
INDUSTRIALISTS

In 1983, Western Pacific Industries attempted to gain control of Cone Mills Corporation of Greensboro, North Carolina. However, the textile giant, which then operated twenty-one plants, employed 10,800 people, and had net sales of more than $608 million, was not interested in the Western Pacific offer. When Cone's legal maneuvers to block the takeover failed, the company's officers and managers responded with a leveraged buyout and returned the corporation to private status. To do this they organized the Management Group, through which they exchanged shares of Cone Mills stock for those of Cone Mills Holding Company. At seventy dollars a share, the move carried a price tag of $385 million.[1]

Among those who sold stock as part of the buyout were third generation descendants of the company's founders, including Ceasar Cone II, a former company president, who personally sold 600,000 shares. Although some family members retained an interest in Cone Mills, their presence and power were much diminished by the sale.[2]

On the surface, the entire transaction was strictly financial, a matter of prudence and profit. Yet in many respects the 1983 buyout of Cone Mills was the culminating event in the remarkable rise of a family, over the course of more than 130 years, from social and economic obscurity to conspicuous affluence and industrial prominence.

The immigrant origins of the Cones and the skillful building of their cotton mill empire are in many ways aspects of a classic American "rags to riches" story, the tale of a poor immigrant and his family who worked hard and achieved success. It is also a story about acceptance and how, as they became wealthy, the Cones consciously and carefully acted in ways that were considered appropriate to their class and place. Wealth certainly conferred a measure of status, but social standing—the desire to "be somebody"—also depended on one's roots, and the Cones worked hard to shed their unwanted immigrant cloak and assimilate within their new community.

Between 1830 and 1880 some 200,000 German Jews immigrated to the United States. One was Herman Kahn, the seventeen-year-old son of a Bavarian merchant. Kahn—who would soon change his name to Cone—joined the exodus in 1846. He had been, with the exception of language classes, a very good student in school, and had demonstrated great industry. In migrating to America, the ambitious youth was hoping to find both economic opportunity and greater civil liberty. He was also seeking to avoid Bavaria's military conscription of eighteen-year-old males, a coercive measure that the country's Jews, already the victims of unequal government laws, particularly disliked.[3]

Beyond politics and economics, Herman Kahn probably received personal encouragement from his sister to emigrate. Some fifteen years older than her youngest brother, Elise Kahn Hirsh had moved to the United States several years before and had established herself in Richmond, Virginia. As might be expected, when Herman arrived in America, he went to live with Elise.

Despite the family ties, Kahn did not stay long with his sister. He soon moved to rural Lunenburg County, located midway between Richmond and Danville, Virginia, and began plying his trade as a peddler. Like other backwoods salesmen of the time, his canvas bags were probably packed with tinware, brightly colored cloth, clocks, nutmeg, leather goods, soaps, and perfumes.

Isolated rural families enjoyed visits from pack peddlers and were quick to push back their chairs and beds to give them a display area near the fireplace. They were also prone to make peddlers the butts of practical jokes. Herman unquestionably was sensitive about his social status. While it would be untrue to say that Kahn had arrived in America a pauper, as a peddler he was at the bottom of the social hierarchy of immigrant Jews. Furthermore, in 1850 he owned no real estate and lived in a boarding house in Lunenburg County. To gain acceptance, he changed his name to Cone, tried to adopt local manners and ways, and did all that he could to become "American" as quickly as possible.[4]

In January 1851, Cone's sister Sophia married Jacob Adler, who had emigrated to America in 1848. Like Herman Kahn, Adler was a man of modest means. The brothers-in-law did what many other relatively poor immigrant Jews of the period did—they pooled their resources and opened a retail business. Sales were slow in Lunenburg and the two soon moved their business to Richmond, where sales were not much better. Jacob's son Samuel later reported that their "wares were not suitable for the market."

The more established Richmond relatives were less than pleased by their return, regarding Cone and Adler, with their "Old World" ways, as socially undesirable. The struggling young men were given a wagon and a load of merchandise and unceremoniously asked to leave town. In 1853, they did so, travelling by rail to Big Lick, (now Roanoke) Virginia. From there they journeyed by covered wagon to Jonesborough, Tennessee.[5]

Jonesborough was an established, stable community, and because it lacked the rigid social structure that characterized much of the antebellum South, it was doubly attractive to wandering immigrants. In fact, when Cone and the Adlers arrived, the town had existed for seventy years. As early as 1834 it had a population of five hundred people, and at mid-century its prospects for continuing growth were excellent. As an auspicious sign, in 1853 surveyors for the East Tennessee and Virginia Railroad placed Jonesborough on the proposed rail route. Townsmen enthusiastically supported the railroad and were ecstatic when they learned that Jonesborough would be on the route.

Beyond economic opportunity, Cone and the Adlers saw in Jonesborough good prospects for social acceptance. Aside from the town's relative social openness, there were "Pennsylvania Dutch" settlers who spoke German. This provided a bond of nationality and made Cone's and the Adlers' foreign accents less unique and not so conspicuous. Jonesborough's first Jewish families soon "made many fast friends."[6]

The two men opened Cone & Adler, a dry goods business, in a two-story brick building opposite the Chester Inn on Main Street. Besides the usual commodities of boots and shoes, hats, groceries, and assorted notions, they were the first merchants in town to sell ready-to-wear clothing. (In most of the antebellum South clothing was made at home from fabric woven at home or purchased over the counter.)

The partners soon gained a reputation as hard working, honest men. To build their business and increase their income, they took turns tending the store and making week-long peddling trips. By pooling resources and labor, they minimized their financial risk and increased the efficiency of their business operations.

It was on one of his many peddling trips that Herman met Helen Guggenheimer. She, too, had emigrated from her native Germany, and was living at Gilmer's Mill, west of Lynchburg, Virginia. Herman married the eighteen-year-old Helen in 1856. Shortly thereafter the newlyweds and the Adlers purchased separate residences, Herman buying a large frame house next door to the business. By 1860, the Cones had two children living at home, three-year-old Moses and one-year-old Ceasar. They also reported real estate and personal property holdings worth $29,365. This was an impressive amount of wealth for antebellum East Tennessee, especially for an immigrant family.[7]

When the Civil War erupted in 1861, Cone and Adler closed their business and jointly purchased adjacent farms outside of town. They quickly took to farming and, in 1863, purchased several slaves. The conversion of their business assets from merchandise, which would have been a tempting target for thieves, to real estate was astute. This was especially true in Washington County, where throughout the war guerrilla raiders committed numerous acts of violence and lawlessness.[8]

Jacob's son Samuel later reported that his father "served the Confederacy," but there is no indication from existing state rosters that he ever joined either army. In the summer of 1863, however, Herman Cone joined McLin's Company of Local Defense Troops, a home guard unit that had been organized to control the depredations of deserters and guerrillas. This was not a front-line regiment and was not sent outside the local area.[9]

When war ended, the two men returned to their retail trade, joined by a new partner. Shelby Shipley had been a loyal Union man during the rebellion. Now, as the new sheriff of Washington County, he was a welcome addition to the firm. Considering the social upheaval that followed the Civil War, having the sheriff for a partner in one's business was an enormous asset. Shipley brought legal and political protection to the business, but he could not compensate for the impoverished state of many local residents. Because capital was especially scarce, the firm of Adler, Cone & Shipley engaged in barter. It also made occasional cash loans and credit sales that were secured by liens.[10]

The three partners occasionally foreclosed on farms, gaining ownership of hundreds of acres of real estate. Among those foreclosed for debts due was former Confederate General Alfred E. Jackson. Before the war, Jackson had been a neighbor of Cone and Adler, having built a successful wholesale produce and mercantile business in Jonesborough. During and after the war, he lost his property and assets in East Tennessee and eventually became a tenant farmer in Virginia.

Though Jackson later returned to Jonesborough, Cone and Adler acquired more than three hundred acres, as well as a house and lot in town, that had belonged to the former general.[11]

While the upheaval of war and reconstruction provided economic opportunities which Cone and Adler seized, the two men lost at least some legal skirmishes. In 1867, Judith Lee sued them over three slaves who were stolen from her on July 28, 1863. Lee never accused her neighbors of the actual theft, but alleged that when she went to the Cone and Adler farm to recover her stolen chattel, she was "run off." At the ensuing trial, the presiding judge ruled that Lee's slaves had been stolen by an unidentified third party. However, because Cone and Adler produced a bill of sale for the slaves, the judge found the two defendants innocent of fraud. Instead, he ordered Cone and Adler to compensate Lee $252 for the "value of hire" that she had lost between the time of the theft and the end of the war. Lee appealed the ruling, but the Tennessee Supreme Court upheld the lower court decision.[12]

Cone's courtroom jousting with Judith Lee was still in progress when several merchants sued him over his handling of the bankrupt Samuel Guggenheim, owner of a dry goods store in the nearby community of Leesburg. The complainants specifically alleged that Cone, as the trustee for Guggenheim, had fraudulently and purposely hindered and delayed their collection of debts. In essence, they accused him of receiving Guggenheim assets, but failing to pay off creditors. The court ruled in favor of the complainants and voided the trustee agreement Cone and Guggenheim had executed in January 1866. The judge also ordered the clerk and master of court to seize and sell at auction the property Cone had received from Guggenheim. In addition, in a later, related suit, Cone was ordered to recover the principal and interest from several notes due to Guggenheim.[13]

While these legal proceedings may have embarrassed Cone and Adler, the two gained far more in their postwar legal encounters than they lost. Although they were not rich, they were far better off than most people in the community. They had also amassed enough wealth that in 1870 Cone moved his family, which by then included seven children, to Baltimore, Maryland. There, in concert with relatives, he opened Guggenheimer, Cone & Company, Wholesale Grocers at #22 Commerce Street.[14]

Cone was making steady progress up the business ladder. He had begun as a lowly peddler, advanced to retail shopkeeping, and had now moved into merchandising and distribution. He continued to use kinship networks to support his entrepreneurial ventures, and he once again exercised prudence and foresight in locating his new business in Baltimore.

As a result of the Civil War, the Maryland city had a decided market advantage over Richmond and other war-torn Southern cities. Large amounts of Southern tobacco, cotton, and grain moved through Baltimore to American and foreign markets. The city had scores of canneries, and it was a financial, distribution, and shipping center.

The city also offered social amenities that complemented the Cones' rising economic status. For example, major universities were located there. Although elder sons Moses and Ceasar had received most of their formal education at local schools in Jonesborough, others of Herman's offspring, soon to number a dozen, would receive college educations. Daughter Claribel later earned her M.D. degree at Woman's Medical College of Baltimore and, in concert with her sister Etta, achieved fame as an art collector. Baltimore was also home of a sizable and prosperous German Jewish community, and it offered the Cones the opportunity to expand their social contacts with fellow Jews and Germans.[15]

In 1873, Jacob Adler joined his brother-in-law's business in Baltimore. The two men worked together as grocery wholesalers for five years, and then the long partnership was permanently dissolved. Although none of the surviving historical accounts say as much, it seems likely that the maturing of both men's children contributed to the dissolution of the old firm. The same year that the firm of Cone & Adler was dissolved, Herman took sons Moses and Ceasar into his business, renaming it H. Cone & Sons. At the same time, the Adler sons went into partnership with their father in Jacob Adler & Company.

For more than two decades the Cone family plied the wholesale trade. Moses and Ceasar were "drummers," as travelling salesmen were then known, and called on customers from Maryland to Alabama. They were described as "affable, friendly men to deal with or know" and in appearance "striking looking, well set up, and healthy."[16]

Now a young man, Moses stood 5'-10" in height and weighed about 180 pounds. Like his father before him, he and Ceasar took their samples and order books into the rural Southern countryside, calling on families and storekeepers. Although most trips proved relatively uneventful, some were memorable indeed. On one, Moses rode his horse off a ferry while crossing the Yadkin River west of Winston-Salem. Plunging into water 15 feet deep, Moses, a non-swimmer, had the presence of mind to hold on to the large gray horse he was riding and managed to make it back to the riverbank.[17]

The brothers were quick studies and perceptive businessmen, ever-alert to expand their business operations. About 1885 Ceasar and his younger brother Monroe formed a partnership with Milton Shields and opened a wholesale grocery business on Gay Street in Knoxville, Tennessee. Besides expanding their wholesale operations into familiar East Tennessee, this venture also provided a training ground for Monroe, who was now in his early twenties and old enough to take his place in the Cone enterprises.[18]

Despite their ambitious and industrious ways, the Cones did not devote all their attentions to business. During the Baltimore period Moses met and wooed Bertha Lindau. In the early 1880s, the Cones moved to Eutaw Place and became neighbors of the Lindaus. Upon meeting the Cones, Bertha's brother Jacob could hardly wait to announce to his own siblings that there was a new family in the neighborhood and that they had "their own baseball nine." This was no exaggeration. The last of Herman and Helen's children had been born in 1878, giving the family a total of nine boys and three girls.

Moses and Bertha probably met at a gathering of the "Sociables," a community social club. Bertha was a small, attractive, and intelligent twenty-six-year-old woman, and she and Moses had much in common. They were both the first-born child of rather large families (there were seven Lindau children). Like Moses, Bertha was also the daughter of German Jewish immigrants. Her father, Max Lindauer, had emigrated from Germany in the 1840s. He soon changed his name to Lindau, and while living in Chicago, met and married Henrietta Ullman, who had come to America from Ulm, Germany. Bertha was born April 1, 1858.[19]

In May 1884, Moses and Bertha began a courtship that was to last nearly four years. As Moses described his first social outing with her:

> I took [sister] Claribel to the races on Tuesday. We enjoyed them so much that I ventured in a new field & invited a young lady (Miss Bertha Lindau) to go with me on Thursday. She

seemed to enjoy the races as well as the compliment and I was equally entertained.[20]

Although Ceasar also courted Bertha, Moses won her affection. On February 15, 1888, Moses and Bertha married.[21]

The matrimonial rivalry did not diminish the close-knit and patriarchal relations of the Cone family. In fact, as the children matured and left home, they seldom moved far. By 1890 Herman, Helen, and their younger offspring resided at 1607 Eutaw Place. Moses and Bertha were a block away at 1524 Eutaw Place, while younger brothers Julius and Solomon later moved to 1616 Eutaw.[22]

By the latter part of the 1880s Moses and Ceasar were urging their father to retire. No doubt, this was an expression of affection and deference, but it was also a sign of the sons' yearnings to prove themselves capable of carrying forward the family business. This was a challenging time for the firm, since rail freight rates had been changed to give old rivals Richmond and Norfolk a competitive advantage over Baltimore. But by now the brothers were looking for business challenges that were larger than grocery wholesaling.[23]

In their extensive travels in the South, the Cone brothers dealt frequently with textile mill owners and company store operators. The merchandise stocked by country and mill village stores was not specialized during the late nineteenth century. Just as Cone and Adler had sold grocery, clothing, and hardware items in their Jonesborough store, H. Cone & Sons specialized in groceries but sold and traded many other items, including fabrics manufactured in Southern textile mills. These experiences introduced them to marketing characteristics and to the culture of the mills.[24]

During the 1880s the brothers began to invest in Southern mills. Returns on such investments tended to be good, and the Cones knew it. Reports circulated that mills "with good, bad and indifferent management were receiving average dividends of 22 percent." Many reported profits of from 30 to 75 percent.[25]

A number of factors contributed to mill growth. Broad popular support was generated by scores of newspaper editors, merchants, and other "New South" boosters who acclaimed mills as the economic salvation for the depressed region. Mills, they said, would enable the South to rise Phoenix-like and achieve through industry what it could not do militarily—defeat the Yankee North. Such rhetoric mobilized community pride and encouraged public subscription to mill building.

Cotton prices in the late nineteenth century were depressed, and the crop-lien system and single-crop agriculture had reduced many yeoman farmers to tenancy and sharecropping. These conditions, coupled with the region's rapid population growth, assured an abundance of inexpensive cotton and a steady supply of cheap labor. These represented the two primary production costs for textile mills, and their ready availability and low cost were critical to the region's mill-building boom.

Advances in industrial technology also contributed significantly to mill prosperity. The new ring spindle doubled the output of the spinner, took up less floor space, and was easier to maintain and repair. More important, the ring spindle required little skill to operate. This meant that the South's displaced agricultural and unskilled labor pool could be successfully tapped.[26]

In the late 1880s, Moses Cone became president of the C.E. Graham Manufacturing Company in Asheville, North Carolina. The textile mill had been built by Charles Edward Graham, a native of Hickory, North Carolina. In 1882 he went to Asheville where, prior to building his mill, he established the Asheville Shoe Company. Graham also had been a customer of H. Cone & Sons and apparently turned to them to assist with the financing of his plant. The Cones had good reason to invest in the western North Carolina mill. In the 1880s Asheville finally got the railroad that its promoters had long wanted, and its population was growing explosively. Thus, it had two key ingredients for industrial development—ready transportation and cheap labor. The mountain city's scenic qualities and its much-touted attributes as a summer resort were probably secondary attractions for the Cones because they were not in town every day or even every week. They continued to travel for their wholesale firm, so that Graham presumably provided the on-site management of the Asheville mill.[27]

At about the time that the brothers were investing in the Graham mill, they also joined Simon Lowman and Charles Burger to open Cone Brothers, Lowman and Burger Clothing Manufacturers at 392 West Baltimore Street, Baltimore. Their contacts with mills had encouraged the Cones to diversify into clothing manufacturing. Because their father and uncle had been the first retailers of ready-to-wear clothing in Jonesborough, entering business with Lowman and

Burger seemed to the Cone sons a natural progression up the production ladder. Their father had begun as a peddler and retailer, then advanced to wholesaler; they were entering manufacturing.[28]

By 1890 Moses and Ceasar Cone were contemplating even grander ventures than clothing manufacture. They had noticed how Southern textile mills produced vast quantities of plaids but did not coordinate their marketing. If someone were to get the region's mill owners to agree to market their entire product line through a single commission house, plaid production could be made more efficient and prices could be manipulated to benefit all mill owners. As it was, each mill produced its own variety of checks and plaids. When the market was glutted with a particular pattern, prices fell. The Cones wanted to assign different patterns to different mills to prevent this from occurring. Surplus fabrics could be exported to foreign markets, and, indeed, Moses saw no reason why the South could not compete directly with Great Britain for the South American export trade. As he put it:

> The inducement for the mills subscribing to the stock is that we propose to carry the accounts of a number of mills making a similar class of goods, with the idea eventually of establishing a uniformity of fabric, where now everything as to qualities is in a chaotic condition. By selling through one channel we are able to stand the expense of looking up [pursuing] the foreign trade, which no single mill could do.[29]

On November 12, 1890, the Cone Export and Commission Company was established. Its stated objectives provided ample entrepreneurial latitude. The company was permitted to purchase and sell cotton goods, advance money, and engage in "any wholesale or retail business pertaining to the manufacture, sale or exporting of cotton or other manufactured or other goods." Capital stock was authorized at $1 million, with 20,000 shares at a par value of fifty dollars. The stockholders at the time of incorporation were Moses H. Cone, Anderson Price, and Jay C. Guggenheimer.[30]

The Cones soon welcomed about forty mills into the so-called "Plaid Trust." Still, this was not enough to gain control of the market. Most mill men were industrial novices who either failed to see the advantages of fixing prices and coordinating production, or who were simply too individualistic to act cooperatively. Also, the number of Southern mills was expanding too rapidly to permit the degree of coordination that was essential for success.[31]

In the end, the Plaid Trust never achieved its ambitious objectives. The late nineteenth century witnessed many mergers and the formation of many successful trusts, none more famous than John D. Rockefeller's Standard Oil combine. Unfortunately for the Cones, the Southern textile industry was not ready for that degree of production and marketing control.

However, Cone Export did not fail completely. The firm had enticed commission contracts from more than four times as many mills as the average commission house. As a result, Cone Export attained overnight financial stability. The company's first annual balance sheet revealed commission sales of more than $72,000, while interest collected amounted to over $13,000. Deducting the cost of salaries, travel, and other expenses, a tidy profit of $33,942 remained.[32]

As commission agents, the Cones marketed and exported the products of the mills they represented. They also made loans to mill owners and provided advice on mill production and management. Many mills bought stock in the Cone company. For example, the owners of Raleigh-based Pilot Mills bought twenty shares of Cone Export stock at fifty dollars per share. In turn, the Cones were given exclusive right to sell Pilot's output of plaids, checks, and stripes, and they received a 3 percent commission on all goods sold.[33]

The Cones were by no means the first commission agents to represent Southern mills in the North. By 1890 fully 65 percent of the region's cotton mills were under contract to New York agents.[34] Though they were novices, the Cones were among the more successful. Commissions for the fiscal year ending November 1, 1894, totalled more than $166,000. This amount, coupled with the interest made on capital loans to mills, provided a substantial capital base.

Although the Cones occasionally sold company stock to increase capital, they never relinquished control of the company. Lists of shareholders for the early years of the company indicate that stock was sold to several dozen mills and individuals, including to B.N. and James Duke, who were amassing a fortune in the tobacco industry, and to the Holt family, established textile barons in Alamance County, North Carolina. With limited exceptions, these sales were small, and Cone family ownership of the company's stock consistently remained above 80 percent.[35]

As assets and retained earnings accumulated, the company

expanded. About 1892, the Cones took over full control and management of the C.E. Graham plant, renaming it the Asheville Cotton Mill. A year later they built the Southern Finishing and Warehouse Company in Greensboro, North Carolina.

In embarking on textile finishing, the Cones once more displayed their extraordinary business savvy. At the time, few Southern mills had the capability of finishing textiles. This process involved bleaching and imparting the desired appearance and handle to the printed cloth. Fabrics with the same colors might be finished differently, for instance, with or without luster, or starched and hardened or made soft. The technology involved was not so advanced that it was beyond the abilities of fledgling Southern mill men. However, a single finishing plant could process, in one day, a week's production from the largest of mills. Southern mills were mostly small and could not afford to integrate finishing into their plant operations. The Cones may well have depended on the output of the several Holt family mills in nearby Alamance County to keep their finishing plant busy. In any event, the primary significance of Southern Finishing is that it established the enduring relationship between Cone Export and Greensboro.[36]

The city offered many advantages to aspiring mill men. Its proximity to Southern cotton fields meant that railroad freight costs were less. Although this advantage would disappear when the rail shipment rates were revised after the turn of the century, during the 1890s shipping costs for cotton transported one hundred miles or less were less than half those for cotton sent from Mississippi or Alabama.[37]

Aside from the city's access to cotton supplies—cotton was a significant agricultural product in North Carolina, though little was grown in Guilford County—Greensboro was centrally located within the state. It was also closer to Baltimore than most other prospective mill sites. This enabled the Cones to travel back and forth quickly and conveniently.

Railroads radiated from the city westward to Winston-Salem and Wilkesboro, southward to Charlotte and Asheville, southeast to Wilmington, and north to Danville, Virginia. By the early 1890s, sixty trains rolled into and out of town daily, helping to earn Greensboro its reputation as "Gate City to the Piedmont." This extensive and heavily used rail network allowed raw cotton to be brought in and finished cloth shipped out. It also facilitated access to Appalachian coal, the fuel used in most of North Carolina's steam-powered cotton mills.[38]

The state offered one other, perhaps decisive, advantage: cheap and abundant labor. Wages in the South were the lowest in the nation, and North Carolina wages were the lowest in the South. The average weekly earnings for unskilled males (above sixteen years of age) working in cotton mills was $4.71 in North Carolina, as compared to $6.09 in Georgia, $8.21 in Massachusetts, and $10.68 in New Jersey. Similar wage differentials existed for female mill workers.[39]

In addition to its economic attributes, Greensboro offered the Cones social acceptance and opportunities for social mobility. Its population had not been part of the Old South's slaveholding aristocracy, and most of its merchants were relative newcomers, young and confident in the city's potential for growth. Most of all, it was a city in which the sons of an immigrant peddler would be accepted according to their business achievement, not their lineage and social connections.[40]

While there were other cities that offered similar economic and social environments, Greensboro had one additional advantage—land at an attractive price. In 1887 several local businessmen had purchased nearly 2,000 acres of land on the north side of town, just outside of the city limits. There they built the North Carolina Steel and Iron Company. Their goal was to tap the iron ore resources in the area and to make the city "the little Pittsburgh of the South." They discovered too late that local ore contained titanium, making it unsuitable for their blast furnace. By the early 1890s, they were trying to unload their defunct enterprise. As fate would have it, the Cone brothers were in the market and looking to buy.[41]

News that the Cones had "closed the deal" for the steel company property must have seemed a godsend to Greensboro residents. In 1890, word that the city was about to become the steel capital of the South had set off a speculative boom. As one resident wrote, "Every man you meet on the street is asking about sales and purchases, and enterprises of every description are springing up."[42] To a local congressman it seemed there was no possibility of failure. "It is," he wrote, "like reading the tales in the Arabian Nights, fortunes are made so easily."[43] Such hopes and high expectations had been dashed by the collapse of the iron and steel company. Now the Cones were stepping in and renewing the city's optimism about its future. In July 1895 they bought the old iron and steel company property—roughly 1,600 acres—for $37,500.[44]

The Cones did not disappoint Greensboro. In the ten years that followed their big land purchase, the brothers built three mills on and near this land, and in the process became one of the largest producers of denim in the world. Proximity, which made blue and brown denims, was constructed in 1895. Revolution, a flannel mill, was built four years later in cooperation with the Sternberger family of South Carolina. The third and largest, White Oak Mills, also a denim plant, was begun in 1902 and completed in 1905.

Proximity was unquestionably the most challenging of the three to build. Even though the Cones had learned much from their oversight of the Asheville Cotton Mill and from their operation of the Southern Finishing and Warehouse Company, and while their four years of experience as commission agents had familiarized them with the operations of dozens of textile mills, Proximity was the first spinning and weaving plant that the Cones designed, built, owned, and managed. It required the brothers to mobilize all their capital and business savvy. As younger brother Bernard later recalled, to muster the necessary capital, Moses and Ceasar "not only put all of their money and all of the money of father's estate that they could spare," but they also borrowed from the Dukes and others.[45]

For technical knowledge, the Cones hired experienced mill men from the North and South. To operate the plant, the brothers recruited R.G. Campbell of Salisbury, North Carolina. He had worked at Vance Cotton Mills and was considered "one of the best all-round cotton mill men in the south."[46]

The main building at Proximity, originally a two-story structure, 380-feet by 80-feet, housed 7,600 spindles and 250 looms. The mill turned a profit immediately and within three years was yielding a return on investment of 25 percent. Not surprisingly, the Cones soon expanded the mill to more than 18,000 spindles and 985 looms. Still other expansions followed. As the *Greensboro Patriot* reported, "The brick layer and carpenter can hardly complete one contract for enlarging Proximity Mills until their ever increasing demand renders another necessary."[47]

Flushed with the success of Proximity, the brothers decided to diversify their product. They persuaded Emanuel and Herman Sternberger of South Carolina to assist them in building a flannel mill in Greensboro. Revolution Cotton Mills was incorporated February 20,

1899, with ten shares owned by Emanuel Sternberger and ten each by Moses and Ceasar Cone. Completed in early 1900, the two-story, 73,080 square feet mill housed 12,000 spindles and 386 looms, making it larger than most North Carolina mills.[48]

As his textile empire grew, Moses thought once again of controlling a market segment. Even though he and Ceasar had been unable to coordinate the South's plaid production in 1891, he now saw the opportunity to control a different kind of fabric. He might yet duplicate, in a modest way, the success of such business tycoons as the Rockefellers and the Guggenheims. In May of 1901 Moses confided to one of his corporate officers, "We, Ceasar and I, are to build another Denim Mill [having] 1,000 looms, the idea being to give us a Denim business of say $2,500,000—and to Control that business in the U.S."[49]

The location for the new mill was at first undecided. Stories surfaced in March 1902 that the Cones were negotiating for an industrial site at Roanoke Rapids, North Carolina. These reports may have been a ruse, deliberately planted in the press to mobilize support in Greensboro. Just a month later, the local newspaper reported that the Cones, "for some time past," had been busy obtaining options on more than 1,500-acres just north of their Proximity plant. "On not more than four individual tracts has the price been fixed at what is considered an exorbitant figure. We cannot conceive," said the newspaper's editor, "of anyone holding out for a price that would for a moment jeopardize the establishment of such a vast industrial enterprise." Clearly, local boosters were not above applying pressure to assure that the Cones got the property they needed at prices they were willing to pay. By July the *Patriot* happily reported that W.A. Watson had a contract to manufacture ten million bricks for the Cones' new mill.[50]

The mammoth new mill was named White Oak because a massive white oak tree grew on the site. Costing an estimated $1.25 million, the mill would boast 60,000 spindles and 2,000 looms. Construction began in the latter half of 1902 and continued for nearly three years. At the peak of construction, 450 laborers and sixty teams of draft animals were employed. A visitor in 1914 gave the dimensions of the weave building as 904 feet by 180 feet. Exclusive of the picker room, warehouses, and office, the mill had more than ten acres of enclosed floor space. By 1907 the big White Oak Mills employed more than

1,000 workers.[51]

Whether or not the Cones were able to manipulate the market as they hoped, they unquestionably captured the dominant share of that market. By 1908, Proximity Manufacturing, including White Oak, was the largest producer of denims in the world.[52] Greensboro officials were quick to laud the brothers for their industrial achievements. The once promising steel mill may have bellied-up, but the Cones had given the city a much-desired and, as time would tell, enduring economic stimulus.[53]

Like other mill owners of the period, the Cones established villages to help speed the transition of their employees from displaced agricultural workers to efficient industrial operatives. The mill village and family labor system also were used to assure a stable and steady labor supply. The communities contained houses, company stores (including bakeries and pharmacies), schools, churches, baseball fields, and gymnasiums. Like masters in the slave system of the Old South, mill owners provided for the material needs of their laborers and expected in return submission, loyalty, and hard work.

Employee houses were the primary component of the mill villages that surrounded each of the three Cone mills. In 1897, the village of Proximity included one hundred tenements. As the mill expanded, so did the number of village houses. In 1899, a contract was let for an additional 250 houses at Proximity.[54]

Whether at Proximity, Revolution, or White Oak, most village houses were single-family, detached, frame structures that sat on relatively narrow lots. Tenants typically paid a small rent, based on the number of rooms the house had (usually from two to six). Residents also provided their own furniture. As might be expected, newcomers usually lived in rather barren houses, but they added items over time. Common furnishings included a center table bearing a large family Bible, a few expensive books, a large "company bed," and wall hangings that included perforated and stitched cardboard mottos (e.g., "God Bless Our Home").[55]

Given their background in the grocery business, the Cones quite naturally operated company stores in each village. These were organized as the Proximity Mercantile Company and initially managed by John J. Phoenix, a long-time grocer and produce dealer and one of the most aggressive and capable business men in Greensboro. Stores carried a wide range of merchandise, including groceries, shoes and clothing, hardware, and furniture. The *Greensboro Patriot* did not exaggerate when it commented that the stores represented "an index of their [village residents] wants from the cradle to the grave."[56]

The Cones took particular pride in ministering to the educational and spiritual needs of their employees. By 1908, 185 students attended school at White Oak, while Proximity was touted as having the best grade school in the state. The Cones also built churches and encouraged employee attendance.

Company schools emphasized the need for discipline, punctuality, reliability, and respect for authority. Likewise, ministers preached "a gospel of work, gratitude for present blessings, and of patience with economic and social maladjustments as temporal and outside the sphere of religious concern." Not coincidentally, the same attributes and values that made good students and devout worshippers also made conscientious and compliant workers.[57]

The Cones provided a gymnasium and other recreational facilities, as well, none more popular than the Cone Athletic Park. Besides mill teams and families, the North Carolina League of Professional Baseball Clubs played there, and from time-to-time so did University of North Carolina teams. In November 1903, a large crowd turned out for a football game between the Tar Heels and the University of Kentucky (which the visitors won, according to a local newspaper, because they were bigger).

On occasion, park users became too boisterous and on a Saturday night in late July 1902 some of the young men from Proximity "roughly handled" a park policeman. This was not the sort of behavior that the Cones tolerated. They assured readers of the *Greensboro Patriot* that there would be no more such disturbances and that the park, henceforth, "shall be entirely free from all semblance of rowdyism."[58]

The Cones also held special celebrations and events. Perhaps because they were the children of immigrants and anxious to demonstrate their American loyalty, their most elaborate and gala occasion was the company's annual Fourth of July picnic. Each year, company store manager John Phoenix prepared mountains of sandwiches and fried chicken and made untold gallons of lemonade. He purchased up to 35,000 pounds of watermelons, nearly as many pounds of bananas, and enough ice cream to fill 20,000 saucers. All this was served by more than one hundred uniformed waiters. Upwards of 12,000 mill employees and their families turned out to eat, watch minstrel shows, take part in foot races and baseball games, and listen to patriotic speeches. The focal point of most picnics was "an immense enclosure, canopied over with denim and decorated with the national colors." Moses, Ceasar, and the supervisors usually circulated among the crowd and took an active and highly visible part in activities.[59]

Despite all the amenities and services—and the Cones were in many respects model mill men—some employees had a difficult time adjusting to factory life and a paternalism that, while usually benevolent, brooked no opposition. Many workers had lived on farms and went to the mills to escape economic hard times brought about by crop failures and the crop lien system. To them, working for wages in a cotton mill—typically referred to as "public work"—was the final misfortune. Many missed farm life and tried to save their wages so that they could return to it. Few ever succeeded.[60]

Dissatisfied workers often migrated from mill to mill, hoping to find one more to their liking. Absenteeism was high, and the Cones were forced to keep a cadre of "spare hands," workers who reported in the mornings prepared to fill the places of those absent.[61]

Some saw labor unions as a route to better working conditions, higher wages, and a greater say over their jobs. In 1900, the National Union of Textile Workers (NUTW) began to organize in Southern mills. By May, a Greensboro local claimed 225 members. When Moses and Ceasar learned that the NUTW was organizing at their mills, they shut down operations and locked out the operatives. According to one newspaper report, "The Messrs. Cone (who are northern men) stated emphatically that they had removed their business to the South chiefly in order to be rid of dictation by labor organization, and utterly refused to deal with any representative of any labor union."[62] In fact, the Cones were not "northern men," at least not by birth and not for most of their childhood, and they certainly did not "remove their business" to the South. They never owned a mill in the North.

Still, the Cones opposed any intervention in their labor relations, whether real or potential, and they could be heavy-handed in their tactics. Following the lockout of Proximity's five hundred employees on May 8, 1900, Ceasar met with a small delegation of mill hands who supported the union. Although the employees vowed respect for Ceasar and loyalty to the company, their boss was not inclined to compromise. He informed them that the mill would remain closed for as long as necessary to defeat the union, and he advised anyone who found fault with that decision to leave the premises and vacate their company houses immediately. A week later, most of the would-be unionists had had enough. They signed an agreement renouncing the union and on May 15 were allowed to return to work. Those who refused were summarily discharged, and with Guilford County sheriff's deputies standing by to make sure there was no trouble, they quietly left the mill village.[63]

When the NUTW attempted to organize mills in neighboring Alamance County later that year, the Holt family followed the Cone lead and used lockouts and evictions to quash the organizing efforts. These tactics worked well because entire families, including children, frequently worked in the mills. A lockout meant that all members of the household lost their wages. Also, employee eviction from company owned houses was an especially powerful management weapon in late fall and winter, when workers quickly tired of huddling in the cold under union furnished tents. Because of the threat of being without any income and homeless, it took unusually motivated workers to buck cotton mill owners.[64]

Although defeated in their attempts to unionize, employees did not always acquiesce in their disputes with management. For example, their tendency to move from mill to mill reflected a personal, if unorganized, form of resistance. Also, employees sometimes took more direct forms of retaliation for grievances, real or imagined. In 1899, vandals knocked out the plate glass door in one home and cut down shade trees on the lawns of other company houses on Summit Avenue where mill managers and department heads lived. While their precise motives remain unknown, former employees of Proximity Mill were charged with the "diabolical crimes."[65]

In a more dramatic incident, former Cone employee Hardin Germany, fired in early 1908 for "shirking his work," decided to get even by a personal attack against Ceasar. He fashioned a small bomb by filling a shallow pine box, little more than six inches by three inches, with eleven ounces of black powder and a bottle half-filled with shot. To set off the powder, Germany arranged matches so that they would ignite by friction when the box was opened. After building and mailing the bomb, Germany had second thoughts. He went to the Cone residence and handed Sol, a visiting brother, an anonymous letter in which Germany said he had overheard two men plotting to mail a bomb and urged Ceasar not to open it. The letter worked, but not as Germany had planned. Within weeks, the reluctant assassin, described by the *Greensboro Patriot* as "possessing the general appearance of a degenerate," was convicted of attempted assault with intent to kill and sentenced to eight years in the state penitentiary in Raleigh.[66]

Such incidents do not mean that the Cones were especially demanding or harsh with their employees, at least by the standards, expectations, and prevailing practices of the time. Indeed, employees sometimes gave them gifts as tokens of their esteem and affection. Even those who disliked factory work or did not care personally for their bosses knew that if they did as they were told and followed the rules, they would stay out of harm's way. The Cones were truly paternalistic and, like stern parents, punished their workers only when they felt personally challenged or undermined.

With equal vigor, the Cones opposed other threats to their complete control of mill operations. When state legislation was proposed to limit the work week to sixty-six hours and to establish minimum ages for child labor, the Cones spoke out. Ceasar opposed it on the grounds that it would be "a bad plan to have any legislation on the labor question. . .the few mills. . .now treating their hands in such manner as require legislation will soon have either no hands or else have to treat them right." He implied that the labor supply was limited and that mill owners, as a consequence, were competing for workers. In reality, labor was relatively plentiful at the turn of the century. Although the situation would soon change, unskilled laborers were, in most years, readily abundant—and readily expendable.[67]

In an attempt to obviate the need for legal controls, Ceasar and four other textile mill owners drafted and circulated a petition asking North Carolina mill men to support a voluntary sixty-six hour work week, with no children under age twelve to work during the school term, unless they were children of widows or physically disabled parents. When the legislature's Judiciary Committee met to consider the matter, Moses testified that the proposed legislation "would disturb in some degree the relations now existing between the employer and employee in the mills." He added that he did not think employees wanted such laws. The General Assembly agreed, and obligingly decided to postpone further consideration until more manufacturers had time to sign the voluntary agreement then being circulated.[68]

Although few said so publicly, mill owners had a practical reason to resist labor legislation. Their workers were on the job an average of sixty-six hours per week, usually working from 6 a.m. to 6 p.m. Monday through Friday, and 6 a.m. to noon on Saturday. In comparison, Massachusetts textile workers, including spinners and weavers, worked an average of fifty-eight hours a week. Thus, North Carolina mill owners worked their employees longer hours for smaller wages. This gave them a competitive advantage that they did not wish to surrender.[69]

Moreover, the Cones, like many of their contemporaries, actually believed that they treated their young employees well. A visitor to Proximity Mill in 1901 reported seeing and talking to twenty boys who were having "a royal good time" laughing, scuffling, and chewing "'backer [tobacco]" while on the job. One "bright chap" commented that he did not care to go to school for fear "the teacher would slap him and the rest of the children would laugh." The visitor reported that there were many such children who enjoyed the relative freedom of mill work and liked learning a trade, earning thirty to forty cents a day, and contributing to the family income.[70]

Aside from the issues of economics and the treatment of working children, labor unions and the prospect of government regulation ran counter to values that the Cones felt deeply. Like other captains of industry, they regarded their rise to elite status as altogether natural and proper. Just as Charles Darwin had advanced the notion of the survival of the fittest in the animal kingdom, so too had families like the Cones risen to the top by virtue of their own abilities and thus considered themselves specially ordained by natural selection to be leaders. As they and most of their contemporaries saw it, there was nothing immoral about resisting outside intervention in their labor relations or, for that matter, in trying to form trusts and manipulate the market. On the contrary, they presumed that no one knew better what was good for business or for workers than nature's own elect. The Cones were simply acting in harmony with the prevailing beliefs of their time and class when they locked out and evicted workers who joined unions and fought legislation to keep children younger than twelve out of the mills. Whether these views are morally defensible is another question.

The point is, they were entirely proper to American industrialists, including Southern mill men, in 1900.

The formative years of the Cone Export and Commission Company were largely a legacy of Cone & Adler and H. Cone & Sons. As the textile company continued to grow well into the twentieth century, the old patriarchal and paternalistic patterns endured, and so did the concern of its officers for social acceptance.

Just as their father had combined his resources with his brother-in-law to form Cone & Adler, Moses and Ceasar relied on kinship ties to supply capital, skill, and emotional support to build their textile empire. When their youngest brother Clarence reached manhood, they acquired an interest in Greensboro's Hucomuga Mill and made him manager. In 1902, the little mill went into receivership, amid charges by minority stockholders that it had been deliberately run at a loss, and was bought in its entirety by the Cones. (One suspects that the Cones did not like answering to stockholders any more than to unions or government regulators).[71]

Moses and Ceasar also brought other relatives into their business operations. Brother Fred managed the Asheville Cotton Mill, while brother-in-law J.W. Lindau became manager of the Coulter & Lowery Finishing Plant, a position he held until 1907. In addition, Moses and Ceasar set up a number of other enterprises in Greensboro and put their relatives to work. In 1896, they established the Merchants' Grocery Company, which purchased and sold canned goods, coffee, leather, tobacco products, and tinware. With brothers Julius as president and Sol as vice president, annual sales at Merchants' Grocery in three years jumped from $150,000 to $500,000.[72]

Greensboro was for the Cone brothers what Jonesborough and Baltimore had been for their father. Success, not Old South lineage, was what counted in Greensboro of the 1890s, and when the brothers became wealthy, they were careful to behave in ways that the well-heeled folk around town expected. They expressed both their business and social attitudes when they acted like affluent industrialists of the period. They managed their empire aggressively, seeking to control a market segment and exercising dominance over their employees, because that was the way others expected them to behave.

Still, it was not enough to wield power. To gain greater public approval, proper industrialists of the time were expected to demonstrate civic responsibility, publicize their good works, and act patriotically and philanthropically. The Cones did exactly that. Just as Herman had been one of Jonesborough's early Masons and made many "fast friends," his sons and other family members took an active role in Greensboro's Chamber of Commerce, joined the local Elks Lodge, became Masons, delivered speeches to business-oriented organizations such as the Industrial and Immigration Association, put on exhibits of their "industrial betterment work," and held "charming receptions" for their many friends.[73]

Like others of their time and social position, the Cones became philanthropists, giving to many organizations. This was all part of an elaborate social code. In the Cones' conservative and rigidly defined world, one behaved in prescribed ways. Workers showed deference, while owners ruled with a complete but benevolent authority that went beyond the mills and extended to the community. The Cones felt this responsibility keenly, which may have been one reason they were so insistent that others abide by the same social rules. As iron-willed and uncompromising as the Cones could be, no one could accuse them of being hypocrites. They shouldered their social responsibilities—as they saw them—and demanded that others do the same.[74]

Succeeding generations of Cones continued the family quest for status. They too joined local civic organizations, belonged to the Greensboro Country Club, and became active in local government. In time, their philanthropy totaled many millions of dollars and extended to scores of organizations.[75]

None acted with any more decorum or exhibited greater concern for status than Moses. The way that he organized and ran the family's textile empire was only one example of how he showed his concern for propriety. As his income and influence grew, Moses began building, at Blowing Rock, what would become one of North Carolina's most elaborate country estates. It would be a showplace in the mountains, one that allowed this immigrant's son to display his hard-won wealth and cultivation, surround himself with the symbols of Colonial America, and live like an antebellum aristocrat. At Blowing Rock, no one would ever be able to tell that Moses Cone was anything other than a long established, native-born American.

CHAPTER 2
HAVEN AND FORTRESS

M oses Cone did not spend all his time shuttling between
Greensboro and New York, planning new mills and scouting
international markets for his commission house. During the 1890s he
acquired and developed a splendid country estate in the mountains of
western North Carolina. Over the course of the decade, he purchased
more than 3,600 acres of land around Blowing Rock and established a
model orchard and stock farm. Displaying artistic talent, this captain
of industry built 25 miles of carefully landscaped carriage roads, manmade lakes, and flower gardens.

In 1900, he crowned his estate with a twenty-three room colonial
revival manor house. Naming his farms and manor after one of the
mountains he had purchased, Cone fashioned "Flat Top" into one of
the largest, best-known country places in the state. It was a fitting
symbol for a wealthy industrialist. Although Flat Top did not equal the
opulence and splendor of George W. Vanderbilt's Biltmore Estate near
Asheville, there is little doubt that Cone patterned his estate after
Biltmore. The similarities were striking enough that newspaper writers
could not resist humorously comparing "Farmer Cone" and "Farmer
Vanderbilt."[76]

Some said that Cone had built his summer country place for the
simple and straightforward reason that he loved nature and wanted a
healthful retreat from the stress and rigors of his myriad business ventures. While this may have been true, other, and more compelling,
motivations had led him to Blowing Rock. In fashioning his grand
estate, Cone was making a powerful social statement about who he
was and how he wished to be viewed by his contemporaries. Just as
Vanderbilt had linked himself with European aristocracy by creating
his sprawling estate—replete with a French chateau—so too had
Moses Cone, an immigrant's-son-turned-industrialist, associated himself with old-line America by building a colonial revival house. Flat
Top Manor may not have rivaled Biltmore in scale or resembled it in
architecture, but the builders of both estates were consciously seeking
to associate themselves with their social betters.

The creation of Flat Top Manor was part of a much larger national
movement. Many other wealthy people were building country estates

during the 1890s. They, too, shared Cone's affinity for nature. In fact, the virtues of rural life were an old and enduring part of American culture. Not only did the Biblical Adam live in a natural paradise, but since Colonial times yeoman farmers had been looked upon as a bulwark of stable and desirable values. No less a figure than Thomas Jefferson advocated agricultural life as the model for the new American republic.[77]

By the late nineteenth century, Americans were embracing these Jeffersonian ideals with fresh enthusiasm. In reaction to the rapid industrialization and urbanization that followed the Civil War, America went "back to nature." In the Gilded Age, people idealized country life as both health-giving and virtuous, simultaneously shunning city life as unhealthy and morally debilitating. North and south, east and west, those who possessed the financial means bought or built retreats in the country. Meat-packing tycoon J. Ogden Armour, for example, acquired the one thousand-acre Mellody Farm near Chicago. At the same time, many of Armour's business peers, including the McCormicks and Swifts, commuted by train to their country retreats in the affluent Chicago suburb of Lake Forest. Other men in other cities did the same. New York merchants embellished the hills of Stamford, Connecticut, with sundry mansions, while Baltimore's elite took to the country and mountains to escape the summer heat and humidity.[78]

It was not simply the popular fascination for nature that motivated wealthy men like Moses Cone to build country estates. Late nineteenth century Americans believed that the environment governed human behavior. They were convinced that living on country places, in properly structured surroundings, not only promoted health, but provided emotional, spiritual, and moral uplift. They built asylums in rural settings because health experts believed that tranquility restored sanity. Fresh air and a properly ordered environment benefited everyone, not just the emotionally ill. According to the prevailing wisdom, thoughtfully planned suburbs, such as Riverside, Illinois, provided escape from urban congestion and furnished the benefits of rural life. Trolleys and trains created a new phenomenon in America—the commuter—and made suburbs possible. In the process, mass transportation bestowed the blessings of nature on those who could not afford the more desirable but distant country places.[79]

While urban parks conferred the blessings of nature on the poor and suburbs provided a refuge for the middle and upper classes, the truly rich built their dazzling retreats by the seashore and in the country. Captains of industry—or "robber barons," as they were more critically labeled—built their fabulous estates and villas not merely to enjoy the much-touted benefits of nature, but also as status symbols. Grand estates served as socially accepted devices for displaying one's wealth. The powerful financiers and industrialists competed for social dominance just as they vied in the market place for economic supremacy. They hired the best architects and built palaces and castles that mimicked those of Europe. In the process, families without aristocratic titles conferred on themselves the trappings of Old-World nobility. It was hardly coincidental that The Elms, the Newport, Rhode Island, home of Pennsylvania coal magnate Edward J. Berwind, resembled a French chateau, or that The Breakers, owned by Berwind's summertime neighbors, the Vanderbilts, looked like an Italian palace. This phenomenon was not limited to well-known places like Newport. In North Carolina, tobacco company and bank president Julian Carr built a substantial villa in Durham in 1887. To turn-of-the-century Americans, great wealth might confer honor, but it took property, the true evidence of riches, to confer esteem.[80]

Of all country places, none equaled in size and opulence the Biltmore Estate at Asheville. More than any other, this was the estate that inspired and served as a model for Moses Cone and Flat Top Manor. Seeking a "refuge from the tumult of the city" and hoping that the mountain climate would benefit his frail health, George W. Vanderbilt III began purchasing land bordering the western North Carolina town in 1888. George was a son of William Henry Vanderbilt, who had expanded the railroad empire founded by his father, Cornelius, and doubled the family fortune to some $200 million. Vanderbilt would eventually spend an estimated $3 million, a sizeable portion of his inheritance, building the largest private residence in the world.[81]

The Biltmore Estate was dominated by a massive, French-style chateau. A true castle in its proportions, Biltmore House boasted 255 rooms and included an indoor bowling alley, swimming pool, and gymnasium, as well as central heating and internal telephone system. The interior decor and furnishings, gathered from Europe, the Orient, and elsewhere around the world, complemented Biltmore's grand exterior and bespoke a royal lifestyle.

Visitors reached the house on a three-mile approach road that, while appearing uncontrived, was carefully designed and landscaped so that the sudden appearance of the main house was breathtaking. Meticulously groomed formal gardens graced the grounds around the house. A 250-acre deer park and a nearby bass pond and boathouse added their own charm to the setting. Beyond the lawns and formal gardens, the estate stretched over more than 125,000 acres of mountains and valley. Altogether, Biltmore demonstrated the wealth and refinement of its owner, a man who spoke eight languages and spent more time travelling and pursuing his interests in art and literature than participating in the family's high-stakes business dealings.[82]

To plan, design, and execute such a grand and complex undertaking, Vanderbilt hired architect Richard Morris Hunt and landscape architect Frederick Law Olmsted. In their respective professions, they were the most eminent men in America. Hunt, who had studied at the Ecole des Beaux Arts in Paris, had designed the base of the Statue of Liberty and the Tribune Building in New York and, before his death in 1895, would design the palatial Vanderbilt family homes in Newport, The Breakers and Marble House. Olmsted's design credits included such familiar landmarks as New York's Central Park, Franklin Park in Boston, the campus of Stanford University in Palo Alto, California, and the World Columbian Exposition, held in 1893 in Chicago.[83]

At Biltmore, Olmsted sited the house and designed the approach road and drives, formal gardens, and deer parks. He also suggested that Vanderbilt undertake the practice of forestry, telling his client that this would be a dignified and appropriately aristocratic undertaking for a country gentleman. Besides, said Olmsted, crops of timber grown scientifically would be profitable and would demonstrate the usefulness of sound conservation and forestry, thereby providing an added public benefit.[84]

Vanderbilt agreed and soon hired New York-born and European-trained Gifford Pinchot, later to become America's chief forester. By replanting harvested areas, controlling erosion, and employing other conservation techniques, Pinchot and his successor, Dr. Carl A. Schenck, proved Olmsted right. The 125,000-acre Biltmore Estate became a model of progressive forestry. To develop a cadre of professional foresters, Schenck established on the estate a school of forestry, the first of its kind in America.[85]

Making a profit, or at least breaking even on his investment, was important to Vanderbilt. At the turn of the century, country estates

were expected to be self-supporting. Indeed, one of the defining characteristics of a country place, as opposed to a villa or other estate, was
that it produced income for the owner. This was one reason that, in
addition to growing and harvesting trees, Vanderbilt established a
dairy and stock farm that featured prize-winning animals. He also
raised sheep and chickens, and he cultivated extensive vegetable gardens. Even in the Gilded Age, opulence and ostentation were tempered
with a degree of practicality. Forestry, stock and dairy farms, and vegetable production did that for George Vanderbilt at Biltmore.

It was also important to Vanderbilt that Biltmore serve as a model.
In promoting his suggestion to implement scientific forestry, Olmsted
told his client that such an undertaking would provide "an inestimable
service" to the country. Vanderbilt no doubt listened intently to this
argument, well aware that one of the social obligations of the wealthy
was to set a good example. He must have been honored when J.
Sterling Morton, secretary of agriculture, declared in 1896 that every
intelligent citizen building an estate would want to make a pilgrimage
to "this Mecca of intensive agriculture and refined taste."[86]

The example Vanderbilt set at Biltmore was not lost on Moses H.
Cone. Living and working in New York City, Cone no doubt read
about George Vanderbilt's activities, which the *New York Times* avidly
reported. More than that, the Cone brothers' Asheville Cotton Mill
stood just a few miles to the north of Biltmore. In 1889, Moses bought
a house very near the mill for his sister, Carrie, and her husband,
Moses D. Long.[87]

There is no evidence that Cone knew Vanderbilt or talked directly
to him about building an estate, but it is obvious that Flat Top was
inspired by, and modeled after, Biltmore. In November 1892, just two
years after Vanderbilt began building his grand estate, Cone bought his
first tract of land near Blowing Rock. Like Biltmore, Flat Top would
ultimately contain carefully constructed carriage roads, a bass lake and
boathouse, deer parks, prize-winning cattle, sheep, chickens, and gardens. True, Flat Top did not feature Biltmore's experiments in progressive forestry, but its apple orchards served the same purpose: to make
the estate profitable and to demonstrate the benefits of growing apples
scientifically. Emulating Vanderbilt was also consistent with Cone's
larger behavior pattern. Because he was sensitive to matters of status
and authority, Cone followed the lead of his social superiors. In fash-

ioning Flat Top after Biltmore, he was doing what he believed to be both practical and entirely proper.

Cone had become familiar with Watauga County, in which Blowing Rock is located, from his early travels as a drummer for H. Cone & Sons, but simple familiarity with the area was not the overriding reason that he chose Blowing Rock as the site for his country estate. Cone had travelled widely and knew other mountain communities just as intimately.

Dozens of towns and villages in the mountain South, like Blowing Rock, touted their scenery and healthful climate. Some offered the additional advantage of warm, mineral spring baths which, advertisers crowed, would eradicate the effects of grippe, malaria, rheumatism, neuralgia, catarrh, blood and skin diseases, kidney and nervous disorders, and chronic and functional derangements. Warm Springs, in Madison County, North Carolina, became a popular resort in the 1830s, and after the Civil War the community was advertised all over the United States.[88]

Blowing Rock had no such springs, but at nearly 4,000 feet elevation, its scenery and summer climate rivaled any in the region. Besides views of blue-hued mountains, daily temperatures in June, July, and August averaged less than seventy degrees. By the 1890s, Blowing Rock had become an established resort, replete with all the comforts pleasure-seeking Victorians could want. Lenoir merchant James Harper built the first summer home there in 1856. After the Civil War, William Morris opened a boarding house that was acclaimed for its deep feather beds, said to be "good for tired legs after a day's wading in the creeks fishing for speckled trout." Other boarding houses and hotels followed. Between 1884 and 1891 the Watauga, Blowing Rock, and Green Park Hotels opened. By the time Moses Cone came looking for land, Blowing Rock's year-round population of two hundred was swelling in summer to more than six hundred.[89]

Visitors whiled away the hours riding horseback, playing tennis, bowling, and attending formal dances and social events. They walked around town in their finery, often carrying magazines and other literature under their arms, where, said one ungentle observer, "most of it stays." Strolling through the village, one might meet North Carolina Senator Matt Ransom, Senator—and former Governor—Zebulon Vance, or the artist Elliott Daingerfield. Businessmen frequently seen included W.W. Stringfellow, an Anniston, Alabama, bank president. In

1892, he and his wife, Suzie, purchased the house and lake owned by Len Estes and renamed the place Chetola, a Cherokee word meaning "haven of rest."[90]

The village furnished all the amenities such well-heeled visitors demanded: hot baths, telephone and telegraph service, newspapers from around the state, and riding stables. Those needing medical services could call on the local doctor or stop by Blackburn's store and purchase a bottle of Hollister's Rocky Mountain Tea, which not only "positively cured" all stomach and digestive disorders, but guaranteed young women "red lips, laughing eyes, sweet breath and good looks!" For a dime a day, one could also order by mail the *Encyclopedia Britannica*.[91] Blowing Rock may have been in the mountains of Appalachia, but it was far from isolated. In addition to local services and accommodations, Henkel, Craig and Company offered daily stage and surrey transportation via the turnpike to Lenoir. There passengers could take the train to various destinations, including Greensboro.[92]

Blowing Rock was a natural choice for a man in Moses Cone's position. Having grown up in Jonesborough, in the second county west of Watauga, he felt at home in western North Carolina. Like others of his time, he believed that wholesome mountain living would promote his physical and emotional well-being and perhaps lengthen his life.[93] Blowing Rock not only escaped the outbreaks of cholera and typhoid that recurrently struck New York and other urban areas, but its cool, fresh air and opportunities for horseback riding, fishing, and other outdoor recreation appealed to someone as active as Moses Cone.

Telegraphs, telephones, and newspapers meant that he could continue to direct his expanding business empire while vacationing in the mountains. Whether proximity to Greensboro figured prominently in his initial thinking is debatable. Cone bought his first property, 31 acres, near Blowing Rock on September 20, 1892. He and Ceasar bought the Southern Finishing Plant, their first in Greensboro, in 1893. The dates are close enough that the brothers may have already negotiated a deal for the plant by late 1892. It is also possible that Cone's early land purchases around Blowing Rock were speculative and that he decided later to assemble a large estate. Interestingly, he waited until September 1893 to make his first major land purchase, the 940-acre Norwood tract on Rich Mountain, and another six years passed before he commenced construction of Flat Top Manor. By the time workmen laid the foundation for the manor, Proximity Manufacturing was in full operation and Revolution Mills was under construction. This made convenient access to Greensboro essential. Thanks to the existing transportation network, Cone could leave Greensboro at 7 a.m. and arrive in Blowing Rock before nightfall, and he could return as quickly. Rail service also connected Greensboro with New York and Baltimore, linking the production mills with the company's sales headquarters, and with family and friends living on Eutaw Place. These must have been major considerations in the decision to build an estate in Watauga County.[94]

As an added enticement, Watauga County land cost relatively little, especially compared to urban real estate markets. Cone paid $29,000 for roughly 3,650 acres of land, for an average per-acre cost of $7.95. As might be expected, prices varied from tract to tract, but largely remained in the range of five to ten dollars.[95]

Finally, Blowing Rock's social atmosphere suited a man of Cone's status. One might pass a senator on the street or meet a piedmont industrialist at an afternoon social, but chances of meeting a Carnegie, Vanderbilt, or Rockefeller were slim. The super-rich had other playgrounds, while the remnants of the blue-blooded, Old South aristocracy were more often found at such places as White Sulphur Springs, West Virginia. Blowing Rock, with its New South bankers and industrialists, offered Cone a comfortable social environment among likeminded, congenial—but not over-awing—company.[96]

At the same time, Blowing Rock's native-born population offered the opportunity to do good works. Just as the Cone brothers exercised a heavy paternalism in their mills and mill villages, in Watauga County they gained the chance to perform "uplift" work among mountaineers. By the 1890s, most Americans regarded Appalachia as a land of ignorant and unchurched hillbillies. Churches and various philanthropic organizations sent missionaries and social workers to polish the mountaineers' manners, wean them from cornbread, and convince them of the superiority of high church religion. In Blowing Rock of the 1890s, Mary Carter, wife of a local physician, held weekly "Mothers' Meetings," where she taught sewing, crafts, and nutrition. At the same time, Carter's neighbor, Suzie Stringfellow, promoted school betterment and civil improvement. Mountaineers did not always greet cultural intervention warmly, no matter how well intended. Episcopal Minister William Savage, who arrived in Blowing Rock in 1902, lamented "the statuesque reserve and stolid indifference" with which his uplift efforts were met.[97] Still, most Americans believed that something needed to be done to make Appalachia more like the rest of the country, and they looked to churches, to social organizations, and to substantial individuals like Moses Cone to get the job done.

Having made the decision to locate his estate at Blowing Rock, Cone quickly set about making Flat Top a reality. Between 1892 and 1908, he assembled the acreage for his estate, tract by tract. He bought parcels as small as one acre and as large as 940 acres. In forty-five real estate transactions, he cobbled together more than 3,600 acres. The estate stretched from the summits of Rich and Flat Top Mountains down across the Yonahlossee Turnpike and downslope to Blowing Rock. In addition, Cone purchased 76 acres below the village in Caldwell County.[98]

Altogether, Flat Top was an impressive holding. Elevations ranged from 4,588 feet at the summit of Flat Top to 2,720 feet on China Creek. The higher elevations afforded some of the most spectacular scenic vistas in the entire vicinity. Even though previous land owners had cleared areas for farms and pastures, much of the land remained heavily forested. Chestnuts, a variety of oaks, tulip poplar, maples, and dozens of other tree species populated the forest canopy, while mountain laurel, rhododendron, and other members of the heath family grew profusely in the understory. The Flannery Fork of the New River and smaller streams flowed down the draws, while numerous springs provided abundant drinking water.[99]

A pragmatic man, Cone went to work beautifying his land and making it profitable. In 1893, only months after purchasing the 76-acre Green Park tract, located just beyond Blowing Rock, Cone hired a manager, J. Lee Hayes, and employed up to twenty men clearing land and planting 1,000 fruit trees. A reporter for the *Watauga Democrat* apparently had not met him, but he applauded the work "Mr. M.H. Cane" [sic] was doing at Green Park, as well as the improvements W.W. Stringfellow was making at Chetola. Such men, said the reporter, "make the prospect of our village brighter, as they are both men of means and will improve the property they have bought."[100]

Despite the initial burst of activity, during 1895 and 1896 Cone bought no land and apparently made few other improvements to the Green Park and Norwood tracts. At that time, building Proximity Mill demanded his full attention and took all the money he and his family could muster. In 1897, he resumed his Blowing Rock real estate purchases with a flurry of transactions, making nine purchases that year and seven the next. This added roughly 1,500 acres to his holdings.

The initial success of Proximity Mill and growing anxiety over his health encouraged Cone to renew his estate building. In 1895, Cone had contracted typhoid fever. Two years later, his father, family patriarch Herman Cone, died. Just three months shy of his fortieth birthday, Moses became increasingly preoccupied with his own health. Bertha later said that her husband hastened the construction at Flat Top because "he knew that he was doomed."[101] The death of his father from heart disease was more than an emotional trauma. It spurred Moses to speed the development of his Flat Top estate.

In September of that year, having acquired the 475-acre Coffey tract, Cone solicited bids to have ten acres of forest cut, and to have stumps, dead trees, and grubs removed from another 200 acres. J.A. Underdown, who owned a nursery in Caldwell County, acted as Cone's agent. He apparently found an acceptable bidder, since by February 1898 he had planted a whopping 20,800 apple trees. By fall of the following year, he had increased that total to 25,100, and had planted another 2,000 peach, pear, plum, and cherry trees. The number of apple trees soon eclipsed 30,000, and the *Greensboro Patriot* speculated that Flat Top Orchards were probably the largest in the state.[102]

Raising apples in such quantities was not something Cone undertook on a whim or without the prospect for realizing a profit. A noted pomologist in 1889 proclaimed western North Carolina's soil and climate among the best in America for growing choice winter apples. By the turn of the century, the state's 4.2 million apple trees produced 7.5 million bushels annually.[103] Growing apples in Watauga County was hardly a novel or high-risk undertaking. On the contrary, one newspaper optimistically predicted that Cone would net a return of $25,000 per year from his orchards. Cone may have based his decision partly on financial rewards, but he did not envision growing substantially richer by selling apples. To be sure, he wanted to recover his costs and in the process to justify his estate as a practical endeavor and not simply a showy extravagance. Cone also wanted a diversion from his business enterprises, and farming helped him do that. Perhaps more important, just as Vanderbilt had shown the advantages of scientific forestry

at Biltmore, Cone wanted to demonstrate the benefits of scientific
pomology. D.A. Tompkins, a textile man like Cone and publisher of
the *Charlotte Daily Observer*, said that Flat Top Orchards represented
"an exhibit of what could and could not be done in horticulture in the
North Carolina mountains," one of "value to the State and to human-
ity."[104] Thus, while the *Asheville News and Hotel Reporter* praised
Vanderbilt for showing the value of "scientific methods of farming,"
other newspapers lauded the work in progress at Blowing Rock.[105]
The descriptions differed from newspaper to newspaper, but the intent
was identical. The *Watauga Democrat* complimented Vanderbilt for
farming that "may prove a source of instruction to others;" the
Greensboro Patriot reminded readers that Cone's undertaking was not
intended for making money but was simply for the public good that
may come of it.[106] Surely, no state had two better known or more publicly applauded "farmers" than did North Carolina with George
Vanderbilt and Moses Cone.

With his orchards well underway, Cone turned his attention to
building a suitable house. This required that he select an architect.
Vanderbilt's architect, Richard Morris Hunt, specialized in designing
homes patterned after European castles, a style Cone could not afford.
Still, Cone planned a substantial house and wanted an accomplished
designer. He first contacted Stanford White, a partner in the New York
firm of McKim, Mead & White and one of the most highly-regarded
architects in America. Bertha met with White but was disappointed
when he told her that unless the Cones were prepared to spend a minimum of $100,000, he would not be interested.[107]

The Cones eventually settled for Orlo Epps of Washington, D.C. A
native of Elkhart, Indiana, and a Cornell graduate, Epps became
acquainted with the Cones when he lived at Greensboro during the
early and mid-1890s. He bought a house in the city in 1890 and
became a professor of physics, mechanics, and applied mathematics at
North Carolina Agricultural and Mechanical College for the Colored
Race (today North Carolina Agricultural and Technical College). Epps
also practiced architecture with the firm of Epps & Hackett, which had
designed Proximity Mill. Even though he had moved to Washington,
D.C., in 1897, the Cones apparently remained acquainted with him.
They certainly knew where to find him when Stanford White turned
them down.[108]

When the Cones met with their architect to discuss details, one critical question had to be answered immediately: what style of house did the Cones want? This is an obviously important decision in any home building, but it was especially so in the late Victorian and early Progressive era. At the turn of the century, houses were believed to reveal the personal qualities of their inhabitants, and socially conscious Americans had developed a strong metaphorical connection between a man and the house he built. As historian Mark Alan Hewitt has observed, "Properly designed, [houses] portrayed human character as precisely as a suit of clothes." In choosing the architectural style for their house, the Cones would be making a powerful public statement about who they were and how they wanted to be regarded by others.[109]

They ultimately decided to build a three-story, twenty-three-room house in the colonial revival style. This architecture emerged in the 1880s and gained popularity in the following decade. Colonial revival art and architecture expressed patriotism and suggested an ancestral rootedness in America. Even though colonial forms borrowed from European traditions, in the popular mind they represented early America and an ethos that was old stock, Anglo-Saxon, and protestant.[110]

While Americans built a number of colonial homes around the turn of the century, larger country estates typically featured French and Italian Renaissance, Georgian, and Gothic houses.[111] That the Cones selected colonial revival strongly suggests that they wanted to be identified with and communicate an established American ancestry that they did not, in fact, possess. In choosing the kind of house that they did, they sought, perhaps subconsciously, to distance themselves from their Old World and religious roots. Economically, Herman Cone had risen from peddler to retailer and, finally, to wholesaler. Moses and Ceasar had ascended the economic ladder one more rung, becoming industrialists.

Socially, the Cone family followed an equally common pattern. Like other immigrant families, the second generation, of which Moses was a part, tried consciously to distance themselves from their own national, ethnic, and religious heritage.[112] Moses built a colonial revival country house for the same reason that he held giant Fourth of July picnics for his millhands in Greensboro and that he otherwise followed faithfully the social code of the proper industrialist: to confirm to others, and perhaps to himself, that he was thoroughly American and deserving of the esteem he yearned for.

There was also a more immediate reason why Cone would want to wrap himself in American imagery. During the 1880s and 1890s immigration from central and eastern Europe soared. Many Americans felt that their way of life was threatened by this immigrant invasion. In 1894, New England leaders and professionals formed the Immigration Restriction League and demanded literacy tests for prospective immigrants. That same year, the anti-Catholic American Protective Association watched its membership surpass 500,000. People feared that aliens would take American jobs, spread the seeds of socialism, and taint the country's social and religious institutions. These anxieties soon hardened into racism. Some suggested that democracy could thrive only among the superior race—"Anglo-Saxons." To forcibly assimilate the hordes of foreigners, a number of states made American history a required course in public schools, while others passed laws forbidding the teaching of foreign languages.[113]

Not surprisingly, a wave of bedrock patriotism accompanied this growing nativism. Lecturers and historians crisscrossed the country giving well-attended addresses on American history. Publishers printed countless biographies of American heroes, while the Daughters of the American Revolution led pilgrimages to national shrines. Civil War veterans attended lachrymose "Blue-Gray" reunions where they sang patriotic airs and, brushing aside the rancor born of four years of bloody war, praised national reconciliation.

People not only reveled in the collective national past, they also searched for and celebrated their own personal roots in American society. Genealogy became a national passion, even though few people seemed to notice or admit that ancestor worship enhanced the prestige of the living more than it honored the dead.[114]

Little wonder, therefore, that Moses and Bertha Cone, eager to distance themselves from their families' immigrant past, adopted the symbols and actions of old-stock Americans. They were anxious to shore up and protect their new-found wealth and status, just as America as a whole was revealing a deep insecurity about its national and cultural identity. Flat Top Manor was their deepest bow to an idealized America that they, like millions of other immigrants, both envied and feared. Within their mountain-top retreat, they would be safe from all inconvenient questions about their own patriotism and national origins. Blowing Rock would be both haven and fortress.

CHAPTER 3

A MANSION IN THE
MOUNTAINS

After he had bought the property he needed and made the critical decisions about architecture, Cone began constructing his massive manor house. In October 1898, wagons laden with tons of nails, tools, and other materials lumbered out of Lenoir en route to Flat Top. Just three months later, the *Watauga Democrat* announced that "Mr. Cone is now preparing to erect a magnificent residence on his estate at a cost of $25,000. It will be on an elevated spot overlooking a lake that will cover 25 acres or more of land." At that time, $100 to $200 would buy a habitable home outside Blowing Rock. Readers could safely assume that this would be no ordinary house.[115]

Skeptics may have thought that the $25,000 estimate was an exaggeration, but if anything, the figure erred on the conservative side. The contractor who had calculated the costs had done a great deal of work for Moses Cone; in fact, W.A. Fries had already moved from Salisbury, North Carolina, to Greensboro, and then to the mill village at Proximity. If not actually in title, he was in fact the Cone's contractor-in-residence. According to published reports, Fries "did all the building at Proximity," presumably including the mill and the village. In any event, he had worked enough for the Cones that when he accompanied his client to Blowing Rock to "figure on" a house, he surely wanted to give the best possible price.[116]

With Fries' estimates in hand, Cone returned again to Blowing Rock at the end of January 1899, this time with his wife and his architect, Orlo Epps. The trio had one purpose for their trip—to select the site for the Cones' country house. Aside from the choice of architectural style, no decision in building a country house was as important as this. Such mundane issues as drainage and water supply had to be addressed, since these, more than anything, determined the sanitary condition of the house. Late Victorians had discovered the microbe and its role in transmitting disease. As a result, they went to great lengths to assure cleanliness and sanitation. Prevailing wisdom was that porous soils and high ground improved drainage and thus contributed to better health.[117]

Beyond health concerns, the Cones and Epps had to consider the relationship of the house to its flower gardens, stable, recreational facilities (such as tennis courts) and, above all, to the layout of the carriage roads and the approach to the house. Aesthetics outweighed convenience in these considerations. To the Cones and their contemporaries, how a house looked to approaching visitors and passers-by was as critical as the way the landscape looked from its windows. This involved not just the approach roads, but also how the house sat within the surrounding landscape. An architect, said one landscaping expert, "must make it appear as though the house could not be moved anywhere else without detriment to its own effect."[118]

The Cones and Epps spent many hours riding and walking over the estate and discussing the advantages of possible sites. In the January cold, with the leaves off the trees, they could read the landscape much better than if they had waited until lush springtime. They finally agreed on a spot about two miles south of the summit of Flat Top Mountain. At 4,000 feet elevation, the house would sit near the edge of a long and steep, though not precipitous, slope. This location afforded an excellent panorama to the south and east and furnished a good view of the landscape downslope from the manor. A small rise of land behind the house site gave room for the laundry building, gardens, and tennis court, and it provided gravity flow for a spring water system.

Anxious to begin construction, Cone ordered 250,000 feet of framing in March, and a month later consummated his building contracts. People around Blowing Rock confidently expected to hear hammer blows echoing from Flat Top come May. Lumber continued to arrive in June, but there was still no work on what promised to be "one of the most splendid structures in Western North Carolina."[119] Finally, in September, Fries' foreman, J.C. Parish, and a squad of carpenters began the long-awaited and much-anticipated construction. In short order, they built four cottages, each with four rooms. The Cones stayed in one of the cottages when they visited, as they often did, to monitor the progress of the work. The others furnished quarters for the horticulturist and grounds foremen Cone planned to hire later.[120]

Once the cottages were finished, the workmen erected a brick, nine-foot-high foundation for the manor house, laid 308 feet of sewer pipe, and began framing the first floor. By January 1900 they had finished framing the first floor and had started on the second. Blowing Rock merchant Will Palmer continued to cut and dress the lumber that went into the house. The *Semi-Weekly News* reported that in the six months prior to January, Palmer had cut 276,000 feet of lumber and had dressed 176,000 feet. As if that weren't impressive enough, the *News* added, he "has his big log splitter ready to cut 300,000 feet more."[121] By the end of the month, the local newspaper informed readers that the workmen were "doing some excellent work" and that the mansion "is being rapidly pushed along."[122]

While carpenters framed the manor house, other workmen began erecting a carriage house and stable, laundry house, and bowling alley. Cone constructed his carriage house, which stood a short distance northeast of the manor house, on three levels. The lower one served as a stable; the main floor housed carriages and harnesses, while the upper one was used for storage. In all, the carriage house and stable exceeded 3,000 square feet of floor space. The stable level included a drive-through shed, which made it convenient to feed horses at midday without unhitching. Architecturally, the building's symmetry and finish harmonized with the main house but did not replicate it. In all, the structure met prevailing tastes for properly designed outbuildings: substantial and well-built, attractive, and labor saving.[123]

The "ten pin" (bowling) alley, a rectangular, board-and-batten building of 864 square feet, was erected on the knoll behind the main house. In early 1900, Cone ordered 931 feet of Number 1 alley stock, a maple flooring that cost him $37.24. The first ball probably rumbled down the lane in August.[124]

Cone located the laundry house immediately behind the house. This building actually served several purposes. As the name implied, the 1,600-square-foot main floor contained a four-tub laundry sink, tables, and other equipment needed to wash the various linens, sheets, and clothing generated by a large country place. Underneath the laundry, in the half-excavated basement, the Cones built two rooms with very specific functions. In the sawdust-insulated ice house they stored food requiring refrigeration. Each winter workmen cut blocks of ice from frozen lakes, hauled them to the ice house, and buried them in sawdust. The location and insulation were so effective that, from one year to the next, farm hands had to remove the old ice before bringing in the new.[125]

The other half of the basement housed what the people around Blowing Rock must have considered one of the more impressive features of Flat Top Manor—a gaslight plant. There was nothing new about this technology, but few people in Watauga County had gas lights in their homes. In fact, it was still newsworthy when the Blackburn Hotel and the Town of Boone installed such lighting in 1908. The Cones ordered their lighting plant, at a cost of $129.60, from the St. Louis, Missouri, Eagle Generator Company, which specialized in automatic acetylene generators. The Model 212 that Cone bought produced gas when water dripped on carbide pellets. As demand increased, so did the volume of water, thus keeping gas pressure constant. The Cones bought their carbide in 1,070-pound drums. The estate's blacksmith operated the plant, performed such repairs as were necessary and, once a week, refilled the glass carbide jars.[126]

Lighting was not the only luxury in Flat Top Manor. As soon as the carpenters began finishing the main floor of the house, Cone installed a telephone system near the kitchen. This phone connected the house with the cottage where the Cones were living temporarily, and with the foremen's houses and apple barn. Telephone lines also ran to Holshouser's store in Blowing Rock. Like gaslight, telephones were well-known and widely used in turn-of-the-century America. The technology had been introduced at the Centennial Exposition in 1876, and by 1897 a telephone line linked Blowing Rock and Boone. When the system went in at Flat Top Manor, Holshouser's store already offered telephone service to more distant points. Cone's crank-type system, ordered from New York, enabled him to keep in touch with the work in progress on his estate and with his textile empire without leaving his house. Few of Cone's neighbors had telephones in their homes and, while the technology may have been familiar, local residents were impressed when they heard that this modern convenience had been installed in Flat Top Manor.[127]

The house also featured a wood-burning central heating system. Vents carried the warmth of the basement furnace throughout the house. High basement walls gave plenty of room for duct-work and stacking wood. This also provided head room, which made it more comfortable in winter for the tenant who lived downstairs and kept the furnace stoked. (Even though the Cones lived in Baltimore and New York during the colder weather months, they heated the house to prevent frozen water pipes and cracked plaster.) Thanks to an exterior basement door, wood could be delivered and ashes removed without disturbing the owners and guests or soiling the main living area.[128]

Local residents were equally impressed by the building materials being used. During the summer and fall of 1900, carpenters installed leaded glass windows over the main stairway and on the sidelights by the front door. They laid maple flooring and put up circular windows, ornately carved mantel-pieces, and decorative Ionic columns. Hundreds of balusters lined the first and second story porches and third floor deck.

At first glance, it might seem odd that such lavish appointments could be found in a house in the mountains of Appalachia. However, the region was not as isolated as many people today believe. In fact, a variety of sashes, doors, and other building supplies could be obtained quickly, cheaply, and, relatively speaking, close-by.

Thanks to new hydraulic presses, steam-powered shapers and scroll saws, and to a well-developed regional rail system that included Lenoir, little more than twenty miles from Blowing Rock, the Cones could obtain almost anything they desired. By 1900 the products of mass production reached even the most remote areas of North Carolina. If the world was not quite at the Cone's door step, it was only a wagon ride away.[129]

Hardware stores as convenient as Blowing Rock and Lenoir supplied many of the materials that went into Flat Top Manor, but the Cones also took advantage of their Greensboro connections, heavily patronizing the Cape Fear Manufacturing Company. Established in 1896 and located on Lewis Street in the city's south side, the company stocked doors, window frames, mantels, and stair work, and it turned out custom work on request. Cape Fear officials advertised their business as one of the largest manufacturers of building materials in the Greensboro area, and boasted, "If you are going to build anything from a hen house to a mansion come to see us. We can fix you up and the price will be right."[130]

The Cone brothers liked to patronize this company. When they built substantial homes on Summit Avenue for their mill supervisors and managers, they bought from Cape Fear. Likewise, the materials that went into the houses in Proximity Village came from the same source.[131]

Nothing purchased from Cape Fear generated more interest among neighbors than the maple flooring that went into the manor. When a rail-car load of the 2-1/4" flooring arrived in Lenoir, the newspaper reported that it had "come all the way from Michigan," was "beautifully worked" and destined for Moses Cones' "fine house at Blowing Rock."[132]

While Parish and his carpenters built most of the manor, J.R. Rich and Son, also of Greensboro, plumbed the house, and Dennis Hall of High Point, North Carolina, plastered it. Subcontracting specialty and skilled jobs like these was a common practice at the time. Rich's two plumbers each worked six days a week for fifteen dollars a day.[133]

By the time Blowing Rock's summer crowd began to depart in the fall of 1900, Flat Top Manor was taking on its final appearance. Its straight lines, flat surfaces, balance, and symmetry reflected the colonial revival style. The portico gave formality to the entrance and visually divided the mass of the house into two wings. Window treatments and balusters on each floor corresponded to those on the other. Design elements matched along the horizonal, as well as the vertical, axis. Elements to the right of the entrance corresponded to those on the left, from the chimneys, to the configuration of the rooms on each floor, to the very basement. The extensive use of custom-cut plate glass and large paired windows not only gave light and views from inside, but reflected light and thereby contributed to the aesthetic quality of the structure. The porte-cochere on the west gave protection from rain and provided a properly dignified point of arrival and departure for carriage and surrey passengers.

In the tradition of country houses, Flat Top Manor had extensive porches and balconies. These extended the full length of the house and wrapped around the sides and back. They not only contributed to the appearance of the house, but became the focus of domestic life and informal social intercourse—a place to sit and enjoy fresh air and views of distant ridges and mountains, and to converse and play bridge with family members and close friends. The porches also provided a buffer between nature and the home's more private interior.

With the exception of interior painting, Flat Top Manor was completed by February 1901. The "elegant mansion," as the *Watauga Democrat* described it, had cost between $60,000 and $75,000. Given its size and luxuries, local residents and visitors probably did not question the veracity of that estimate. No house around town quite compared with Flat Top.[134]

Neither did any estate in western North Carolina quite measure up to the size, landscaping, and farms that Cone was developing at Flat Top—except, of course, Biltmore. While workmen were busily erecting the big house, other crews toiled away, cutting down trees, burning brush, building and landscaping roads, and planting orchards and gardens. Cone initially hired J.A. Underdown to take bids for the land clearing that he initiated in 1897. Underdown owned Caldwell Nurseries, where Cone bought much of his nursery stock. Apparently Underdown had no desire to give up his nursery business and work for Cone full-time, but his son and business partner, twenty-three-year-old Edward, became a foreman at Flat Top in 1899.

Although the younger Underdown knew a great deal about orchards and gardening, he lacked the high level of training that Cone desired. Just as Pinchot did with progressive forestry at Biltmore, Flat Top Orchards were to serve as an experiment and a demonstration in what could be achieved through scientifically practiced horticulture and stock farming. Publisher Tompkins suggested that Cone keep records of his farming activities. These, he said, might serve as a "standard work" on pomology in western North Carolina. This kind of careful management required a person with proper training and credentials. In the fall of 1899, he found just such a person in thirty-year-old New Jersey native Freeman L. Mulford.[135]

With Mulford as manager, the younger Underdown supervised one group of laborers; Jefferson Davis Brown headed up another. Brown was a Blowing Rock farmer who had sold his place to the Cones. Whether he had bartered a job in exchange for selling his land is not known, but he went to work on the estate about 1899.

Although Cone had hired hands to begin the work on his estate, he soon adopted a labor system that resembled the one used in his mill villages in Greensboro. In time, he recruited and negotiated signed agreements with some thirty tenants. These families lived rent-free in small frame houses that Cone began to erect in 1897. Each received pasturage for one cow, a half-acre garden plot, and, typically, seven-and-a-half cents per hour for his labor. In return, the tenant agreed "to give his entire time to the Work of M.H.C. [Moses H. Cone] if not Providential [sic] hindred [sic]," and further, "to give possession of the House he Now lives in if he has a cause to Stop Work during the Year."

The tenants also understood that they would behave in a manner approved by the Cones or face dismissal.[136]

Cone provided shelter and paid a small wage. In return, employees worked hard and followed the boss's rules. Those who questioned that system or failed to act in the approved way—whether talking to a union representative, showing a fondness for booze, or demonstrating questionable morals—lost their jobs, and they and their family were evicted from their houses. More independent and high-spirited factory and farm hands may have bridled at such a system of dependency, but most acquiesced. Given the options of unemployment and homelessness, and considering the sharecropping and debt peonage that existed in large parts of the South, it is little wonder that they did. The security of a home and the steady, if meager, wages of Cone's mill and estate exerted an attraction too powerful for many to resist.

By the fall of 1899, Cone had seventeen hands in his employ. He also had retained the services of J.M. Wolfe, a Greensboro contractor, to build carriage roads. Carefully laid out and landscaped roads were a vital part of any country place. At Biltmore, Olmsted had laid out and directed the construction of Vanderbilt's roads. He cut down all "undesirable" trees along his 18-foot wide lanes and interspersed those that he kept, including hickories, sourwoods, chestnuts, and beech, with transplanted rhododendron, azaleas, and other flowering plants. By selective clearing and artful planting, Olmsted created a landscape that gave the illusion of being uncontrived and natural. Cone had no Olmsted in his employ, but he tried to copy at Flat Top what America's premier landscape architect had done at Biltmore.[137]

Whether Cone personally and singlehandedly laid out all the roads on Flat Top is unknown. Clearly, it was not Mulford, because Cone did not hire him until road construction was well underway. It seems likely that Moses, Bertha, and architect Epps determined the routing at the time they chose the site for their house in January 1899. This would have been the most logical approach. Typically, country place owners sited their house and the other parts of the estate only after carefully considering and mapping the location of roads and paths. No element of an estate was planned without consideration for all the other elements. The house and gardens, roads, lakes, pastures, and orchards represented a single composition. Each had to be evaluated for its relationship and impact on the other.

It is also likely that Wolfe influenced the design. He was a man who, said a Lenoir newspaper reporter, "knows his business." Others apparently thought so, too. Just months before taking on the job at Flat Top, Wolfe had completed a building contract in England. He also possessed a diverse and odd combination of talents that hinted at artistic sensitivity. Besides being a contractor, he later became a U.S. Commissioner in Greensboro and "poet laureate" of Guilford County.[138]

By May 1899, Wolfe and a sizeable force were at work in Blowing Rock, under the watchful eyes of Moses and Bertha, who arrived late in the month to spend a few weeks. Work progressed rapidly despite the steep and rocky terrain, which sometimes required the use of dynamite to excavate. By summer's end, Wolfe had completed nearly 22 miles of carriage roads. Made mostly of hard-packed dirt surfaces, these lanes were 12 to 15 feet in width, sufficiently broad to permit surreys travelling in opposite directions to pass. Some of the carefully graded lanes snaked their way along the steep slopes in a series of switchbacks. These had several purposes. They helped to keep grades at no more than five percent, which made riding and hiking more pleasurable. Gentler slopes also made it easier to haul apples, farm produce, and equipment. In addition, they were intended to reduce washouts that would result from steeper slopes.[139]

Some, such as the Duncan Road, took their names from estate workers and supervisors. Others designated former property owners. This included the Stringfellow Road, which was named for W.W. and Suzie Stringfellow, who lived just below the Cones at Chetola. Moses and Bertha had a good reason to honor their neighbors—the Stringfellows sold 140 acres to them for "a valuable consideration."[140]

While carriage roads served an important practical function, their aesthetic quality played the dominant role in their design and layout. Cone planted double rows of sugar and scarlet maples near the estate entrance at Blowing Rock, set out thousands of rhododendron, and planted groves of balsams. He consciously and carefully controlled the landscape to reveal views in sequence and to provide color and texture from season to season. In spring, apple blossoms and wildflowers delighted riders on the estate. In early summer, catawba rhododendron added their pinks and purple, while in July and August white rhododendron blossomed in profusion. Fall displays included the bright red berries of dogwood, ripe red apples, and the varied hues of the estates' abundant hardwoods changing from green to yellow, gold, red, and russet. This procession of colorful displays was carefully orchestrated. Like other elements of the estate, Cone selected plants not so much for their individual charm, but for their contribution to the total picture he desired. He also considered how the landscape would look in sunlight and in shadow, in morning and in afternoon, and from season to season.

This attention to detail and composition was equally apparent in the way Cone arranged his views sequentially. Riders wound their way through tree-lined and colorful corridors to a series of "lookouts." Good design demanded that each important view be developed as a pictorial composition, separate from, yet harmonious with, the whole. Road segments passed through formally planted avenues of trees, skirted orchards and pastures, and entered deep woods, then suddenly emerged at carefully constructed lookouts that revealed distant peaks.[141]

Casual visitors may not have noticed the detailed planning that Cone had put into his roads, but they liked what they saw. A newspaper reporter who was one of the first to sample the product of Cone's and Wolfe's design and labor described the roads as "laid out with great skill." They "afford grand mountain views at every turn. The roads are built without regard to cost and a team can trot either way over them. Some of the finest views east of the Rocky Mountains can be had from these drives." He glowingly concluded, "Everyone visiting Blowing Rock should avail themselves of the opportunity to go over these roads." Other visitors were equally impressed. Before long, postcards depicted the carriage roads at Flat Top.[142]

Impressive though they were, roads represented only one of Flat Top's notable landscape features. Cone also built two lakes: Trout Lake, below Rich Mountain at Flannery Fork Road, and Bass Lake, located between Flat Top Manor and the village. At 15 acres, Trout Lake was the smaller. As the name suggests, Cone regularly stocked it with up to 8,000 rainbow trout. He also stocked Bass Lake, which was 21 acres in size and more than 30 feet deep, with black bass. He built a boathouse by the northern shore, though he rarely launched the several boats he kept inside. Like European aristocracy of old, he did not extend fishing or, for that matter, hunting privileges to the public or to his tenants, except when the tenants fished to supply the table at Flat Top Manor.[143]

As was true with his carriage roads, Cone's lakes served an aesthetic, not simply a recreational or practical, purpose. In the 1893 Columbian Exposition at Chicago, Olmsted had demonstrated how a great reflecting lagoon could dramatize and unify buildings. On a lesser scale, he used Bass Lake at Biltmore Estate to show how a small body of water could be used to accent the setting of a great country place. Once again, Cone had followed the Biltmore lead. He planted hydrangea bushes around his Bass Lake. Fragrant water lilies, with their showy blossoms, grew in the shallows, while ducks added their own color and life to the scene. Just above the lake he built a small heart-shaped pool and planted flowers around it. Grassy areas were kept neatly mowed and bushes regularly pruned.

Cone prohibited swimming. This may have been because, like hunting and fishing, he reserved such privileges for himself and his guests. Others said this was because Bertha, as a child, had been aboard a ship that sank in the Atlantic and, ever since, had feared the water. In any case, those who dared to swim in Bass or Trout Lakes risked a stern Cone rebuke.[144]

For visitors entering the estate from Blowing Rock, as most did, Bass Lake provided an excellent reflective foreground for viewing Flat Top Manor, which stood sentinel-like nearly 1,000 feet above the lake. Likewise, from the porch of the manor, the flat, uniform surface of the lake provided a visual focal point and unified the landscape. The nearby rows of maple trees, the hydrangeas, water lilies, and manicured lawn each contributed to the visual effect and provided texture and color that the water mirrored. Thanks to its thoughtful design and careful landscaping, Bass Lake soon became know as "one of the picture places of the mountains."[145]

Deer parks added another dimension to the estate's landscape. Just as Vanderbilt and Olmsted did at Biltmore, Cone constructed enclosures to house deer. He built the first in 1899 above Bass Lake near the carriage road. Occupying fifteen acres and surrounded by a wire fence, the park contained about twenty deer that in time became very tame. In 1908, Cone added a 200-acre deer park to the side of Rich Mountain above Trout Lake. This one he enclosed with a paling fence.[146]

To complement the impressive vistas from the summit of Rich Mountain, Cone built a walled, grassy observation platform. On top of neighboring Flat Top Mountain he constructed a tower. Made of chestnut and costing the then significant sum of $53.75 (this included clean-up), the Flat Top tower gave a 360-degree view that was as spectacular as any around.[147]

Landscaping close to the manor house took on a special significance. While Cone did not replicate the elaborate formal gardens that framed the chateau at Biltmore, he did plant flower and vegetable gardens that were large enough to require four men to tend. He also installed a water fountain and, to facilitate watering the plants, hydrants. Below the carriage house and stable he planted a rose garden. Flower gardens not only added seasonal beauty out-of-doors, but provided a continuous supply of blooms to grace the hallways and rooms of the house.

Vegetables were deemed an absolute necessity for those desiring country place luxury. Among the scores of vegetables grown and served at Flat Top Manor were asparagus, peas, radishes, lettuce, corn, cabbage, spinach, cauliflower, Brussels sprouts, tomatoes, and celery. The Cones also enjoyed strawberries and raspberries, as well as pears, peaches, plums, nectarines, cherries, chestnuts and walnuts and, of course, lots of apples.[148]

A five-acre lawn surrounded the house. One of the first pieces of equipment Cone had transported from Lenoir was a mowing machine. By the turn of the century manicured lawns had become a fetish. According to E.P. Powell, author of the 1904 work, *The Country Home*, "Your handsome lawn means that you can think handsomely; your clean orchards and gardens mean that you can feel purely."[149]

While such meticulous landscaping provided the family with personal enjoyment, dazzled visitors and, in the process, elevated the Cones' social status, Flat Top married utility with beauty. Scientific apple growing allowed Cone to put his wealth to work for the public good and make a profit on his labor and investment. Even if he did not realize $25,000 per year from apples, as some speculated, he wanted to break-even. If he could do that, he told his tenants, he would be satisfied.[150]

Cone planted more than 32,000 apple trees in four orchards. As already noted, Green Park was about two miles removed from the main estate, by the Blowing Rock to Lenoir Turnpike. China Orchard received its unusual name because it lay on "the other side of the world." In fact, China was only as far away as the steep slope located on the south side of Yonahlossee Turnpike (now U.S. Highway 221). Flat Top Orchard spread downslope from the manor house to near Bass Lake. Anyone calling on the Cones or sitting on their porch looked directly down on this more than eighty-acre orchard. The smallest orchard, twenty-five-acre Saw Mill Place, occupied the slopes above Chetola and north of Bass Lake. Altogether Cone's orchards embraced perhaps three hundred acres.[151]

Consistent with good horticultural practice, Cone planted his trees about thirty-five feet apart, interspersing rows of permanent trees with fillers. While some growers allowed livestock to graze their orchards, tenants mowed the Cone groves. This is hardly surprising, given the emphasis on aesthetics at Flat Top.[152]

Planting and maintaining orchards demanded a relentless cycle of chores. In winter, Mulford directed planting and transplanting operations. Pruning commenced in February and continued until May. During the growing season, tenants sprayed each tree two to three times with Dry Bordeaux or other fungicides. They also hoed under each tree two to three times. The busiest season came in September and October when the crop matured. All tenants and, when the harvest was good, their wives and children pitched in during fall. In exceptional years, Mulford and Underdown hired extra hands to pick and pack apples.[153]

Workers hauled the apples to five barns—or apple houses, as the tenants often called them—which were strategically located in the orchards. The main apple barn, which still stands at Saw Mill Place, totaled more than 7,000 square feet, including its basement, main floor, and loft. Here the tenants graded the apples as firsts, seconds, or culls, and packed them for shipment. They exercised great care in packing the fruit, as bruised apples spoiled more easily and brought less at market.

Not all apples sold immediately. To keep those in storage chilled, Cone kept large barrels of cool spring water inside the fruit barns and insulated the crop with wood shavings. He also floored his main barn, no doubt to discourage mice and rats.[154]

True to his goal of providing a demonstration in applied pomology, Cone had Mulford plant some seventy-five varieties, including many that are now considered rare. His commercial crop he restricted to sixteen varieties, among them Albemarle Pippin, York Imperial, and

Virginia Beauty. He also grew large quantities of Ben Davis apples. In all cases, he tried to select cultivars best suited for the slope and exposure of his orchards.[155]

While the records of farm income are too incomplete to permit a thorough analysis, Flat Top Orchards probably netted Cone a small profit. Moses grew apples until his death in 1908, and Bertha carried on until she died nearly four decades later. It is unlikely that they would have kept the orchards had they operated at a loss. They certainly scaled back their livestock farm once it proved unprofitable, even though at first, this rivaled apple growing in importance.

Cone entered the livestock business with ample motivation and high hopes. He had watched Vanderbilt's stock farm grow to include hundreds of head of cattle, sheep, and hogs, as well as large numbers of chickens and other fowl. Vanderbilt had also developed a reputation for breeding prize-winning stock. A proper country place, by definition, featured independent, self-sufficient living, and no place could have that without a variety of stock.

By the fall of 1899, Blowing Rock's biggest farmer had turned 400 acres of Flat Top and Rich Mountains into prime grazing land. He planted fescue, blue grass, and clover, erected fences, and set about buying his stock. Within a few months he had amassed a cattle herd of ninety-nine head and had purchased the first of what would grow to be nearly three hundred Shropshire sheep. He also added two horses and an ox for work stock. Below the carriage house Cone built a hennery, where he kept brown leghorns and other breeds. He also raised and sold turkeys.[156]

By 1902, the *Greensboro Patriot* reported that Cone took "particular pride" in his cattle and that he was "developing some of the finest beef cattle ever grown in the state." This was no mean accomplishment, considering that Cone's experience with farming was limited to his childhood years, when his father and uncle farmed at Jonesborough. As in so many endeavors, Cone taught himself much of what he knew. He subscribed to various farm magazines and acquired technical reports, and took advantage of societies and organizations that possessed and shared the information he needed. Indeed, the *Patriot* noted that Cone was the only North Carolina member of the American Hereford Cattle Breeders' Association. Despite his personal commitment and the newspaper's glowing pronouncement, Cone did have one complaint about raising cattle: he paid more for fodder than he received at market. Given his business acumen, it is not surprising that Cone ultimately deemphasized cattle breeding.[157]

He and Bertha continued to raise, shear, and sell sheep. With the vicissitudes of market prices, cattle and sheep may not have generated a consistent profit, but they always provided a source of fresh meat for the family.

Beyond his poor return on cattle, Cone faced many vexations in sculpting his estate. For one, the carriage roads that touted contractor J.M. Wolfe built looked wonderful, but they washed and rutted horribly after heavy rains. In a dispute that erupted over this issue, Cone bought much of Wolfe's equipment, including his road scraper, then used his own crews to make and modify roads. In 1901 and 1902, Cone contracted with D.D. Gaston and T.H. Hughes of Cherokee, North Carolina, for additional construction work. He also loaned the contractors $2,000. When they defaulted, Cone took possession of a large quantity of scrapers, wagons, hand tools, drills, and pumps, as well as a road roller and thirteen mules. Whether by accident or design, Cone now had the equipment he needed to make and repair roads with his own crews.[158]

Cone did not always win his legal skirmishes. When he contested the work being done on Bass Lake dam, he and H.C. Coffey, the builder, posted bonds of $2,500 and agreed to binding arbitration. Coffey had sold to Cone the tract of land that included the Bass Lake site and, being from Blowing Rock, may have felt that he had an edge in the proceedings. On the other hand, Cone was buying lumber and supplies from at least two of the four arbitrators, W.J. Palmer of Blowing Rock, and J.M. Bernhardt of Lenoir. He probably figured that this gave him an advantage. In the end, Coffey was awarded more than $500 and all contracts between him and Cone were annulled. The newspaper report of the case noted that, "We hear that Mr. Coffey is very well pleased with the result."[159]

Other challenges were not so public and, individually, not terribly significant. But taken together they show that running a well-ordered country place required patience and perseverance. For instance, rabbits ate the saplings in the orchards. Mulford wrote in his diary that he set traps on January 30, 1900. Two days later he lamented, "Not making much progress with the rabbits." Later that year, Mulford reported two mules sick with distemper and three cows dead from "milk poison."

Even healthy animals could be a nuisance. One cow "has taken to being unruly again, goes over stake fences or anything else." Neighbors' hogs got loose and damaged China Orchard.[160]

The roaming dogs that attacked and killed sheep were a recurring concern. Local newspapers advocated poisoning canines to eliminate the problem. "One good sheep is easily worth all the dogs in the community," said one; "a liberal use" of strychnine would remedy the problem, said another.[161]

Foxes also frequented the estate, causing Cone concern. Even though he usually forbade hunting, he made exceptions for them. In 1904 he instructed foreman J.D. Brown, "Kill off foxes or have it done. No objection to hunters after foxes."[162]

Weather, as always, helped to produce bumper apple crops or, in some years, virtually no crop at all. When the harvest was exceptionally bountiful, Mulford and Underdown scoured the countryside for extra hands to help with picking. They also pushed their laborers to gather the apples before frost. A visitor in mid-October wrote that with a third of the crop still in the field and a heavy frost expected any night, apple picking, "has now risen to a feverish pitch." Relatively speaking, a shortage of hands and hurrying to beat the frost were good problems to have. Some years, late spring and early summer cold snaps and inordinately dry or wet weather devastated the crop, so that tenant labor was more than sufficient to do the picking.[163]

Cone made sure that his tenants kept the farm, its landscaping, and carriage roads in top condition. "It was all kept so beautifully," said one tenant.

> All the leaves were taken out of the ditches in the fall. . .all the trees were properly trimmed; anything that was dead was taken out. All the fences were kept in perfect repair. Everything was just . . . You just can't believe how pretty it was. The grass was all kept mowed, and most of this was done by hand.[164]

Cone had developed a showplace of the mountains and he intended to keep it that way. He let admiring visitors ride the carriage roads and picnic on the summit of his mountains. The estate became a popular destination for Blowing Rock's seasonal residents. They came to enjoy the apple blossoms and wildflowers in spring, the mountain laurel and rhododendron in early and mid-summer, and the red and yellow apples and the brilliant leaves in the fall. Some thought the views from Flat

Top were unmatched, even by Biltmore. As D.A. Tompkins said in the *Greensboro Patriot*, "The altitude [4,500'] of Mr. Cone's development is more than twice that of the Vanderbilt undertaking near Asheville and his landscape [panoramas and long vistas] from three to five times as extensive." John Preston Arthur styled Cone's estate "one of the picture places of the mountains," and "second only to that of George W. Vanderbilt" at Asheville.[165]

Whether the scenery at Flat Top surpassed or came in second to Biltmore, Cone had to have been pleased by such comparisons. He had tried to model his estate after Vanderbilt's, and many knowledgeable people pronounced him successful. It was as important to Cone to be compared to Vanderbilt as it was for Biltmore's famous owner to be likened to European royalty. Each took his cues from his social superiors. In doing so, both sought to elevate their own status. With the completion of his Blowing Rock estate, Cone had literally made it to the summit—socially, aesthetically, and financially. No doubt, he greatly enjoyed the view from the top.

CHAPTER 4
EVEN THEIR BEDS WERE GOLD

A s impressive as the exterior of their home was, the Cones wanted the finish and furnishings inside to be even more so. Here they entertained friends and business associates and, in the process, revealed their personal tastes and values more completely and candidly than they did to the outside world. Anyone could drive a carriage past Flat Top Manor, but only those who possessed social standing gained admission to the manor's interior. These people of means were the ones the Cones esteemed and wanted to dazzle most.[166]

In the Victorian era, homes and their interiors embodied ideals, not just styles. Furnishings and decor served as signs and symbols that contemporaries could read as completely and unambiguously as a book. The manor's interior represented culture in a tangible form, and the Cones, like other families of the time, took pains to ensure that their possessions sent the signals that were appropriate to their social class. At Flat Top the intended message was straightforward and unmistakable: this was the home of a modern but rooted, refined, and thoroughly American family.[167]

From the beginning to the conclusion of their visit, favored callers received a carefully orchestrated set of visual and behavioral cues. Disembarking their carriage at the porte-cochere, they crossed the broad, brown-painted porch, past fashionable rattan chairs and lounges to the front door. To announce themselves, they tapped the ring on a shining, brass American eagle knocker that was fastened to the front door. Visitors could not fail to note the obvious symbolism. Though a seemingly small act, knocking on the manor door initiated contact with the home's occupants, and it involved touching a quintessential American image. By comparison, at Biltmore, Vanderbilt's guests were greeted by a highly polished brass lion's head, which conveyed the impression of power and prestige that estate's owner sought. Though their messages differed, the Cones and Vanderbilt both employed symbolism to inform their guests. At Flat Top, the American eagle linked the Cones with colonial America and subtly but powerfully reinforced the manor's thoroughly colonial revival facade.[168]

In keeping with the mythical tradition of the aristocratic and slaveholding Old South, a black butler, replete with buttoned white jacket, dark trousers, and highly polished shoes, always answered the door. If he failed to recognize the visitor, he might inquire, "What name, if you please, ma'am [or sir]?" He would then proceed to the library or upstairs living hall and announce the caller to Bertha or Moses.[169]

Waiting visitors may have been seated in the wide central hallway that separated the parlor and library. At the end of the hall, opposite the front door, a small but formal sitting room was arranged around a red-brick hearth, with ornate mantel. This room was not intended for regular use or extended social intercourse. Callers were either invited into other parts of the house or soon departed. The sitting room's red horsehair sofa and chairs were hard and prickly, but they possessed a satin sheen that was considered formal and that Victorians prized. A huge bronze vase, four to five feet tall, and large Oriental rug gave the space an international flavor and helped to mark the boundary of this open room.[170]

Matching Sheraton card tables flanked the sides of the main hall. With their round, hinged tops folded in the upright position, they supported and provided a backdrop for vases of flame colored gladioluses and wildflowers.[171]

A hallstand or nearby table very likely held a silver tray for receiving calling cards. The practice of leaving cards, well established in America by the 1850s, persisted into the twentieth century and no doubt took place at Flat Top Manor in the early 1900s. Customarily carried on by women, this ritual helped establish, maintain, and sever relationships. Because of its social importance, the practice was governed by formal and scrupulously observed rules. For example, cards were left only at certain times—usually from 3 to 5 p.m. Women left a card for the mistress and each of the daughters in the household. They also left their husband's card for the master of the house. Proper ladies, married or single, never left cards for bachelors. To violate the rules, warned one etiquette advisor, "would result in the probable loss of desired acquaintanceships, or the risk of being characterized as ill-bred."[172]

Halls served as a transitional zone between the public exterior and the more private rooms on the interior. Some visitors probably left cards, but never saw more of Flat Top Manor than the hall. Still, they could readily comprehend the colonial associations and images of high style that the Cones projected. This was not simply because of the colonial tables and other furnishings. To be sure, hall furnishings mattered greatly, but the entrance conveyed other impressions. To Bertha's grandnieces, who as children spent many summers at Flat Top, "The general look of the house when you walked in was of glittering cleanliness—the shiny waxed floors that showed around the edges of the rugs, and the brass everywhere just shining, everything just immaculate, as clean as the mountain air was." From the door hardware, to the fender by the hall fireplace, to the brass gasoliers that hung from the ceiling, there was certainly no shortage of gleaming things. Even the shovel, poker, and tongs that stood beside the fireplace were polished.[173]

Because Flat Top Manor was a summer home and had a central heating system, the fireplace, like others throughout the house, was seldom used. Rather, framed by a pair of Ionic columns, it provided a focal point for the entry and lent an air of culture, domestic comfort, and family togetherness. Though the Cones never passed a winter's evening warming themselves by a crackling fire in this hearth, it was the suggestion of comfort and family unity that counted. The prominence of a hearth in so visible a location indicates the importance that the Cones attached to its symbolism.[174]

The facade of culture and comfort carried over to the parlor and library, located, respectively, to the left and right of the entrance. Of the two, the parlor was by far the more formal, reserved for receptions and teas for governors, for business and social elites, and for such somber ceremonies as funeral eulogies and services. This was where the Cones, like others of their generation, put on their best public face. Indicative of this, the furnishings in the manor parlor featured a French sofa, mahogany book cases, and a grand piano. Although hardly colonial, French furniture conveyed an ambience of high style. France had long been considered the center of courtly design, and having such furnishings inherently communicated refinement and good taste. Whether the Cones' greenish-gray sofa was, in fact, European made, or whether its design precisely matched French styles mattered very little. Its pastel upholstery and overall effect were French and, therefore, resonated with high style. The books, in their free-standing cases with diamond patterned glass doors, reinforced this impression of refinement, as did the ebony Steinway piano, with its massive fluted legs.[175]

Ostensibly, the library was the room where Moses and Bertha read and entertained, although, in fact, they usually did this in the living hall upstairs or in their bedroom. They used the library to receive and converse with acquaintances and visitors who were closer to the family than those who were greeted in the parlor. The room's furnishings included a large and a small rug, a mahogany pedestal center table, a small sofa and matching chairs, and built-in book cases that ran nearly the length of two of the room's four walls. On top of the mantel sat a girandole, or branched candleholder, while the tops of the bookcases were lined with Oriental art objects, including jars, vases, and bronze Buddhas. Other art, including a Picasso drawing, hung from the room's picture rails.[176]

Though the objects differed from those in the parlor, they contributed their own ambiance of culture and hinted at an educational level that exceeded Moses' and Bertha's actual attainment. While Bertha may have attended finishing school, neither she nor Moses was college-educated. This was not unusual for the time. A relatively small percentage of women attended college during the 1870s, when Bertha would have completed secondary school. Also, many captains of industry, like Cone, were hardly men of letters. They prospered because of their considerable entrepreneurial skills and persistence, not because they were highly or formally trained. While success in business and wealth gave them an undeniable measure of status, these did not confer the aura of gentility that country place owners desired. Books and art objects helped do that. By design and decor, the Cones assured that their library placed them in a positive light. In it, and largely throughout the downstairs rooms, they created a scene, a stage set. Objects functioned as props that made it easy for visitors to imagine the Cones seated at the center table enjoying scholarly pursuits, while surrounded by an array of art.[177]

The display of Oriental materials was not confined to the library. Many of the rugs that served as hallway runners and that helped provide focal points for rooms and major pieces of furniture were Oriental. The Cones probably collected most of these, and their scroll art, ceramics, and bronzes, during a lengthy world tour that began in 1906 and included travels in India, China, Japan, and other Eastern countries. Displaying such objects in a colonial revival home was not as aesthetically inconsistent and contradictory as it might seem. On the contrary, to antique collectors and interior designers of the day, "Good hand-loom Oriental rugs of satisfactory vegetable dyes, fit any date and go with any style of furniture; and this whether the rugs are old or of modern make."[178] The same principles applied to other art objects. The lines, quality, and artistic impression were what mattered. Whether the object came from India or Japan was irrelevant. Indeed, few people differentiated Oriental cultures and art. An ornate Indian incense container fit as comfortably in Flat Top Manor as a marble Buddha from Japan.

Despite the occasional pieces of French furniture, Oriental art and floor coverings, visitors could not mistake the manor's colonial ambience. White paint, wooden floors, and mahogany furniture were defining elements of the colonial, and Flat Top Manor had all three. Even though the walls were painted an eggshell or antique white, and although runners and carpets were scattered throughout, the overwhelming impression was of bright walls and shining wood floors. Similarly, while some of the antique and reproduction furniture may have blended designs from both the eighteenth and nineteenth centuries, the effect was colonial, as Americans of the period understood it. Usually persnickety Victorians did not make sharp distinctions when it came to things colonial.[179]

Architectural details and hardware helped to define the home's interior just as much as the individual items that occupied its rooms. At Flat Top Manor, the walls were not merely an off-white color but, in the colonial tradition, they were as unrelentingly symmetrical as the house's exterior. Paneled wainscoting, picture rails, and cornices effectively divided the walls into thirds. Mantels were adorned with Ionic columns and decorated with egg-and-dart and ribbon and wreath motifs, and with friezes depicting classical scenes. The main stairway featured paneled colonial newels and turned balusters, and was lighted by a large, leaded glass Palladian window, a hallmark of colonial design.

Equally in the colonial tradition, main floor window treatments consisted of white sheer curtains, tied back. Opaque pull shades provided privacy in the evenings, but remained inconspicuously rolled and out of sight during the day. Flat Top Manor had none of the elaborate wallpaper and heavy drapes found in many Victorian homes. Nor was it cluttered. As true colonial revivalists, the Cones rejected the overstuffed and ornate furniture that was popular throughout much of the mid and late nineteenth century and refused to crowd their homes with furniture. If not stark, the rooms at Flat Top Manor were at least spare.[180]

The spatial arrangement of rooms also revealed the colonial aesthetic and a high degree of formality. For example, each room had a single purpose. The Cones ate in the dining room and entertained formally either in the parlor or library, according to the occasion and the social standing of their guests. Unlike many of their contemporaries, the Cones had no all-purpose living room.

Other rooms were similarly specialized. The billiard room, located next to the parlor but accessible only from the stairs hall, was dedicated exclusively to games and light entertainment. The billiard table, a Brunswick-Balke-Collinder "Monarch," sat parallel with the fireplace and occupied the center of the room. Cues stood upright against one wall, while fourteen woven-bottom chairs lined two other walls. Other than a clock on the mantel and a Victrola, probably added after 1908, the billiard room had no other furniture. It was designed, furnished, and used for a single purpose.[181]

Double pocket doors allowed the Cones to limit access to each room. In addition, this feature allowed them to slide the doors into the walls and out of sight, so that they did not intrude visually upon the room and interfere with its decoration. When closed, the doors gave complete privacy. Indicative of the value placed on formality, the parlor, the manor's most formal room, had only one access. Also, the sliding doors that separated the library and dining room usually stayed closed, thus creating two distinct rooms.

When entertaining a very large number of guests, the Cones no doubt opened the doors that separated the library and dining room. With the parlor doors also open, as they usually were, this united three of the four front rooms and created an open area more than 65 feet in length.

In a sense, the precise order of their home reflected the precision and social distinctions that the Cones expected in their larger personal universe. They believed that as wealthy people they were obliged to act in established ways, no less than mill hands and tenants followed rules that were prescribed for them. Just as people lived by regulated relationships, material things demanded order. By carefully structuring and arranging their home, as well as their personal relationships, the Cones gained—and communicated to others—a feeling of stability and permanence. This was especially important to them, since they were nouveau riche, not scions of an old, aristocratic family.[182]

The blend of formality, colonial association, high style, and good manners was most evident in the Cone dining room. In all cultures and societies eating is invested with meaning. The act itself promotes bonding and is used to initiate and maintain relationships. What is consumed also reveals tradition and values. Champagne celebrations, birthday cakes, and unleavened bread are examples of these continuing associations and food customs. For Victorians, meals served as the focal point for social intercourse, and Moses and Bertha hosted many dinner parties. Though these hardly rivaled the lavish affairs put on by the Astors and Rockefellers, the always proper Cones and their guests meticulously observed the complex rituals that governed dining.[183]

At the turn of the century, dinner guests were expected to arrive on time. At Flat Top, that usually meant at 1 p.m. The men customarily wore coats and ties, while the women dressed in fashionably long dresses with long sleeves. To expose arms or legs, especially at the dinner table, would have violated a basic rule of good manners. In addition, Bertha, in her role as hostess, was probably careful to wear subdued tones so as not to upstage any of her guests. When it was time to eat, the butler entered the library or parlor and quietly announced dinner or, better yet, simply caught Bertha's eye and bowed.[184]

Guests may have noticed the claw-and-ball feet of the Cones' Centennial reproduction Chippendale table, but they could not see the many leaves that enabled the table to be extended to a full fifteen-foot length. This was because a spotless white damask table cloth covered the table and hung well over the sides. Each place setting included a large, white damask napkin, monogrammed with a "C." These were typically folded, although for some occasions they may have enclosed a large slice of bread. The center piece consisted of flowers that were placed in a large, low-rimmed silver bowl, which sat on an embroidered runner.[185]

The silver service for each place included a number of forks and knives, all arrayed in precise order. For breakfast and informal suppers, the Cones used simple, oval pattern silver. For dinner, they brought out their best—a floral pattern repoussé which Moses' brother Sol had given them as a wedding present. As the occasion warranted, the Cones also employed a variety of specialized silver pieces, including butter picks, fruit knives, and fish servers.[186]

The Cones owned separate sets of china which they alternated according to the meal. At dinner they used a white, gilt-rimmed porcelain made by Charles Field Haviland at Limoges, France. Although readily available through Montgomery Ward, Haviland china was acknowledged to be quality made and desirable. The Cones also owned a complete set of Haviland china fish plates. Crystal goblets or cut glass—the Cones had both—complemented the china and completed the setting.[187]

Meals were conducted with a dignity and formality that matched the table setting. The butler, assisted as needed by other male servants, served each course. In the social pecking order of domestic workers, males were accorded higher status and, therefore, not only greeted callers, but also performed all of the more visible tasks. Each course was brought out separately, or " à la Russe" (the Russian style). This reduced the passing of food from one diner to the next and left room on the table for the elaborate place settings and flowers.[188]

Dinners at Flat Top began with a fruit serving; then came soup. This was followed by the main course (lamb was a favorite) and as many as ten vegetables, including stewed tomatoes, mashed potatoes, corn (off the cob), carrots (sliced, lightly cooked, and served in butter), lima beans, and eggplant. Salads and dessert followed the main course. Home baked bread was usually on the table before the diners took their seats and, thus, did not constitute a separate course. Altogether, manor fare was distinctly country, and the Cones probably took pride in knowing that most of what they served came from their own estate.[189]

There was nothing country or bucolic about the etiquette and behavior that the Cones and their guests displayed. Diners ate slowly, drank noiselessly, and avoided two-handed eating. They never ate with their knives, but cut their meat, then shifted their fork to the opposite hand. Diners did not touch their food, as this might spread germs. To remove a fish bone or fruit pit, they discreetly covered their mouths with their napkins. If, despite all their caution, they spilled their drink or upset their plate, no one, especially the hostess, commented or otherwise appeared to notice.[190]

The task of directing conversation fell to Bertha. As hostess, she tried to keep the subject matter light. Controversial topics and deep discussions had no place at the dinner table, nor did loud or boisterous talk. The butler and others serving were expected to say little or nothing. Also, no matter how delightful the meal, diners never commented on the quality of the food. That would have suggested sensuality and animal gratification, something Victorians were loath to acknowledge.[191]

Hostesses typically bowed to signal the end of the dinner. The men might remain at the table to talk and smoke cigars, or the entire party might adjourn to converse in the library for an hour or so. Upon parting, guests would never regale Moses and Bertha with thanks. Reciprocation was deemed more appropriate and cultured than simple verbal acknowledgement.[192]

The entire ritual demonstrated control and symbolized the diners' commitment to social order and constraint. Good manners were emblematic of higher civilization. To Victorians, it was not "You are what you eat," but "You are how you eat." As excruciating as this "ordeal by fork" could be to the insecure, passing the rigid test of table manners confirmed the refinement, character, and good breeding of guests, host, and hostess.[193] Even children were groomed in the social graces. Upon finishing their dessert, Bertha's grandnieces "were taught that we should dip our fingers into the finger bowl, just touch our lips with our wet fingers, then wipe our lips and our fingers."[194]

Victorians also practiced a high degree of symbolism in the furnishing and objects that they displayed and used in the dining room. Guidebooks and furniture manufacturers recommended organizing these rooms around a central theme, with associations that could be perceived only gradually. At Flat Top Manor the Cones provided cues that could be discerned and interpreted by the observant.

Besides the Chippendale table and its shield-backed chairs, a serpentine colonial sideboard stood opposite the fireplace. Surmounted by a rectangular and rather plain gilt mirror, the sideboard provided a backdrop to the meal. It was used for storing fancy silver and may have displayed some of the Cones' most prized dining room porcelain, although when not in use, most of the gilt china stayed in a built-in corner cabinet. At larger dinners, the sideboard also supplied another surface from which to serve food and drink.[195]

Ordinarily, the butler kept his silver water ewer and other frequently used items on a table that sat to the right of the pantry entrance. A decorative Chinese serving tray, with elaborate mother-of-pearl inlay, sat upright on the back of the table and lent an international touch. Over the fireplace hung a large print of Ben Franklin at the French court, while directly beneath it on the mantel stood a brass and marble candelabrum with a fishing motif.[196]

These items, together with the silver and china service already described, comprised the room's essential decor. The meaning that they collectively embodied would not have been difficult for guests to discern. Like the parlor, objects in the dining room combined colonial and French elements to convey a unified sense of substance and culture and to suggest a linkage with old stock America. The antique colonial sideboard reinforced this impression. Victorians regarded the sideboard as the principal piece in any dining room, and they assessed its style and ornamentation carefully. It was no accident that the Cone's Hepplewhite sideboard was a valuable antique. Whether made in this country or in Europe, it was without question American.

The French associations were only slightly less obvious than the colonial. Damask table cloths and napkins, white, gilt-trimmed china, and repoussé silver all bespoke French styles. So too did the relief carving on the mantel. Just as much as certain fabrics and colors, the mantel's ribbon and bowknot motifs signified France.

The framed print provided a visual focal point and neatly combined the room's two themes. In the panoply of America's founding fathers and revered patriots, few stood higher than inventor, patriot and diplomat, Benjamin Franklin. In choosing this print of Franklin in France, the Cones simultaneously distanced themselves from their immigrant origins and indirectly linked themselves with French royalty. As an industrialist, Moses also may have found pleasure in showing off a particularly inventive and technically inclined patriot.

Callers rarely witnessed the actual work that went into preparing the fancy dinners or that kept the maple floors and brass gasoliers gleaming. Excluding the butler, the Cones' staff of perhaps seven to ten servants stayed discreetly behind the scenes, working and living with little intrusion on the family's daily activities.[197]

In the small room that adjoined the dining room toward the rear of the house, the butler readied food for serving by transferring vegetables and meats from pots to plates, pouring beverages, and adding garnishes. After the meal he donned a full blue apron and washed and put away the china and silver. He also made sure that the silver retained its luster, polishing it regularly.

The butler's pantry was a model of turn-of-the-century cleanliness. By 1900, Americans had discovered the microbe and its role in transmitting disease. Crusades for public sanitation helped to create municipal and state boards of health and standards for sewage disposal, water supplies, and garbage collection. The public health movement also influenced the design of homes, as reformers advocated smooth, easy-to-wash surfaces for walls and floors, and abundant sunshine. To many reformers, cleanliness and aesthetics were inseparable.[198] As a *House Beautiful* writer put it, "Where beauty at its highest dwells, he [the microbe] has no place."[199]

Concern over the microbe clearly influenced the design of Flat Top Manor. It was not by chance that the butler's sink and drain board stood directly beneath a pair of windows. These gave light, which made it easier to detect spots and smudges on the porcelain and silver, and, in the eyes of health reformers, added nature's most potent disinfectant—sunshine. The butler also walked on a white ceramic tile floor. The tile's smooth surface and light color facilitated thorough cleaning. It also reflected light, making the room brighter and, to Victorians, inherently more healthful.[200]

Flat Top Manor was a thoroughly modern house, even though its furnishings and architectural details were predominantly colonial. Besides its central heating system, up-to-date gas lights and telephone, the manor embodied many of the designs and principles that domestic scientists of the period encouraged. The goal of these reformers was to create households that would run "as quietly and productively as a machine."[201]

Thus, Flat Top's butler enjoyed the convenience of storage shelves that were built-in to his sink. Consistent with the recommendations of experts, the cabinet that held the everyday china stood against the opposite wall. To save steps, a small marble water fountain was located immediately beside the entrance to the dining room. Also for convenience, the door that separated the pantry and dining room was hinged to swing.

The positioning of the pantry between the dining room and kitchen gave the butler ready access to both rooms and economized the time and motion required to stage and serve the meal. This location also allowed the pantry to buffer the heat, noise, and odors of the kitchen. No matter how hectic and hurried things became in the pantry and kitchen, thanks to this strategic placement of rooms and doors, guests dined undisturbed. A harried butler could pause, compose himself, and then step into the dining room as if under perfect control.

Efficiency and cleanliness also ruled the kitchen and its separate pantry. A large wood-burning steel range, which the Cones purchased in Baltimore for $132, occupied the center of the room. The sink and drain board, flanked by a pair of windows, stood against the opposite wall, while a nearby cabinet provided storage for utensils and frequently used foods. Bulk supplies stayed in the kitchen pantry. Reached by way of the butler's pantry, this small room contained wall-mounted shelves for orderly storage, and durable linoleum floors for good sanitation. To make sure that meals were ready on time, an H. Cone & Sons clock was mounted on one kitchen wall.[202]

Laying and maintaining a fire in a wood-burning stove took a considerable amount of time and effort. The cook or her assistant, properly called a scullery maid, arose early in the morning to dispose of the remains of the last fire and remove ashes. If the Cones' range operated like most, the maid then closed the stove doors and drafts, started a fire with kindling and paper, reopened the drafts, added larger pieces of wood, and closed the damper. Complicated and temperamental dampers required almost constant attention. Operating and maintaining a wood stove also required carrying fuel and regular cleaning of the stove top and oven.

Even in Blowing Rock's cool climate, cooking on a large range made the kitchen uncomfortably warm. As Bertha's grandnieces recalled, the kitchen was always "about ninety degrees," and the cook stood at the range "dripping sweat."[203] The cook at least had all the modern conveniences of the time. Although iron skillets and pans were still common, Bertha furnished her cook with a variety of onyx pans and kettles, enameled spoons, mixing bowls and muffin pans, a sifter, and a Dove brand egg beater. Specialized cookware, including fancy molds, made cooking easier and allowed for a more elaborate presentation of food.[204]

Bertha very likely set the menus, provided the recipes, and controlled the quality of the cooking. Women of her generation were defined by their domesticity. The way that they decorated their homes, kept house, and cooked reflected on their reputation as ladies and largely determined their status. Culinary arts were so important that women regularly scoured such publications as *New England Kitchen Magazine* for recipes and hints on cookery. Special cooking schools, such as the one founded at Boston in 1879, promoted a "nobler cuisine." Cooking school principal and lecturer Fanny Farmer spoke for many when she said, "Progress in civilization has been accompanied by progress in cookery." Conscientious women like Bertha were not about to delegate the responsibility for their own reputations, much less the progress of civilization, to their cooks.[205]

Bertha may have met with her cook and the rest of her domestic staff in a small servants' hall that adjoined the kitchen and back porch. This room was originally intended as a laundry, but when the Cones decided to build a separate laundry and ice house behind the manor, they made this a place where servants—or the "help" as the Cones preferred to call them—waited and socialized when between chores. Besides a large oak table and seven chairs, the servants' hall had a telephone that was mounted low on the back wall, along with a small shelf. A single chair sat beneath the telephone.[206]

Both the servant's hall and kitchen opened onto the back porch. The domestic staff used these doors and connecting stairs and walks to come and go from the laundry and their cottages, which were located behind the manor. They also brought in supplies and reached their designated rest room by way of the back porch. In addition, interior stairways let servants carry laundry and cleaning supplies and otherwise move between the basement and third floor without entering the family portion of the house.

The Cones also had an office on the back side of the main floor near the billiard room. Business associates could reach the office by way of the front door and hall, without entering any of the main rooms. The office also had a door that opened onto the side porch. This provided access for the farm foremen and other employees, and kept them out of the more formal and visible entrance hall.

In a sense, the manor was three houses in one. The main floor front rooms—hall, parlor, library, billiard, and dining rooms—were the public and ceremonial spaces. There the Cones entertained and revealed themselves to their neighbors and associates as they wished to be seen. The upstairs living hall and bedrooms were essentially their private domain. Family and intimate friends had access to this space; casual acquaintances and social unequals did not. The pantries, kitchen, servants' hall, basement, exterior laundry, and office were all service and work areas. This sharply defined use of space reflects the Cones' social views and values just as powerfully as their mill and tenant labor relations. Simply put, they lived in a world of clear distinctions and hierarchical relationships, and they showed it in the way that they organized their house.[207]

Although more private and less lavish, the second floor still reflected the trappings of formality and an allocation of space based on status. Five bedrooms occupied the front of the house. The master bedroom, located directly over the dining room, was a corner room and commanded views to the south and east. A wicker table, covered with an embroidered white cloth and graced by a vase of flowers, stood in front of the fireplace, while a bureau, surmounted by an oval mirror, stood against the opposite wall. Bertha's Governor Winthrop style desk and chair, where she composed her letters, was located to the right of the room's south-facing paired windows. The Cones could recline and read on a chaise lounge, which was covered with a floral cretonne (drapery print) slipcover. This backless, rolled arm sofa sat immediately in front of the paired windows, giving a scenic view of Flat Top Orchard and Bass Lake. Moses and Bertha also had a pair of walk-in closets.[208]

Their private bath, complete with shower, included extensive built-in shelves with mirrored doors. The master bath, like the guest bathrooms, also had a white wicker table and chair, a plain plush carpet, and monogrammed Turkish towels.

All front bedrooms shared certain features. For one, they were about the same size—roughly 17 feet across the front and 20 feet deep. While hardly palatial, their large windows and thin white drapes, high ceilings, shiny maple floors, and scattered Oriental rugs gave them an open and airy feeling. A chaise lounge, like the one in the master bedroom, sat beneath the south-facing windows.[209]

Brass bedsteads were another common feature. Although found in many colonial revival homes, these were apparently unfamiliar to the Cone tenants. As Bertha's nephew recalled, for years after the beds were hauled up from Lenoir, "The mountain folk spoke in awed tones of the 'gold' beds in the Cone mansion."[210] Considering the many fine furnishings that went into the house and the Cones' appreciable wealth, such tales must have seemed plausible, even to skeptics. At a distance, it was hard to tell what was gilt and what was gold.

The Cones built two guest bathrooms on the back side of the house. Getting from bedroom to bath required crossing the common hall that ran nearly the length of the second floor. This was less convenient than having bedrooms and baths that adjoined, but Ceasar had suggested this arrangement, saying that the view from the front was simply too beautiful to waste on bathrooms.[211]

The manor's bathrooms were as up-to-date as its kitchen and

pantries. The enameled fixtures, including comfortably large bathtubs that were appropriately adorned with claw-and-ball feet, appealed to late Victorians because they were durable and easy to clean. The showers were equally modern but apparently saw limited use. Baths were more traditional, and residents and guests so preferred them that as late as the 1930s Bertha's grandnieces regarded the showers as a curiosity. The syphon jet water closets, with tanks that mounted high on the wall, were also the latest design. The white ceramic tile floors and walls further testified to the Cones' modernity and commitment to germ-free living.[212]

As functional and utilitarian as these bathroom materials were, they were chosen and installed with full regard for style. White was not only synonymous with purity, but also the color most associated with colonial homes. Furthermore, each wall had a single horizontal band of color tile that visually divided the wall, just as the dado did in the halls and main floor rooms. These decorative tiles had relief ribbon-and-bead motifs that aesthetically corresponded to those established on the fireplace mantels. Many guests may have overlooked such small details, but symmetry helped define the colonial style. Even casual observers could not fail to notice the consistent way in which elements and lines corresponded and were repeated.[213]

Just as the manor's entrance featured a formal, if little used, hall parlor, so too did the upstairs hall have its own living area. Although the Cones never referred to it as other than a hall room, it was effectively the manor's sitting room, a turn of the century equivalent of today's living room or den. This was where the family, close friends and overnight guests typically read, played bridge, and otherwise amused themselves. Located at the top of the stairs and arranged around the fireplace, this open room was nearly 16 feet square. A round mahogany table sat in the center of the room on a large pink rug. Wicker chairs with cushions stood beside the windows that flanked the polished brass fenders around the fireplace. A row of free-standing mahogany book cases lined the walls of the hall, holding works by such authors as Robert Louis Stevenson. (Not coincidentally, these volumes were red-backed and coordinated well with the room's pink rug.)[214]

A sofa, with Empire and Sheraton motifs and upholstered in tan damask, sat against the hall wall between the bookcases. Opposite the stairway, against the room's west wall, sat a slant-top table similar to the one in the master bedroom. Portraits of relatives and other works of art were spaced around the walls. These included an 1897 Renoir lithograph, *Le Chapeau epinglé*, which may have been a gift of Moses' art collecting sisters, Claribel and Etta.[215]

On cloudy days and in the evenings, the room's centrally located gasolier distributed an even light throughout the room. People who tired of reading or wanted a quick diversion from card games and other amusements could walk through the doorway at the end of the hall and onto the balcony that wrapped around the second floor. Americans of the day praised the salubrious effects of fresh air, and the manor balcony provided plenty of that, as well as outstanding views.

The hall sitting room, like the bedrooms and, for that matter, the entire house, stayed spotlessly clean and orderly. To Victorians, being a perfect housekeeper was an essential step in the all-important goal of establishing one's self as a lady. A home's furnishings and housekeeping reflected both a family's status and degree of cultivation. Bertha understood this intuitively. As her grandnieces recalled, "Nothing was ever disorderly in that house—nothing. The general effect was of beautiful order." No one left their clothes on the bed or about the room. "If you took off a garment, you hung it up."[216] Other visitors could not help but notice, sometimes to their discomfort, just how fastidious Bertha was. Gertrude Weil informed her mother that the mistress of Flat Top was "an immaculate housekeeper. . .so I am kept in a constant state of fear lest I leave something around where it ought not to be." In a light-hearted but revealing afterthought she added, "It's a good thing I was so well brought up, isn't it."[217]

Although responsibility for the appearance of the manor fell to Bertha, she did not perform the actual labor. She was more of an administrator. Since she and Moses traveled frequently to Greensboro, Baltimore, and New York, she probably retained a housekeeper during the early 1900s. This employee would have directed the servant staff, following instructions given by Bertha. Regardless of who exercised immediate control, the duties of the servant staff were as sharply defined and specialized as the rooms in the manor.

Besides the highly visible butler, the parlor maid cleaned the hall, stairway, and front rooms on the main floor, while the chambermaid tended the bedrooms. The laundress washed, starched, and ironed. This work required a sturdy back and strong arms. Most washing machines of the time had hand-pumped agitators, while ironing was performed with several heavy flatirons that were heated and used in rotation. The laundress also had to be skilled. Cottons and various fine fabrics needed to be washed in different temperatures and with different combinations of cleaning compounds, bleach, and starch. A mistake might ruin an expensive table cloth or a guest's wardrobe, and that might entail unpleasant relations with the mistress of the manor.

In the early years of the estate, the coachman may have helped with household chores, as the chauffeur did later. But if so, this was only occasionally; he spent most of his time washing and touching up carriages and keeping the carriage house neat and orderly. The coachman polished harnesses, burnished steel-tined forks, and painted shovels and rakes. Using hooks and shelves, he carefully arranged these items on the walls. Country place owners took seriously the appearance of their carriage barns, and lazy coachmen seldom remained employed for long.

Firing the help was not something that the Cones or anyone at the turn of the century did without careful consideration. For one thing, demand for domestic workers exceeded supply nationwide. Because of the legacy of slavery, many African Americans were loathe to become servants. Also, they, like white domestic workers, detested always being on call. They could tolerate the usual ten-hour workdays, but they wanted some time to do as they wished. Finding servants was particularly difficult around Blowing Rock, which had a small black population. Because of this, the Cones usually recruited and brought servants with them from Baltimore. The staff often changed from summer to summer, and recruitment was a never-ending challenge. In later years, Bertha and her sisters kept a diary and noted the names and addresses of good prospects.[218]

The manor's design suggests that Moses had a valet and Bertha a lady's maid to help them with grooming, to run errands, and otherwise to act as personal assistants. On the back side of the house's second floor, the Cones built two bedrooms that were less than half the size of the five on the front. The size, location, and proximity to the service stairs all suggest that the Cones intended these rooms for white body servants. (In the turn-of-the-century South, black servants very rarely lived in their employer's house.)[219] If the Cones elected not to retain a valet and lady's maid, then these rooms may have served as guest bedrooms for the body servants of well-to-do visitors.[220]

The manor's third floor contained four more bedrooms and

another bath. These were spare rooms that variously accommodated the children of visiting relatives and friends, nursemaids, and other body servants of guests. They were designed for utility, not to impress or even be seen by most callers. Their tongue-and-groove "carsiding" paneling, lower ceilings, and small dormer windows indicate the less formal use and lower status of these rooms. Also, these rooms could be reached only by the service stairs, at the top of which was a large open area for the storage of trunks and household supplies. The smell of Ivory Soap, purchased and stored in bulk, permeated the entrance to the third floor.[221]

In building a colonial revival house and furnishing it with objects associated with the same style and period, the Cones mirrored the fashionable tastes of the times. This is not to suggest that they had no choice or that the style they chose was universally approved.[222] Colonial revival was only one of many styles that were popular at the turn of the century. Thanks to technological advances in saws, sanders, and other tools, furniture manufacturers were turning out a wide variety of furniture, which they mass marketed through department stores and furniture rooms, and by mail order catalogs. Americans of 1900 could readily purchase elaborately turned Elizabethan chairs, overstuffed "Turkish" sofas, and massive Grecian bedsteads. Those who yearned for the simple, handcrafted look, yet wanted to be fashionably up-to-date, could decorate their homes with Arts and Crafts furniture. Still others preferred the sinuous curves that characterized the Art Nouveau style.[223]

The point is, people had choices, and those who, like the Cones, picked the colonial style made a statement about themselves and their contemporaries. In the larger sense, the colonial revival appealed to people who felt America had suddenly become too big and too complex. Antiques reminded them of an idealized preindustrial time, when production centered in the home and around the hearth. Americans also looked to the early days of the Republic for a sense of moral superiority.

The Cones' colonial furnishings obviously matched and were an extension of the manor's overall architecture. One might logically expect to find those kinds of objects in a colonial style house. There was nothing unusual about that or about the class-conscious way they used the space in their home and emphasized proper behavior. What is striking is the amount of care that the Cones devoted to impression management and, beyond that, the unswerving consistency with which they modeled proper behavior and decorum. Their furnishings, like the manor's architecture, the estate itself, and even the Cones' mill labor relations, were part of a much larger and recognizable pattern of behavior. The Cones cared deeply about the way others perceived them. Because they were so status conscious, they surrounded themselves with possessions and practiced etiquette that portrayed them in the best light. At the turn of the century, that meant appearing to be tasteful, well-bred, and rooted Americans. The interior of Flat Top Manor suggested all these things, and, as such, reflected the image that the Cones most wanted to present to the outside world.

CHAPTER 5
THE PROPER COUNTRY GENTLEMAN

The emphasis on form and ritual was not confined to Flat Top Manor's exterior or interior design and furnishings. Like other country estate owners, the Cones adopted prescribed social forms and graces. Just as Vanderbilt did at Biltmore, Moses and Bertha entertained guests and managed their estate like well-heeled aristocrats. They not only hosted formal dinner parties, but also treated callers to carriage rides, tennis, bowling, and croquet.

To show off their accomplishments, the Cones let visitors enjoy the fine views from their carriage roads, and they entered their apples in state and world expositions. These award-winning exhibits demonstrated the region's potential for scientifically grown apples and elevated Flat Top to a model of progressive farming. Like Old South gentry, the Cones also exercised a paternalistic authority over their tenants, providing job security and free housing for those who were loyal and behaved according to their bosses' rules. Finally, to show community concern and to win public approval, the Cones generously supported local schools and crusaded aggressively for the control of alcoholic beverages. Altogether, life at Flat Top Manor was a model of country place propriety. From social graces to labor relations, its master and mistress scrupulously observed the established forms and protocols.

Although his business pursuits would not let him spend the entire spring and summer at Flat Top, Moses stayed there as much as possible from April to November. With the help of her housekeeper and servants, Bertha managed the household, while Moses oversaw the orchard and stock farm and otherwise followed "the peaceful pursuits of a farmer."[224] The Cones delighted in living at Flat Top. Moses once commented, "Now, I don't believe there is a citizen of this country who loves his lands any more than I do mine, or one who would rather live on them than anywhere on earth."[225]

Moses and Bertha shared their enjoyment with friends and business associates from near and far. Callers to Flat Top occasionally included the governor of North Carolina, the Secretary of the Navy, the president of the Southern Railroad, and noted author Gertrude Stein, a close friend of Moses' sisters. But more often than not, visitors were Greensboro businessmen, community leaders, and close relatives. Dinner was sometimes served to as many as twenty guests, among them Greensboro Mayor L.J. Brandt, insurance company executive Julian Price, attorney R.R. King, and various members of the Greensboro Elks Club and Chamber of Commerce. Moses' brothers also visited frequently, as did members of Bertha's family, especially "the Misses Lindau," Bertha's spinster sisters, Sophia and Clementine.[226]

In addition to the formal dinners and games of billiards, guests played tennis and bowled on the courts and in the ten-pin alley that were just behind the house. For more subdued gatherings, a carriage ride or a game of bridge followed dinner. There was also plenty of serious discussion and amiable chatting. Both Moses and Bertha were good conversationalists, although by most accounts he was the more talkative and personable. His years as a traveling salesman and his experience in speaking at banquets and other public occasions served him well in social intercourse. He was variously described as a "fluent talker" who, despite being very direct and frank, had an "exceedingly engaging" personality. After hearing him speak at a Chamber of Commerce banquet, where Cone was the guest of honor, one listener remarked,

> He is unquestionably a man of most attractive personality, and he held his audience as well as the most skilled orator could have done. The expressions of good feeling towards him were really equal to eulogies, or, as he [Cone] expressed it, 'such things are usually said about a man after he is dead'.[227]

Carriage rides gave the Cones an opportunity to show off their delightful views and landscaping. This was a popular activity in Blowing Rock, and fine carriages often rolled down the village streets and along the roads on Flat Top. The Cones' buggies tended to be two-seat, fringed-top affairs drawn by the relatively small team of two horses. These vehicles could be purchased in Greensboro for less than $150. The horses were Morgans and fast trotters, which added to the overall appearance of the ensemble. A coachman helped load and unload passengers at the porte-cochere, or side porch. His appearance and skill also added to the elegance of the riding experience. Coachmen were typically uniformed with coats and high-top boots.[228]

Bowling appealed to youthful as well as adult visitors. On occasion, the Cones hosted bowling parties for young people from Blowing Rock. However, not everyone approved of that activity or of billiards, which was played in the room reserved for that game. In a letter to the Lenoir newspaper, P.H. Pardue lamented the sudden popularity of tenpins and pool. Because of such "evils," he said, youths "appear to have lost all interest in anything good or building up a Christian character."[229] On the other hand, tennis and croquet had few detractors. The former, it was said, created "litheness of body," while the latter taught accuracy of judgment.[230]

Sports-minded guests could also fish in the two lakes and go boating on Bass Lake. Both lakes were well-stocked and fishing was good. Because of Bertha's fear of water, no one swam and children were not permitted to go boating. To Alfred Lindau, a nephew who visited as a child, Bertha's lingering anxieties, "used to plague us in Blowing Rock when we wanted to go boating on the lake."[231]

Women visitors also participated in sports; some of them played tennis, croquet, and otherwise took part in the whole range of outdoor recreational activities that Flat Top offered. For their part, Bertha and her sisters preferred good conversation, a bit of bridge, or a walk on the carriage road just south of the house. Clementine liked to watch birds and enjoyed reading, as did her sisters.

When the Cones opened their carriage roads to Blowing Rock residents and summer guests, many commented on the beauty of the estate's vistas and the showy apple blossoms, which reached their floral peak in late April and early May. Come September and October, guests were equally pleased by the color and sweet smell of the ripened and yellow Albemarle Pippins, the deep red Virginia Beauties, and other equally colorful varieties. The Cones even made special trips to Flat Top in the spring to enjoy the apple blossoms. In a letter to a friend in September 1912, Bertha wrote, "The apples are a show, as they are turning now and add much to the joy of everyone driving through the place."[232]

In allowing visitors to enjoy his fine views, Cone once more mimicked George Vanderbilt. At Biltmore visitors could obtain passes to ride and drive in carriages on the estate's roughly seventy miles of roads. Both Cone and Vanderbilt prohibited unauthorized hunting and patrolled their property to prevent guests from harvesting timber, picking wildflowers, or fishing. The *Lenoir Topic* reported that Vanderbilt employed five men—all "good riders" and "dead shots"—to keep out poachers and timber thieves.[233] The tenants at Flat Top likewise knew the rules and saw to it that the public followed them. There is no indication that they ever shot at transgressors, but then most visitors were happy to do as they were asked in exchange for enjoying the fine views at Flat Top. As H.C. Martin commented:

> Many large land owners have conspicuous signs at the entrances of their estate on which the word 'Private' prevents the sight seers from entering, but not so with Mr. Cone, he is broader minded and his fine drives are open to the public so long as no trespassing is done. There are prominent sign boards requesting visitors not to pluck flowers, fish or hunt.[234]

Cone appreciated such public expressions of gratitude. He had built a model estate, and one of his major purposes was to show others what he had done, and what could be done, especially with the scientific growing of apples and animal husbandry. A model farm could hardly achieve its purpose if it had no audience. The public appreciation shown by visitors elevated Moses Cone's own status in the community, something to which he was always sensitive.

Like a feudal lord, Cone tightly controlled the range of recreational activities permitted on his estate. He not only prohibited hunting, a traditional activity in the mountains, but also barred visitors from walking off the carriage roads.[235] In addition, he protected his privacy by not permitting visitors to ride or walk on the road immediately in front of the manor house and on the short "private road" located just to the west. Although now overgrown, this road was "perfectly level, perfectly kept, and perfectly private." It was favored by Bertha and her sisters for short walks.[236]

Not content merely to garner community approval while guarding his own privacy, Cone took steps to advertise his good works outside the local area. He particularly liked to enter apples in state fairs, shows, and international expositions. Such fairs and expositions were extremely popular in the late nineteenth and early twentieth centuries. The North Carolina Exposition, which celebrated the state's agriculture, opened in 1884 outside Raleigh and was proclaimed magnificently successful.

Moses and his brothers recognized the advertising, marketing, and status potential of both agricultural and industrial exhibitions. In the 1899 Firemen's Tournament at Greensboro, they exhibited textile ticking, sheeting, and plaids, and they set up a loom and wove Proximity denims. The following year, Ceasar Cone was appointed a vice president of the Central Carolina Fair Association and, in 1902, the *Patriot* reported that "Farmer Cone" had come from Blowing Rock to attend the state fair.[237]

Once again, Cone may have been inspired by Vanderbilt's activities at Biltmore. In 1893, long before Cone's first exposition entry, Pinchot prepared an exhibit of Biltmore forestry experiments for the World Columbian Exposition. Cone may also have been motivated by others who had entered western North Carolina apples in various shows. For example, in 1897 the *Watauga Democrat* reported that a Haywood County resident had stopped by Boone en route to New York, where he was entering apples in a show at Madison Square Garden.[238]

In 1899, Cone began gathering Watauga County apples for an exhibit of his own to be entered in the 1900 Paris Exposition. He visited orchards from Banner Elk to Cove Creek, selecting the best specimens of Virginia Beauty, Ben Davis, and Red Limbertwig. His apples were among the more than ten tons of agricultural products shipped by the state's Department of Agriculture to the 1900 Exposition. The efforts paid off. The following summer Cone was awarded second place for his apple exhibit. The local and Greensboro newspapers praised the achievement for showing "the great possibilities of Watauga as an apple-growing section." The Paris show had drawn upwards of a half-million visitors a day.[239]

Cone also entered state fairs and, in 1902, received a check for twenty-eight dollars for his apple entry at the North Carolina Fair. When asked about his modest prize, the proud Cone said that he would not take $250 for his check. Tending 33,000 trees took a lot of work, he said, but the occasional recognition and the prospects for large harvests made the labor worthwhile. Cone grandly predicted that in ten years he would be shipping 100,000 bushels of apples annually at fifty cents a bushel.[240]

In 1904, Cone entered an apple exhibit at the World Exposition in St. Louis. As before, he scoured the county for the best specimens. In a letter to the editor of the *Watauga Democrat*, he announced plans for his exhibit and promised local growers a fair price for specimen fruit. Fearing that other growers might handle the fruit carelessly, he asked that the apples be left on the trees. That way he could pick and pack them himself. Despite his characteristic attention to detail, Cone's St. Louis exhibit netted only a bronze medal. That was hardly something to be ashamed of, but in light of his second place prize at Paris, it must have been a disappointment.[241]

Undaunted, Cone entered other exhibitions, but his only first place finish was in December 1908 at the National Apple Show in Spokane, Washington. Ironically, the show ended less than a week after Moses Cone died.

Cone's varied awards helped earn him a reputation for growing fine apples—never mind that much of the exhibited fruit came from neighbor's orchards. Contemporaries could not resist comparing Cone's model orchards with Vanderbilt's scientific forestry. As the *Charlotte Chronicle* put it:

> Farmer Vanderbilt, at Asheville, pays most of his attention to forestry and science effects. Farmer Cone, at Blowing Rock, is devoting his efforts to supplying the country with apples. Both are doing a great work for the state, but we believe that for real promotion of mountain interests, Farmer Cone stands a head [sic] of Farmer Vanderbilt.[242]

Managing a model farm and country estate required that the owner establish proper labor relations with tenants and employees. At Flat Top, these relations not only resembled those at Proximity and White Oak Villages, but also evoked images of the Old South. Tenants demonstrated a deference that might be expected of workers who were psychologically and socially dominated. No "uppity" hands worked at Flat Top—not for long, anyway. Similarly, as in the antebellum South, Flat Top's domestic servants were black—the butler, the cooks, the laundress, the housekeepers—all. The tenant field hands were, to the man, woman, and child, white.

The organization of labor along strict racial lines was not restricted to Flat Top. When the labor supply was plentiful, most Southern cotton mills used white workers exclusively. Indeed, mill owners often manipulated white workers by threatening to replace them with blacks, and they quelled efforts at unionization by equating organized labor with "niggers," "yankees," and—after World War I—"communists." Moreover, by 1900, Southern legislatures had largely disfranchised blacks and institutionalized segregation. In the Jim Crow era, it would have been more remarkable had the Cones not segregated their workers.

The housing that Cone provided his workers was modest, even for the times. Most of the nicer residences, including some that were two-story, had been built by previous land owners. The majority of those that Cone constructed for his employees were single-story, board-and-batten affairs, containing two to three rooms. These were relatively cheap to erect. Cone paid local builders about forty dollars per house; the records are unclear as to whether this included building materials or merely labor. In either case, it was a bargain. Most mill village houses of the time had two to five rooms and cost between $250 and $450.[243]

Scattered over the estate, the gray tenant houses typically sat in draws and away from summits. This sheltered them from winter winds and prevented them from intruding on the carefully contrived landscape. The houses were also built near springs, which supplied the residents with water. There was no indoor plumbing, and the homes tended to be cold and drafty in winter. Even pre-existing houses, including a brick house near Chetola, were not known for their warmth. When Omer Coffey reflected about the estate house he grew up in, he sighed, "It was a cold, old house, I'm telling you." When the original shingle roof was replaced with a tin one, the house became even colder. Coffey occasionally woke up to find that snow had drifted onto his bed.[244]

Tenants supplied their own furnishings, purchasing most items in Boone and Blowing Rock. Although people today associate Appalachia with crafts, most Flat Top employees showed a decided preference for machine-made furniture and had relatively few hand-made items in their homes.

For the workers, estate life required plenty of toil, but it also provided appreciable rewards. Like Proximity and White Oak Mill hands, Blowing Rock tenants typically worked Monday through Saturday. The length of the workday varied slightly from season to season and according to the amount of work to be performed. Ten hours a day was the norm. During inclement weather, crews did not work and were not paid. Those who missed work because of sickness also did not get paid, although the Cones made exceptions, presumably based on hardship. Only the foremen and farm manager were salaried. In 1900, J.D. Brown received $22.50 a month, Underdown $25, and Mulford $50.

The Cones usually provided enough work in the winter months to assure that their tenants received wages regularly. The practice also benefitted the Cones by helping them retain their laborers from year to year.[245]

Workers could earn extra money by taking on work outside of their regular chores and by providing room and board to the skilled craftsmen the Cones hired from time to time to augment their tenant labor. For instance, Caesar Pons, the estate gardener, earned extra pay when he lodged a party of Italian stone masons. Interestingly, Pons himself was Italian-born, indicating that not all Flat Top's farmhands were native mountaineers.[246]

While tenants could earn extra money by performing additional services, they also had to pay for the farm products they used. Foremen made payroll deductions for such sundry purchases as chickens, apples, hay, and firewood. Because the houses tended to be cold, winter firewood purchases cut significantly into workers' pay. Many men bought ten or more cords of wood a season, at a cost of a dollar and a half per cord. That was a hefty sum for men earning less than fifteen dollars a month.[247]

Work was hardest and most intense at harvest time. Tenants gathered apples by mounting ladders and filling cloth bags that hung at their sides. They emptied the filled bags into crates, which were then transported by sled and wagon to the apple barns. Other seasons had less rigorous, but still difficult, regimens. During the growing season, workers applied pesticides and fungicides by donning backpack sprayers or manning hose reels attached to larger, cart-mounted, barrel sprayers. Some jobs demanded year-round attention, such as feeding and caring for cattle, sheep, chickens, and other livestock, smoothing and grooming roads, and repairing buildings.[248]

There was no shortage of on-the-job hazards. Hefty populations of timber rattlesnakes inhabited rocky China Orchard. Excluding fright, the snakes apparently never inflicted any casualties, although they did not fare as well themselves. Workers usually dispatched any rattler that showed itself.

Cutting ice from Bass Lake to fill the ice house entailed cold, hard work. Although there is no indication any worker ever fell through, it was almost impossible not to get wet. Likewise, sorting and packing apples in wintertime exposed workers to prolonged chilly temperatures. One orchardist was treated for rheumatism, contracted, it was said, while superintending the packing of fruit over the winter.[249]

Apple houses also involved other dangers. Silvio Pons, one of the gardener's seven children, got his left hand caught in the cog wheels of an elevator. His little finger was cut off and another finger mangled and amputated. The doctor who treated the boy reported that, "The little fellow bore up under the strain heroically," and that he was progressing well.[250]

Despite the Cones' demanding paternalism, meager wages, drafty houses, and taxing and occasionally dangerous work, most tenants were pleased to live at Flat Top. They may not have owned the land, but they were still farmers and they could keep chickens and ducks, and perhaps a cow or a hog. They planted fruit trees around their houses and grew cabbage, potatoes, corn, and beans in their half-acre gardens. They also developed a strong camaraderie. Workers often teased, played practical jokes, and gave one another friendly nicknames.

Many expressed respect and admiration for the Cones, though they rarely mentioned affection. The social distance was too great for them to develop close emotional ties. When Bertha's carriage approached, men stepped out of the road and doffed their hats. And the carriage rolled on.[251]

Some workers, however, could not adapt to the paternalistic system in place at Flat Top. Though they rarely confronted the Cones directly with their grievances, they deliberately broke the rules. Some hunted, others fished in Bass Lake. Considering that killing a single squirrel meant dismissal, the tenants did not engage in these activities lightly. With roughly thirty families living at Flat Top, it would have been exceedingly difficult to hunt and fish without being seen. That the tenants still did so strongly suggests that they trusted and were loyal to each other. Some tenants took more direct action. A few quit in anger, while others simply packed up and left.[252]

Despite occasional departures, the Cones maintained a nucleus of families that worked for them for decades. A number of children were born, grew up, and spent much of their adult lives on the estate. To them, Flat Top was an "'A-Number-One' place" to live.[253] The estate was beautiful, a house and steady work were assured, and families could remain close to their homes and their agricultural roots. Besides that, the Cones treated their employees like stern but loving parents.

This paternalism was practiced at countless other estates of the period. According to the prevailing country-place social code, like medieval vassals and lords, employees gave deference and obedience and the land owner reciprocated by looking after the welfare of his charges. Besides furnishing housing and steady wages, Cone met his paternalistic obligations in ways that aided both his employees and the larger local community. First and foremost he supported public education.

On a cold, blustery day in the winter of 1898-1899, B.B. Dougherty visited Cone at his cottage in Blowing Rock. After introducing himself and explaining that he and his brother were building an academy at Boone, Dougherty asked Cone for a donation. Ever the cautious businessman, Cone said he would consider the request if Dougherty would send him a catalog. Dougherty obliged and in short order received Cone's check for fifty dollars. This was the first of many contributions Cone would make to local education.[254]

Four years later, Cone played a key role in the conversion of Watauga Academy to the state-supported Appalachian Training School, forerunner of Appalachian State University. Cone lobbied hard for the 1903 legislation that authorized the training school and later served as one of its original trustees. He was also a leading proponent of locating the school either at Blowing Rock or Boone. The authorizing legislation had only specified that the school be located in one of North Carolina's seven northwestern counties, and a number of communities competed vigorously for it.

On May 15, 1903, the school's trustees and county school superintendents met at Blowing Rock to decide where the new training school would be located. The meeting was well attended and spirited, as representatives argued the advantages of their respective communities. Like high-stakes gamblers, they promised varying sums of money, facilities, and sites for the privilege of landing the school. When J.B. Clark offered a choice site in Blowing Rock, Cone sweetened the deal, saying that he would contribute $1,500 to have the school there. But Boone carried the day when its representative made a ringing speech touting the advantages of the town, offered the use of Watauga Academy, and pledged $1,500. For his part, Cone said he would contribute $500 in support of the Boone location, provided the town and county raise their $1,500 first.[255]

When public subscriptions reached $1,500, Cone, true to his

pledge, sent his check. His support was unquestionably wholehearted. He had inspected and pronounced himself pleased with the facilities at Watauga Academy, and he was convinced that the new state institution would "add much to the county's moral, intellectual and financial development."[256]

Cone's support was duly acknowledged. The *Watauga Democrat* commented, "Mr. Cone has done much along educational lines and the people appreciate it to the fullest extent."[257] Because of his public esteem—and perhaps because Dougherty knew how to court the school's benefactors—Cone was invited to speak at least once each year to the assembled student body. In 1904, he spoke on business education, a topic he certainly knew well. One listener commented, "His address may not have been as flowery as that of some others, but no man has ever given to our people more thought and good common sense than did Mr. Cone."[258]

Cone also supported primary education, and in a way that provided more immediate benefits to his tenants. Because of his support of local education, and with Dougherty's recommendation, Cone was named a committeeman for the Watauga County Schools around 1901. Committeemen took censuses of students, retained teachers, and expended county funds which were awarded on a per capita basis.

With characteristic energy, Committeeman Cone set out to improve Sandy Flat School, which adjoined his estate. He "put new life" into the school, calling the people in the district together and urging their support of education.[259] Not content merely to improve the existing school, in 1905, Cone led efforts to build a new facility at the intersection of Shull's Mill Road and the Yonahlossee Turnpike. Generously, he and Bertha sold a three-acre tract to Watauga County for one dollar, with the stipulation that if the school ever permanently closed, the Cones could buy back the property for $300. Grateful county officials took title to the site that November.[260]

Cone also contributed the lion's share of the money to pay for building the school and augmented teachers' salaries to extend the academic year from a customary four months to eight. Of the school's estimated $1,800 construction cost, the county furnished $300, Cone $1,500. Apparently not all of Cone's share came out of his own pocket. He requested donations from his tenants and made deductions from the wages of those who agreed to contribute. These amounts tended to be small, and more than likely Cone solicited them as a matter of principle. To late Victorians, philanthropy was not a gift to the weak or undeserving—that would pervert the Darwinist notion of the "survival of the fittest." Instead, it was a way to assist those who were worthy and motivated but without means. One way to demonstrate one's worthiness was to contribute to the cause, no matter how meager that support might be.[261]

The finished two-room school was dubbed "the best public school house in the county" and became a source of local pride. Instead of the usual benches and tables, Sandy Flat's fifty-plus students sat at individual desks which had steel legs that bolted to the floor. The sliding doors that separated the two large classrooms could be opened to create an auditorium capable of accommodating five-hundred people. This was intended as a "lecture hall to which will be invited men and women who have a message to the people." Not surprisingly, one of those who had occasional messages for the people was Moses Cone.[262]

To a Blowing Rock neighbor, Cone seemed to get "as much pleasure out of building and furnishing the new school house as some other financiers do in manipulating stocks and bonds." That may have been an exaggeration, but considering all of Cone's contributions, it was not much of one. Little wonder that some people around Blowing Rock began referring to Sandy Flat as the Cone School.[263]

Typical of the times, Sandy Flat teachers stressed reading, writing, and math. They augmented their instruction with lessons in geography, history, and beginning agriculture. They also taught public speaking, as students sometimes entered local "declamation contests." To conclude each school year, an "entertainment" was held. This usually featured an address by a local community leader or educator, such as I.G. Greer of the Appalachian Training School.[264]

Despite the large, well-equipped classrooms, which were heated and well-lighted, and even with the conscientious instruction, a local teacher complained that some students attended only one or two days a week. The reason, said the teacher, was simple and familiar enough: they "have an aversion to hard study and therefore would prefer to stay away." Still, Sandy Flat was a model rural school that effectively served the children of Cone's tenants and their neighbors.[265]

Cone's philanthropy did not end with the two local schools or with his school building in Proximity Village. He and Ceasar also contributed $1,000 to the Methodist Protestant College of Greensboro and another $1,000 to the Greensboro Female College. On occasion, they tempered their benevolence with a healthy dose of pragmatism. For example, when Greensboro's aldermen were considering possible sites for the Carnegie Library, the Cones offered a free lot, provided the city would open and surface Greene Street through the brothers' mill property.[266]

Most Cone philanthropy was not so overtly conditional. In 1906, the brothers gave $1,000 to help the victims of the San Francisco earthquake. Not only was the gift sent without strings, it was the first and largest gift from North Carolina. The *Greensboro Patriot* applauded the brothers, commenting that there was no more "generous, patriotic or public spirited men in the state," and that "The Cones always rise to the occasion."[267]

The Cones also rose to the occasion in defending and enforcing community morals. This was especially so when it came to the consumption of alcohol. Although he occasionally imbibed, Moses had little tolerance for those who did so to excess or drank too openly. After buying the old Norwood place on Rich Mountain, Cone apparently leased the house to R.O. Colt. Colt built a barn and put up fences, minor improvements that probably met with Cone's approval. Colt also built a whiskey still by the stream that coursed down Rich Mountain. This did not set well with the landlord, and neither did Colt's reputation for hosting rowdy parties. Cone told Colt that he would evict him, even if he had to build a church next door.[268] Eventually, Colt yielded. He accepted a $210 payment for his barn and moved to Charlotte, although not before tearing some of Cone's buildings "all to pieces."[269]

Cone was equally vigilant in policing violations of local charters and ordinances that governed the sale of alcohol. Just months after settling his dispute with Colt, Cone became involved in a minor but hot legal skirmish between two Skyland Institute teachers and a local entrepreneur named Eli Miller.[270] According to a newspaper account, the teachers had observed two bottles of whiskey in Miller's buggy. He was evidently trying to sell the liquor near the school, even though the charter for the female institute prohibited such sales within two miles of the school. The incensed teachers took it upon themselves to empty and smash the bottles of whiskey; Miller, in retaliation, took out warrants against the two. When the case came before the local magistrate, Moses Cone represented the teachers. By the time he had finished examining the first witness, the plaintiff Miller, the court had heard enough and ruled in favor of the defendants. "So much for the whiskey business," said the Lenoir newspaper, "The Ladies and the better class of people at the Rock [Blowing Rock] are determined to break this business up; it should have been done long ago."[271]

Cone's support of temperance extended beyond Flat Top and Blowing Rock. In Greensboro, he opposed the establishment of "dispensaries." Like later-day alcoholic beverage control boards, the dispensary board governed and monitored sales of spirituous beverages. Although the North Carolina General Assembly authorized the dispensaries in 1899, Greensboro opponents, who included Moses and Ceasar Cone, successfully lobbied the legislature to repeal the law the following year.[272]

On a more personal basis, Moses supervised the recovery of David Dreyfuss, an officer in the Cone Export and Commission Company, who was treated at Greensboro's Keeley Institute for alcoholism. Cone was asked to watch over his ward and to report it if he found Dreyfuss "taking a drink." Perhaps Cone also encouraged Dreyfuss to publicly confess the error of his ways. In a statement to a local newspaper, a contrite Dreyfuss lamented the "hopeless failures" brought on by lack of will-power and drinking to excess, and recommended the Keeley treatment as a way to restore one's integrity and influence.[273]

The crusade against the distribution and abuse of alcohol was only one of the moral causes Cone embraced. A pillar of the community, in Victorian times especially, found many vices to battle. Sometimes they were uncomfortably close to home. It no doubt pained Moses deeply when his brothers Sol and Julius were charged with gambling and fined $500 each. Even though the wayward pair persuaded the judge to reduce the assessment to $400 apiece, Moses had to have been mortified by such behavior—reported, no less, on the front page of the *Greensboro Patriot*.[274]

Julius' transgression could be excused. He had always shown a streak of independence. As a young man he had run away from home and refused to join the Cone Company. After proving to himself that he could earn a living without relying on his brothers' largess, Julius returned to the Cone fold. Outside of his one indiscretion for gambling, he apparently caused his family little embarrassment.[275]

Sol was another matter. He had a habit of gambling, chasing after women, and making unreasonable promises to Cone Company clients and customers. Sister Claribel blamed Sol's troubles on "accidents of Heredity and Environment." Putting the best face on it, she admitted that, "Yes—Sol is erratic," but, "Deep down in his nature I believe dear Sol possesses the same excellent fundament of the Cone Constitution." Moses was not as understanding. He and Ceasar ultimately bought Sol's Cone Company stock just to be rid of him.[276]

Then there was Monroe, the third eldest of the Cone brothers and, during the 1880s, one of the partners in H. Cone & Sons. He, too, was especially fond of women, but his passion cost him more than embarrassment. In 1891, only months before his thirtieth birthday, he died of complications from syphilis.[277] The Cone family never created a public memorial to honor Monroe and rarely referred to him in their correspondence. This may seem surprising considering that he was a partner in the family business and the first adult family member to die. But if the Cone moral code demanded that their factory workers and Flat Top farm hands walk the straight and narrow, then they demanded no less of one another.

This was especially so of Moses. As the eldest son, he was dominant. All the Cone children showed deference by referring to their elders as "brother" or "sister." Thus, while Moses always addressed his brothers and sisters by their first names, they always called him "Brother Moses." This was not simply a matter of form, but symbolic of the hierarchical relationship that existed between them. Moses took the lead in both business and family matters. He served as president and made the key decisions regarding the Cone Export and Commission Company. Moses also decided what career fields his younger brothers and sisters would follow and otherwise exercised a firm authority over family matters.[278] When he died, Ceasar, who became the eldest surviving brother, inherited that role. Those who did as Moses (and later Ceasar) expected were rewarded; those who did not paid the price. Relationships were based on position and power. Moses demanded that those below him in the social pecking order show deference and a willingness to abide by his rules. Mill workers and Flat Top tenants who did so received steady employment, shelter, and fatherly concern. Compliant family members received high posts in the Cone company, gifts, and Moses' approval and love. By the same token, Moses brooked no opposition and accepted no breaches of the rules.

R.O. Colt was not the first or the last person to discover what that meant. Depending on the nature of the infraction, recalcitrant employees were either sternly warned, discreetly dismissed, intimidated into leaving, or fired on the spot. Wayward siblings were quietly bought out of the Cone company and relegated to oblivion. This is not to suggest that Moses developed a lingering hostility toward any of his family, Sol included. The Cones were emotionally close, but they could not overlook repeated violations of their behavioral code, whether by others or by themselves. Considering the family's social dynamics and values, it could be argued that no mill man, no country estate owner, ever came by his paternalism more honestly than Moses Cone.

Moses did not see himself as immune from the power relationships that governed his interpersonal dealings. Cone took his cues from his social and economic superiors, which included the Vanderbilts. Moses may have been the eldest son and he may have climbed the ladder of success, but he did not stand at the social pinnacle. While he had achieved more than most of his contemporaries, there were others who stood above him. And he looked to them for guidance, just as he expected those of lower rank to look to him.

Cone's social views were common at the turn of the century. Magazines regularly featured biographies of great individuals such as Napoleon and Oliver Cromwell. They also extolled manly and moral business men who had struggled up the competitive ladder of power and influence and who "fight the battles of life. . .in the markets of the world."[279] People liked to read about the captains of industry and how they had succeeded by the strength of their individual will, forcefulness, and power. Many Americans agreed with Andrew Carnegie when he said, "The bigger system grows bigger men, and it is by the big men that the standard of the race is raised."[280]

When a Blowing Rock resident extolled Flat Top as "another great school" for mountaineers, neighbors knew exactly what she was talking about.[281] The estate existed not merely for the pleasure of its owners but to set a good example. Like conscientious parents concerned about the welfare of their children, Moses and Bertha improved education and taught citizenship, and they showed local residents how to grow prize-winning livestock and apples. They also demonstrated proper etiquette and practiced the accepted labor and social relations. In the process, they not only gave ambitious mountaineers something to aspire to, but they also proved themselves worthy of their high social standing. To the Cones, like others of their generation and class, the trappings of landed aristocracy conferred a mantle of responsibility and obligation. The Cones wore it faithfully and proudly.

1. Flat Top Manor House today. *Blue Ridge Parkway photo.*

2. Proximity Mills and Manufacturing Company about 1908. The first of three textile mills built in Greensboro by the Cone brothers, Proximity proved profitable from the start and paved the way for the Cones to become world leaders in denim manufacturing.

Photo courtesy of North Carolina Division of Archives and History.

3. By 1907, massive White Oak Mills, one of the largest denim mills anywhere, housed an impressive 60,000 spindles. *Photo courtesy of North Carolina Division of Archives and History.*

4. As model mill men, the Cones sponsored baseball teams and provided recreational facilities and welfare programs for their employees.

Photo courtesy of Greensboro Historical Museum.

5. Moses Cone. By the turn of the century, he was a prosperous and powerful manufacturer, respected member of the community, and builder of one of North Carolina's premier country estates. *Blue Ridge Parkway Archives photo.*

6. Bertha Lindau. Wooed by both Moses and Ceasar Cone, she ultimately married Moses on February 15, 1888. *Photo courtesy of Judith Lindau McConnell.*

7. Flat Top Manor at about the time of its completion in 1901. *Blue Ridge Parkway Archives photo.*

8. Flat Top Manor's picturesque setting and carefully groomed carriage roads soon became the subject of picture postcards. *Photo courtesy of Perkins Library, Duke University.*

9. The scenic view from the expansive porch of the manor house showing Flat Top Orchard (foreground), Bass Lake, and portions of Blowing Rock. *Blue Ridge Parkway Archives photo.*

10. The family's world tour of 1906-1907 included stops in India and a ride on an elephant. Moses is behind Bertha (left) and sisters Etta and Claribel Cones. *Photo courtesy of the Cone Archives, Baltimore Museum of Art.*

11. From left, Claribel Cone, Gertrude Stein, and Etta Cone on a visit to Italy in June 1903. Stein introduced the art collecting Cone sisters to many prominent artists. *Photo courtesy of the Cone Archives, Baltimore Museum of Art.*

12. While on their world tour, the Cones purchased a number of Oriental art objects, many of which found their way to Flat Top Manor. *Photo by the author.*

13. As grocery wholesalers, H. Cone & Sons gave clocks to their best customers. This one, which still keeps time after more than a century, hung in the
kitchen at Flat Top Manor. *Photo by the author.*

14. Formal meals at Flat Top Manor featured this gilt china and repoussé silver. *Photo by the author.*

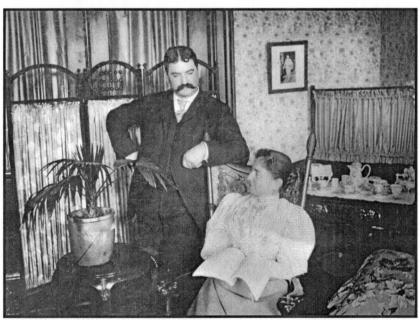

15. Moses and Bertha cone, location and date unknown. This photo may have been taken at their residence in Baltimore or New York. The furnishings and wall covering suggest that this was not at Flat Top Manor. *Blue Ridge Parkway Archives photo.*

16. The laundry and ice house, which stood immediately behind the manor house, also accommodated the carbide generator that produced gaslight for the manor. This structure was one of more than 50 buildings that were removed from the estate during the 1950s. *Blue Ridge Parkway Archives photo.*

17. Baltimore's Lindau sisters—Clementine, Sophie, and Bertha. Date and location unknown. *Photo courtesy of Judith Lindau McConnell.*

18. Judith (left) and Nancy Lindau, daughters of Bertha's favored nephew Norman and wife Margaret Kelton Lindau, spent their childhood summers in the late 1920s and 1930s at Flat Top Manor. Dressed in white, a Sunday tradition at Flat Top, they stand on the second floor porch of the manor house about 1934. *Photo courtesy of Judith Lindau McConnell.*

19. For nearly four decades following her husband's death, Bertha Cone skillfully managed Flat Top Manor. Wearing a white silk dress with amethyst pin, Bertha sits in the hall family room on the second floor of the manor house about 1940. *Photo courtesy of Judith Lindau McConnell.*

20. Bertha and spinster sisters Clementine and Sophie were lifelong friends and, following Moses' death, constant companions. Here they converse on the side porch of Flat Top Manor about 1940. *Photo courtesy of Judith Lindau McConnell.*

21. Built in 1906 with substantial support by Moses Cone, Sandy Flat School operated until 1927. It became a Baptist church the following year. These students were among those who attended the school around 1920. *Photo courtesy of Ruby Moody Walters.*

22. Present day view of Flat Top Manor from across Bass Lake. *Photo by Mike Booher.*

23. The Cones' once fancy parlor became the home of a Pioneer Museum following acquisition of the estate by the National Park Service. *Blue Ridge Parkway Archives photo.*

24. A typical tenant house on the estate. The houses varied in size but were commonly of board-and-batten construction. *Blue Ridge Parkway Archives photo.*

Cone Park Carriage Trails

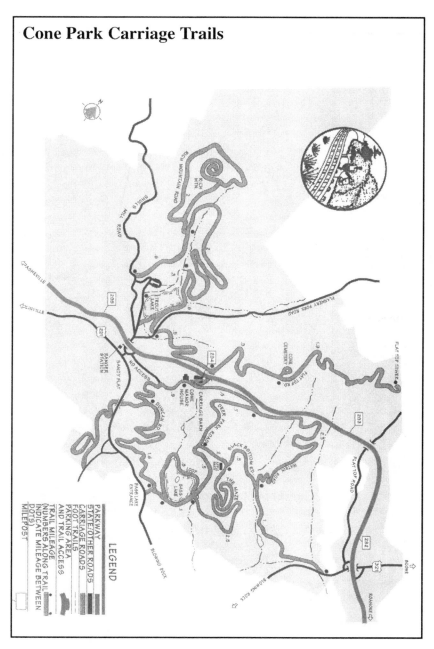

25. The estate's carriage roads, now part of the Moses H. Cone Memorial Park, are heavily used by hikers and horseback riders. *Blue Ridge Parkway map.*

CHAPTER 6

A BRIEF REIGN AT THE PINNACLE

Moses Cone's power and influence extended far beyond the Blowing Rock community and his sprawling textile mills. Having arrived as a captain of industry and a country gentleman, he publicly defended financiers and trusts, supported such business organizations as the Greensboro Chamber of Commerce, and championed local economic development. His interests and influence also extended to the world of art. Money from his fast-growing Cone Company made it possible for his sisters, Claribel and Etta, to amass a premier art collection. Like other well-to-do businessmen, Cone also traveled extensively, taking his family on a year-long tour of Europe, the Mediterranean, and the Orient.

Financiers and industry tycoons had few defenders any stauncher than Cone. For example, he praised banker and railroad magnate J.P. Morgan, even though the U.S. Supreme Court in 1904 had ruled that the company Morgan had set up to control key railroads violated the Sherman Anti-Trust Act. Demonstrating his loyalty to business interests, Cone argued that through his investments Morgan had done more for the Southern Railroad "than any fifty men." And he publicly chastised those who blamed "the man of means" for economic downturns. The country did not need more anti-trust legislation or government regulation. That, said Cone, sounding like conservatives of a later generation, was what strangled free enterprise.[282]

The Lenoir newspaper supported Cone and his sentiments. When the state legislature considered anti-trust measures that threatened the Cone textile empire, the editor railed:

> We think the Legislature can find more useful employment for its valuable time than legislating such men as Moses H. Cone out of the State. North Carolina needs men of wealth and energy to help develop her latin [sic] resources, and our lawmakers should go slow on the proposed legislation that will cause such men to leave our borders. Trusts and combines are not hurting North Carolina half as much as calamity howlers and demagogues.[283]

While Cone savored such support, he also lashed out at those newspapers that advocated controls over business. Even when times were good and jobs plentiful, he said, "Newspapers were criticizing the rich men and the corporations, and [wanting] to regulate everything." Such talk, Cone said, precipitated economic panics.[284]

Like other industrialists, Cone supported conservative monetary policies. In the controversy over whether the country should remain on the gold standard or convert to silver, Cone was ardently pro-gold. The value of silver fluctuated too much, he warned, and adopting it as the nation's standard would "require five times as much capital to do business."[285] Although Cone had once styled himself a Democrat, the controversy over the monetary standard impelled him to support Republican Congressman Thomas Settle in his unsuccessful bid for reelection.

Although his candidate lost, Cone pressed the case for gold in other, more controversial ways. In June 1896, he decided to pay his finishing mill employees in Mexican silver dollars. These coins had a bullion value of fifty-four cents, and Cone handed them out as fifty-cent pieces. His goal was "to demonstrate in a practical way the inconveniences of a dollar that does not represent a hundred cents." Puzzled local merchants were not so impressed by Cone's tactics, although they were probably reluctant to refuse the coins, since the Cones were so powerful. In the end, some merchants redeemed the coins at fifty cents, others unwittingly took a loss and redeemed them at their face value of one dollar. The *Greensboro Patriot* reported, in what was probably an understatement, "Opinions are divided as to the success of his scheme."[286]

If Cone's tactics seem extreme, perhaps it is because few reform issues in the 1890s generated more controversy than proposals for the unlimited coinage of silver. Opponents regarded silverites as "anarchy's spearhead." Many substantial citizens adamantly opposed "cheap money," fearing that it would imperil the nation's credit.[287] To them and to most monetary conservatives, gold represented stability. They associated silver with upstart Populists and the common people. The passion with which Moses Cone embraced the gold cause suggests that he had psychological, as well as pragmatic, motives. By supporting the gold cause, he associated himself with elite financiers and industrialists. Besides that, he owned and managed an export company and no doubt worried about any policy that might disrupt international exchange.[288]

Cone also spoke out on an issue that generated considerable controversy in western North Carolina—the proposal to establish a federal Appalachian Forest Reserve. By the early twentieth century, timber companies had logged vast tracts of Appalachia. In the process, they paid little attention to conservation. As a result, wildfires were common and erosion scarred the denuded mountain slopes. Advocates of the forest reserve argued that government ownership would help restore the productivity of the land and alleviate many of the problems caused by careless harvesting. Cone spoke out for the proposed reserve, maintaining that it would provide fire protection, promote mountain beauty, lead to better roads, and encourage industrial development. He also knew, though he did not say, that forests were vital to conserving the region's water resources, which in turn were essential to the operation of cotton mills. It was no coincidence that Cone's friend and industrial promoter, D.A. Tompkins, was president of the Appalachian National Forest Association.[289] Other supporters included the *Lenoir News* editor, who told readers, "What M.H. Cone is doing at Blowing Rock and George Vanderbilt is doing at Asheville in the way of protecting the forests, stocking the streams with fish, and making roads, on a small scale, the General Government will do on an extensive scale, when the Appalachian Forest Reserve is established."[290]

Many mountaineers were less enthusiastic about the proposed reserve. Joe T. Ray, replying to a letter to the editor written by Cone, said succinctly, "We don't want to sell; it don't suit us to leave the mountains." Efforts to create a federal forest reserve, Ray said, grew "out of that same old idea that the people of the mountains are a kind of half savage tribe that ought to be kicked out of the way to give room for nice folks a hunting ground," and to make "a playground for the rich."[291] Although the 1907 reserve proposal was defeated, eventually millions of acres of western North Carolina would become national forests.[292]

Cone expressed his many opinions in a variety of forums. He lectured students at Appalachian Training School about the "ways and habits" of businessmen, including their character traits, industry and economy, and perseverance. He also addressed students at schools in Greensboro, as well as Blowing Rock, and wrote articles about business and finance for the *Charlotte Observer*. He spoke to the Elks and other clubs and organizations in Greensboro. As evidence of his popularity, more than two hundred people attended a banquet held in his honor by the city's Chamber of Commerce. The Business Men's Organization, formed to "protect the morals of Greensboro and likewise look after the best interests of the City from a business standpoint," expressed their appreciation of Cone by offering to buy him a gift. Clearly this was a man whose opinions counted.[293]

Cone's influence also extended indirectly to the world of art. Although he never became a serious collector, he and his brothers subsidized and encouraged their sisters Claribel and Etta. In time, the two Cone women assembled an extraordinary collection of paintings, sculpture, textiles, and miscellaneous objets d'art. Although Claribel died in 1929, Etta continued adding to the collection until her death twenty years later. By then, the Cone Collection had grown to more than three thousand items and included works by Renoir, Picasso, van Gogh, Gauguin, Pissarro, Courbet, and Delacroix. It also boasted forty-two oils, thirty-six drawings, and eighteen sculptures by the sisters' close friend, Henri Matisse. Valued at $3 million in 1949, the sisters bequeathed their collection to the Baltimore Museum of Art, where much of it is exhibited today in the Cone wing.[294]

The two women began their art collecting humbly enough. In 1898 Moses gave Etta $300 to buy some paintings to decorate their mother's parlor. At the time, twenty-seven-year-old Etta was still living at home, having taken over as her mother's helper after the eldest Cone sister, Carrie, married. On a visit to New York, Etta, with Bertha, had visited an exhibition from the estate of painter Theodore Robinson. She liked the work and, through a bidder, bought five pieces. Bertha did not attend the auction—she went to a concert instead—but she assured her sister-in-law that the pieces her agent bought "will make your parlor the delightful room you want." More serious art collecting did not begin until seven years later when Gertrude Stein and her brother Leo, living in Paris, introduced Etta and Claribel to Picasso, Matisse, and other artists living there at the time.[295]

The Cone women had met Gertrude and her family in 1892 when the Steins moved to Baltimore from San Francisco. Gertrude was later a student at Johns Hopkins Medical School, where Claribel pursued postgraduate research. Claribel was impressed by Gertrude's regal bearing and autocratic manner, and she often invited the Steins to socials at the Cone home. Besides their common study of medicine,

Claribel was, like Gertrude, strong-willed and outspoken. She never hesitated to challenge authority or to contradict her male acquaintances. She was also highly intelligent. In 1890, Claribel graduated at the top of her class at Woman's Medical College of Baltimore. She subsequently pursued postgraduate studies in gynecology and pathology at several colleges and institutions in America and Europe.[296]

Etta also was attracted to Gertrude, though she was not as academically inclined as her sister or as intellectually gifted as Stein. Her formal education stopped with graduation from high school. More reserved and orthodox than her older sister, Etta seemed content to be the family's housekeeper and to do many of the domestic chores that Claribel declined.[297]

The three women shared other things in common, including similarities in appearance. For one, all three were large. Ernest Hemingway, one of the Steins' coterie of intellectual friends, said Gertrude reminded him of a heavily built peasant woman. She had, he said, beautiful eyes, a "mobile face" and "lovely, thick, alive immigrant hair." Hemingway later had a disagreement and parted ways with his erstwhile mentor. After that he described Stein less charitably, as resembling "a Roman emperor and that was fine if you liked your women to look like Roman emperors." Perhaps Stein took comfort in having been elevated in Hemingway's eyes from peasant to emperor. Dr. Claribel, at 5'-3", was several inches shorter than her sister. She was also heavier and, by most accounts, more handsome than Etta. Both the Cones had dark hair. As she aged, Etta's hair turned very white, which contrasted strikingly with her heavy black eyebrows. Although Etta was the more conservative, both she and the doctor liked to wear Moroccan djellabas (loose-fitting outer robes) and black Victorian dresses which they adorned with Renaissance jewelry.[298]

The Cones and Steins visited and traveled together often at the turn of the century. In 1901, Leo, one of Gertrude's brothers, spent nearly a month showing Etta and two of her friends around Naples, Italy. Etta later visited the Steins in Paris and, with Claribel, rendezvoused with Gertrude in Florence. Etta also sailed with Gertrude to Europe in 1904.[299]

The friendship blossomed to such an extent that the following year Etta rented an apartment in Paris near the Steins. Between her piano lessons and forays around town, Etta, ever anxious to please, typed the handwritten manuscript of Gertrude's most important early literary work, *Three Lives*. It was also during this time that Gertrude introduced Etta to artists who were destined to become some of the most influential of the twentieth century.

In late 1905 and early 1906, Gertrude and her sister-in-law Sarah took Etta and, less often, Claribel to call on gifted but struggling artists Pablo Picasso and Henri Matisse. The Steins liked the work of these contemporary artists and hoped that the well-to-do Cones might help them financially by buying their work. Etta quickly obliged, choosing a variety of drawings and etchings. Most of these early acquisitions were small, and Etta paid as little as two dollars for her first Picasso drawings. Although this probably had a modest impact on the financial means of the artists, these initial purchases established the foundations and set the pattern for the systematic collecting that the Cone sisters undertook after World War I.[300]

The sisters did not mind playing the role of wealthy collectors. Etta once wrote to Gertrude, "By the way, don't you need some more cash, don't hesitate. You need'nt [sic] luxuriate in the feeling of poverty, for it's no use to." Etta could afford to make such offers—and she and Claribel could buy thousands of works of art—thanks to their family's grocery and textile money. Moses not only paid for the initial Robinson works, but he and Ceasar gave their inheritance from their parents' estate to Claribel and Etta. The family patriarch, Herman, also willed each of the two daughters $5,000. As substantial as these gifts were, most of the money that supported the sisters and their art purchases came from dividends from their stock in the Cone Export and Commission Company and Proximity Mills. In 1930, as America sank into the Great Depression, Etta's adjusted income totalled more than $55,000. Of that sum, Cone Company dividends accounted for more than $46,000. Little wonder Etta could offer Gertrude extra cash, or that Claribel could put down more than $18,000 to buy their most expensive single work, Paul Cézanne's *Mont Sainte-Victoire Seen from the Bibemus Quarry*.[301]

Although mutually beneficial, the intimate friendship between Etta and Gertrude did not endure. Alice Toklas, member of a mercantile family from San Francisco, moved into the Stein apartment at 27 rue de Fleurus in 1909. This was after Gertrude had proposed that they spend the rest of their lives together. Toklas was jealous of Etta and tried, apparently with success, to undermine the long and close relationship between her and Gertrude. The Stein-Cone ties were further strained when Gertrude fell out with her brother Leo over his decision to marry a model. Etta was especially fond of Leo and appreciated his expansive knowledge of art, which he willingly shared with her. As a sign of her high regard for him—and to the detriment of her relationship with Gertrude—Etta sided with Leo in his squabble with his sister.[302]

Despite the widening rift with Etta, Gertrude was instrumental in the origins and early development of the Cone Collection. She introduced the two women to influential artists and encouraged them to buy works that were avant-garde. While most wealthy collectors used agents and invested in works by old masters, the Cones, with Stein's urging, patronized radical artists. They especially liked and bought the works of Matisse, who startled critics by using subject matter merely as a framework for harmonizing and contrasting colors, lines, and textures. Though his style and his use of distortion would have a revolutionary impact on modern art, at the time Matisse's creations were derided as savage and outrageous. Defenders of conservative taste referred to artists like Matisse as the "Fauves" or wild beasts.[303]

Even the sisters refused to buy the most daring Fauve works, including some of the more controversial creations by Matisse, whom they greatly admired.[304] Although Claribel was bolder than her sister, the Cone Collection reveals a decided bias toward traditional and realistically portrayed subjects. The sisters may have patronized radical artists, but they passed up the most controversial and, in some instances, most important creations. This is not surprising. The Cones were collectors, not trained artists or art critics. They bought things that appealed to them aesthetically. Etta began collecting because she wanted to decorate her mother's parlor. Even though the Cones' knowledge of art and the breadth of their collection grew over time, they selected works that appealed to their personal tastes and that they thought would look good in their Marlborough apartments in Baltimore.[305]

Acquiring art was for the Cone women akin to Moses' building a country estate. Both added to their status and lent respectability to the Cone name. Succeeding in business and possessing wealth conferred a certain amount of public approval, but it did not indicate refinement or culture, or lend the patina of lineage and permanence. Country estates and art collecting did that. This involved more than having a large house and vast acreage, or amassing thousands of works of art. Just as Moses entertained formally and exercised power and influence in his community, the Cone sisters traveled extensively, attended plays and symphonies, and enjoyed associating with rising literary talents and artists. Claribel gaily informed Etta that she was "thinking of giving up Paris" and staying in Munich, where she enjoyed "music-music-music every evening-& theater." Similarly, Etta delighted in Matisse's esteem and maintained a long relationship with Gertrude Stein despite feeling hurt and angry over Stein's relationship with Toklas.[306]

To demonstrate their wealth, the sisters also engaged in conspicuous consumption. This was especially true of Claribel who had to have two or three of everything. At the theater she always bought two front row aisle seats—one for herself, one for her packages. She also refused to travel second class. If first-class accommodations were unavailable, Claribel simply waited for the next ship or train. On her trans-Atlantic voyages she booked two staterooms for herself, unless travelling with a companion, in which case she took three. During World War I, Claribel remained in Germany because, she said, she could not get a private compartment on a train or space in the baggage car for her trunks. Even in death, Claribel travelled first-class. In deference to the doctor's memory, the Cones chartered a special train to take her coffin from Lausanne to Paris.[307]

For all their public displays of wealth, the Cone sisters worried about money. They kept detailed lists of prices paid and noted the value of complimentary catalogues given by art dealers. They also fretted over whether they were spending too much. Some of this may have been because they were both compulsive. For instance, Etta always sailed on the *Statendam* and, in Paris, always stayed at the Hôtel Lutétia. Rules and ritual determined when she rose, bathed, and dressed, when she retired, and even how she shopped. Claribel always travelled with an extraordinary number of possessions, even though she never opened many of the trunks she took with her to and from Europe.[308]

The support Moses gave his sisters in their art collecting may seem unusual.[309] After all, he was an industrialist and, one might suspect, too busy directing his business empire and building his country estate to have much interest in art. This was not so. Many business tycoons and financiers added the luster of culture to their fortunes by amassing substantial art collections and establishing and endowing galleries and museums. In 1870, banker William W. Corcoran gave seventy-nine of his personally owned paintings and built the gallery in Washington, D.C., that bears his name. More than sixty years later, financier Andrew William Mellon donated his massive art collection and gave $15 million to build the National Gallery of Art.[310]

Moses did not have to look as far away as Washington, D.C., to find affluent men supporting and collecting art. George Vanderbilt adorned his Biltmore chateau with art and decorative objects he had inherited from his father and that he collected. The tapestries, rugs, and other textiles, sculpture, and paintings at Biltmore came from around the world. Vanderbilt often travelled abroad and on those many trips obtained much of the art and decorative objects that he showcased at Biltmore.[311]

Just how directly Vanderbilt's globetrotting influenced Cone is debatable. Then, as now, vacationing in distant lands was one of the things that rich people did. Having joined the ranks of the affluent, Cone decided that he needed to travel. In May 1906, he and Bertha joined Etta and Claribel in Europe to kick off a world tour that lasted for more than a year. Their itinerary included stops in Italy, France, Germany, Austria, Egypt, Turkey, Ceylon, India, China, and Japan. They shopped and bought souvenirs, sent postcards to friends and relatives, visited museums, and partook of local customs and culture. They rode elephants in India, and in Egypt took a trip up the Nile that, said Etta, was "most comfy and beautiful."[312]

But "There was a great deal of being led around by the nose." Etta and Bertha tired of that and sometimes decided to "play hooky" and have fun with the locals. The more driven and achievement-oriented Moses and Claribel, intent on learning as much as possible, kept to the busy schedule of tours. In the ancient Egyptian temples and tombs, the elder Cones, said Etta, "were drinking in chunks of information wholesale."[313]

Like many people visiting exotic places, the Cones picked up souvenirs to give to friends and influential acquaintances when they returned home. Moses, for example, purchased a "Hotei," which he later gave to J.P. Caldwell, a Charlotte newspaper man. The small statue, Moses explained, was a Buddhist "God of Good Luck" and a symbol of hospitality and good humor. Moses thought that was an appropriate gift for Caldwell, whose upbeat editorials Cone liked.[314]

The four also bought oriental statues, prints, wood carvings, and textiles that ultimately found their way onto the walls and tables at the Cone home at Blowing Rock and to the sisters' Baltimore apartments. Etta told Gertrude Stein, not altogether facetiously, "I fear the Cone Export's got to declare an extra dividend for me if it expects me to keep my head above water at this rate."[315]

Despite their long journey and being together continuously, the Cones got along well. More than halfway through the trip Etta reported that the four comprised a happy family. "I don't believe that we are going to have the traveller's [sic] 'fighting illness' this trip." That may have been a reflection on Bertha's ability to get along with her sisters-in-law. And it undoubtedly was a commentary on Etta's tendency to be accommodating. "Somehow," said Etta, "I never did mind being bossed by my biggest brother."[316]

For all the wonderful sightseeing and family harmony, Moses grew homesick. By March 1907, Etta noticed that her brother had developed "strong hankerings after Blowing Rock and I suspect he will never get far from its sheltering arms when he once gets back to it." Moses himself told the editor of the *Lenoir News* that, for all his travels, there was no place like his home at Blowing Rock, and that he regretted that he could not return to it until August.[317]

Moses also longed to be home because he was worried about his health. Early in the tour he had developed stomach distress. He wondered if perhaps they were all eating too many canned foods, since Etta also had developed stomach pain. They were troubled enough that in Vienna, Austria, they sought treatment at Dr. Van Noorden's sanitorium. He was said to be the "big gun authority on all disorders of the abdominal care." The treatment there consisted of a diet that included sauerkraut, cabbage, sausage, and currants with stems. Moses apparently followed the doctor's orders, but not Etta. "I stood it just two days," she said, "and refused point blank to eat a bite they put before me." However much she may have objected, Etta admitted that her "bum gut" had improved.[318]

Moses continued to be plagued with stomach distress, and, more disturbingly, he suffered headaches and chest pain. Because his father had died of coronary disease, Moses may have recognized these symptoms. If so, his desire to get home probably stemmed from a nagging fear that his illness was caused by something more than poor diet. Perhaps he thought that familiar surroundings and the invigorating mountain climate would restore his health. He was certainly anxious to find out.[319]

Cone received a warm reception when he returned to North Carolina. At well-attended banquets in Greensboro, leading citizens lauded Cone for his contributions to the city. In return, the flattered honoree modestly acknowledged the praise and entertained his listeners with tales of his world tour. Though he may not have recognized it as he stood in front of his admiring audiences, Moses Cone was at the height of his power and popularity. In New York, the Southern-born-and-raised Cone may have been little known. There, he was only one of many prosperous exporters and industrialists. But North Carolina was another story. From the mountains to the piedmont, businessmen, merchants, and editors sang his praises. They found much to applaud.[320]

By July of 1907 Proximity and White Oak Mills were turning out more blue denim than all other Southern cotton mills combined, and one-fourth of total world production. When a three-story yarn mill was added to Proximity Mill early the following year, a Greensboro newspaper reported that the Cones' Greensboro plants had 106,000 spindles and 3,100 looms. They also employed 2,500 people. The Cones owned other textile mills and did a brisk export business as well, but Proximity Manufacturing Company was their flagship. It had become the largest denim maker in the United States.[321]

Moses Cone also showed his business acumen in other ways. In 1904, he and several other investors, including a North Carolina congressman, formed the Tallulah River Lumber Company. They reportedly bought 100,000 acres of "the finest hardwood timber forests" in North Georgia and Clay County, North Carolina. The *Watauga Democrat* reported the purchase price as two dollars per acre. A year later the company sold 48,000 acres of its holdings for some $250,000, a price per acre of more than five dollars. That was a good return on investment by anyone's calculations.[322]

Cone did not always reap such handsome returns. In 1905, he, W.C. Coffey, and J.W. Farthing incorporated the Watauga Railroad Company, with the intention of building and operating a line between

Lenoir and Boone. But the rugged Blue Ridge proved to be too formidable a barrier for the capital they could raise. Undaunted, Cone continued his efforts to improve local transportation, serving on the board of directors and investing in efforts to macadamize the rough and frequently muddy Lenoir-Blowing Rock Turnpike. In 1900, the editor of the local newspaper had proclaimed that there was "nothing Watauga needs more than a railroad." Cone did his best to secure one. By 1908, when the first automobile sputtered down Boone's main street, good roads were being touted as the community's "only hope" for economic growth. Once more Moses Cone lent his support.[323]

The public accolades that Moses enjoyed in August 1907 may have buoyed his spirits, but physically he felt increasingly weak. Bertha was worried about her husband and anxious to dispense with social affairs in Greensboro. She wanted them to go back to Flat Top, where she hoped that Moses' former vigor would return. Apparently he did improve, for he resumed the day-to-day management of his estate and continued active in the management of his textile and business empire. There were ample challenges in both areas.[324]

A heavy frost in early June, followed several weeks later by a rare summer snowfall, had all but destroyed the apple crop. Ed Underdown, by now an experienced hand, assessed the situation in early August and predicted that Flat Top would not produce one hundred bushels of apples on all its trees. As if that were not disappointment enough, Cone also found that his handsome house required major repairs. He was unsure if the problem resulted from defective material or construction, but the woodwork was rotting and removing and replacing it would cost "considerable money."[325]

Developments in the Cone Export and Commission Company were even more distressing. Cone discovered that Company Treasurer Reuben Lindheim and Secretary David Dreyfuss had variously pledged $60,000 of company bonds as collateral for personal loans, speculated in cotton by using company assets, and falsified books. Lindheim pleaded for forgiveness, admitting that to cover his poker debts he had speculated twice with Cone assets. Lindheim was candid and contrite in confessing his transgressions, but that carried little weight with the boss. Moses Cone's overwhelming sense of propriety made him intolerant, especially of deliberate violations of trust. He abided by the rules and he demanded that those under him do the same. Whether Dreyfuss also made a fruitless plea for leniency is unknown. People around Greensboro must have wondered what was behind the scenes when they read in December 1907 that the popular Dreyfuss, exalted ruler of the local Elks, was thinking about leaving town.[326]

Moses relieved the two offending officers of their duties and began negotiations to buy their company stock. He also revised the company's by-laws, specifying that no act of the secretary or treasurer would be binding without the consent and approval of the president or vice president. In the future, Moses or Ceasar would approve all decisions.[327]

The bitter dispute resurfaced in an emotional confrontation at the annual stockholders meeting held early in November 1908 at Jersey City. Expecting to have the meeting to themselves, the Cones were surprised when Lindheim and his son Norvin walked in. Moses did not wait to hear their grievances but launched into a spirited denunciation of the criminal behavior that Lindheim and Dreyfuss had committed against the company. Moses' blistering charges went unanswered and the meeting proceeded. When Bernard Cone made a motion to adjourn, Norvin jumped up and demanded that the proper order of business called for reports. A heated argument broke out. Norvin charged that the rights of the minority stockholders had been violated and that company books had been manipulated so that the directors could declare a smaller dividend. Moses shot back that Lindheim's terrible management had consumed the profits and that he had no intention of discussing the matter further. With that the meeting closed, but the confrontation continued.

Julius Cone, simmering over the allegations, approached Reuben to ask about a personal debt owed by Lindheim. When Norvin joined the argument, fisticuffs erupted. Bernard Cone stepped in to stop the fracas, but Moses tried to keep him from it. The fray finally ended when people from an adjoining office, hearing the row, burst in to see what was happening. Seething, Moses shook his finger in Norvin's face and told him that he and his father had better keep their mouths shut or else Julius would take care of him and he [Moses] would take care of Reuben.[328]

For all the heated and salty rhetoric, no one had been seriously injured. It was the kind of affair that, with time, might have made for good storytelling. The Cones could certainly boast that they were not people that one challenged with impunity. Tragically, for Moses Cone there would be little time for such reflection.

He had not been feeling well prior to the meeting. Etta and Claribel were concerned enough about his health to cut short a trip to Europe and come home to look after their brother. Writing from Blowing Rock in early October, Etta reported that "Brother Mosie is in fair shape right now, but I fear I shall always be nervous about him when I am not on the spot." She had reason to worry.[329]

In early November Moses was admitted to the hospital at Johns Hopkins, near his brothers' and sisters' homes in Baltimore. He told Dr. Fulcher, who treated him, that he had become enraged at a recent business meeting and had experienced pain around his heart and a sudden headache. This was apparently a reference to the altercation with the Lindheims. In any case, Cone told the doctor that he simply had not been himself since that meeting. He also complained of continuing headaches, intermittent indigestion, and mental strain caused by fifteen years of intense business endeavors. The diagnosis was worse than he might have expected. Fulcher told him he had myocarditis, an inflammation of the muscular part of the wall of the heart; pulmonary edema, a swelling and accumulation of fluids in the lungs; arteriosclerosis, a thickening and hardening of the walls of the arteries; and chronic nephritis, an inflammation of the kidneys. These conditions were aggravated by high blood pressure. His systolic reading at admission was a dangerously high 230. Cone was a gravely ill man.[330]

Curiously, Fulcher prescribed a "milk diet" for his patient. This evidently was an accepted medical treatment of the time. In 1898, the *Greensboro Patriot* reported that a man who had severe indigestion had gone to Johns Hopkins, where he was directed to drink milk exclusively. After 2-1/2 years of this regimen, the indigestion had disappeared, but the patient reported that he was "unfitted for manual labor" and that a half-hour's work "undoes him."[331]

Moses improved in late November, but he still worried about his condition and the continuing attacks of indigestion. A week later he took a sudden turn for the worse, experiencing difficulty breathing and frothy coughing. At 4:30 p.m. on Tuesday, December 8, he suddenly stopped breathing. Efforts to revive him with artificial respiration failed, and at 4:45 Moses Cone was pronounced dead.[332]

The news of Cone's death shocked his friends and associates. Many knew that he had entered the hospital, but few suspected that his condition was so critical. Up on Flat Top Mountain, workmen began to excavate the grave-site that Cone had chosen years before. In Greensboro, the Chamber of Commerce passed a resolution noting that in its infancy the Chamber had depended on the "wise counsel and generous subscriptions" of Moses Cone. Chamber members asked that, as a show of respect, all Greensboro businesses suspend operations during the funeral services that were scheduled for 4 p.m. Friday, December 11, at Blowing Rock. Ceasar closed the mills and the village schools at Proximity and White Oak until after the funeral.[333]

On Wednesday evening, December 9, Bertha and close relatives boarded Southern Railway train Number 37 in Baltimore, riding in the special section that they had reserved to carry Moses' body to Lenoir. When the train entered Greensboro on Thursday morning, local citizens crowded the depot. About seventy-five grieving relatives and friends boarded the special car, which was now coupled to Number 37. These included Cone Company employees, representatives from the Greensboro and Guilford County governments, and members of the Chamber of Commerce, Merchants and Manufacturers' Club, and local Elks lodge. After the train trip to Lenoir, where once more large crowds had gathered at the station, wagons and coaches bore Moses Cone and the entourage up the mountain to Blowing Rock.[334]

At 4 p.m. the next day, as bells tolled in Greensboro, the family and closest friends gathered inside Flat Top Manor, where Rabbi Guttmacher of Baltimore conducted the funeral services. Afterwards, the funeral party journeyed in a pouring rain to the graveside. There, despite the foul and gloomy weather, a large number of people had assembled. The only color came from the astounding array of flowers that surrounded the grave. In all, there were four wagonloads of floral arrangements, the largest such tribute ever seen around Watauga County. The services at the grave were brief. The rabbi gave a short chant and Moses Cone was laid to rest on the side of the mountain that he had grown to love.[335]

On Monday morning following the funeral, the more than three hundred students at the Watauga Training School gathered in the chapel for special services honoring Cone. The featured speaker, B.B. Dougherty, recounted his deceased friend's support of education and the local community, and noted that Cone had spent an estimated one-half million dollars in building his beautiful country estate at Blowing Rock. He also lauded Cone for his outspokenness. He was, said the schoolmaster, a man of courage who "would contend for what he believed to be right."[336]

The *Charlotte Daily Observer* called Cone's death a blow to North Carolina and the entire South. Materially, said the *Observer*, he had made lasting contributions to the "uplifting of his state." That was unquestionably true. Not only did his giant textile mills in Greensboro attest to Cone's achievements in industry, but the Cone Export and Commission Company had assets in 1908 of more than $3,388,000. The company's balance sheet showed an undistributed surplus of nearly $842,000.[337]

Beyond Cone's achievements in the business world, the Charlotte newspaper, like Dougherty, also praised Cone's character and, especially, his generosity and philanthropy. Morally, said the *Observer*, he had been a "benefactor of the best type" and had done much in "uplifting his employees and others around him and making their lives worth while."[338]

Moses Cone had lived an exemplary life. He had been a model mill man, a proper country gentleman, and a conscientious community leader. As such, he had won the respect and esteem of those he valued most and sought to imitate. By their measure and, hence, by his own, Moses Cone had been a most successful man.

CHAPTER 7
CARRYING ON

B y all appearances, Bertha was a fortunate, if bereaved, widow. Acquaintances around Blowing Rock could only assume that Moses had left her well-off and with his financial affairs settled and in order. Considering the size of Moses' textile empire, his fancy estate, his always conscientious ways, and his long-time concerns about his health, it is surprising that he left no will. Although Bertha would never suffer any material discomfort, settling the estate required her to negotiate with the Cone brothers and sisters who were the other heirs, and to make profound and irreversible personal decisions at a time when she was still emotionally distressed.

As uncharacteristic as it may have seemed, Moses did not die intestate by accident. According to his nephew, Moses did not want his widow to inherit all his property, but he could not bring himself to tell her that or to make the difficult decisions as to which of his heirs would inherit what. By leaving no will, he left his survivors and the State of North Carolina with the necessity of coming to terms.[339]

It took time and thought to settle an estate as sizeable as Moses Cone's. Flat Top Manor and its 3,600-acre farm were valued at just over $48,000, while Cone's textile holdings totalled nearly $375,000. In addition, Moses' life insurance policies paid more than $52,600. The considerable value of the estate was only one reason that it took Bertha and Ceasar, as court-appointed administrators, two-and-a-half years to negotiate an acceptable settlement.[340]

Dividing the property involved sensitive issues that required careful and tactful consideration. For one, the Cone men apparently did not want Bertha to participate in the management of the Cone Export and Commission Company, which, if she obtained all of her deceased husband's stock, she would have had every right to do. No one objected to her having the run of Flat Top, and all the Cones wanted to assure that Bertha enjoyed financial security. In short, the Cone siblings were willing to concede to Bertha the domestic realm and the management of her estate, but not the world of high-stakes business. As delicate and potentially contentious as this issue was, there was one point on which the entire family agreed: they wanted to honor Moses' memory. The binding legal agreement, or indenture, that the heirs signed in May 1911 to settle the estate accomplished all these objectives.[341]

Under the agreement, Bertha conveyed her Cone Company stock to the proposed Moses H. Cone Memorial Hospital, Inc. Greensboro needed a hospital and the Cones thought that building one there, in honor of Moses, would be a fitting gesture. During her lifetime, Bertha would continue to receive the income and dividends from Moses' company stock. When she died, these assets would be used to build and endow the hospital. To emphasize the hospital's charitable origins, the Cones specified in its charter that indigent patients would not be refused treatment.[342]

Bertha also conveyed to the hospital trustees the entire Cone estate at Blowing Rock, excluding only the seventy-two acre Green Park Orchard and several smaller tracts that she had purchased after her husband's death. During her lifetime, Bertha would continue to own the estate. Upon her death, the hospital trustees would convert Flat Top to a public park and pleasure-ground for the "free use and enjoyment of all." Designated The Moses H. Cone Memorial Park, it would be an "everlasting memorial" to its namesake. In addition, because of Moses' fondness for the Appalachian Training School, the heirs agreed to give $250 a year to the Boone institution.[343]

For their part, the Cone brothers and sisters agreed to surrender to Bertha their interests in Moses' real and personal property. They probably were delighted to do this, since the indenture had given them everything they wanted. It left Bertha materially comfortable, excluded her from the management of the Cone Company, and assured that Moses would be appropriately honored.

However, both the memorial hospital and park would be created only after Bertha's death. In 1911 she was a middle-aged woman of fifty-three and in good health. Chances were good that she would live another decade, perhaps two. This was not a problem as far as the establishment of the Cone Park. Bertha had no intention of stopping public horseback riding and the other recreational activities that had gone on at Flat Top since its inception. The hospital was another matter. Leaders in Greensboro were reluctant to start a facility on their own, knowing that the Cone Hospital would be constructed upon Bertha's death. As it turned out, Greensboro would wait a long time for its hospital.

While Bertha negotiated the complex and time-consuming settlement of her deceased husband's estate, she also had to confront her grief and take over the operation and management of a considerable country estate. Both tasks were difficult and burdensome.

Bertha had depended on Moses and by all accounts loved him deeply. His death plunged her and the household at Flat Top Manor into a dark and brooding period. To display her grief, Bertha for many years used mourning stationery, which had a wide black border. She also made sure that the estate tenants kept her husband's grave mowed and raked. Every Friday, summer after summer, Carl Hollers groomed the cemetery, and he knew that he had better do the job right, otherwise he would "hear (about) it" from Mrs. Cone.[344]

Emotional distress may have contributed to an eye infection that Bertha suffered in 1909. The inflammation was severe enough to prevent her from reading for weeks. Bertha also experienced other illnesses for several years after 1908. A visiting physician and friend of the family thought that some of Bertha's illnesses were emotionally induced. "She is ill from the psychic side," he said, "and as long as that persists she will imagine herself ill from the physical." Bertha eventually recovered from her emotional trauma and accompanying illnesses. Still, for years after Moses' death, she had a difficult time coping.[345]

So did Etta. To help Bertha and to deal with her own sense of loss, Etta spent several summers after her brother's death at Flat Top Manor. Her letters to Gertrude Stein reveal a depression that bordered on the suicidal. In July 1909 she wrote that she was miserable. "I know that I ought to pull out of this, but somehow there does'nt [sic] seem any reason to and I know that is nonsense too." Several weeks later she confided, "Honestly Gertrude you cannot possibly know how unhappy I am & you could not have realized how I fought hard against depending on him [Moses] & his exaggerated approval & love for me." Her life now seemed "almost without aim." Two years later, still battling her grief, she told Stein that her makeup was a "desperate one" and that she "would like to go to sleep & not awaken." Etta also seemed obsessed with the desire to be near her brother. As she told Claribel, "Brother Mosie just seems so alone up here and it is as though he were beckoning one Cone to stay."[346]

Bertha, more than Etta, felt the power of Moses' influence and was determined to carry on his work at Flat Top. Only weeks after Moses died, Ceasar informed a reporter for the *Lenoir Topic* that the estate at Blowing Rock would be "conducted in the future just as he [Moses] has been conducting it in the past." That had been Moses' wish, and few widows were more loyal and conscientious than Bertha Cone in carrying out their deceased spouse's desires.[347]

Managing the estate proved to be a taxing undertaking, one that required Bertha to fill a role for which she had not been groomed or socially conditioned. She had always run the household at Flat Top, setting menus and directing the work of her housekeepers and domestic servants, but supervising the tenants, overseeing the maintenance of roads, houses, and dams, and marketing the produce of a large farm were outside her familiar domestic experience.

Fortunately, Bertha was a determined and strong-willed woman. The role she assumed may have been unfamiliar, but she was not easily daunted or deterred. Despite being "as unhappy as a human can be," she was soon "working almost wildly over the running" of Flat Top. Each morning after breakfast she met with her foreman and cook in the office at Flat Top Manor. With a portrait of Moses watching over the proceedings, she reviewed the farm work to be done and menus for the day. She also went over the mail and took care of estate correspondence.[348]

Each year she gathered the tenant men at the carriage house to review her goals for the season. As one workman recalled, she frequently said that she "wanted to carry out what Mr. Cone wanted; she'd always refer to what he had wanted done."[349] To the tenants, Bertha seemed demanding and aloof, but she also impressed them as being fair. She often rode around the estate to check on her tenant's work. She may have been insecure, but she was hardly shy or retiring. Without mincing words, she would tell her employees "just what she wanted, how she wanted it, [and] if we was [sic] doing alright." With her, said one, "it was all, all business." Bertha impressed tenants with her knowledge of farm practices. One confessed that even "as a woman" Bertha knew about farming. Not only could she talk intelligently about cattle and general farm operations, but in every sense of the expression, "She knowed [sic] what was going on." To Etta, it was "remarkable to see how well Sister Bertha manages this place in every detail. She has wonderful executive ability and the men respect her immensely & do her bidding."[350]

Bertha occasionally stopped by the main apple barn to select and wrap apples, which she sent to friends, as well as buyers. In the fall of 1909, Etta mentioned to Gertrude Stein that she and Bertha were planning to wrap "some beautiful apples." Apparently referring to her and

Bertha's continuing grief, Etta wrote, "This will at least keep our fingers busy."[351]

Bertha had developed a basic familiarity with farm operations before Moses died. She added to that knowledge by her first-hand observations and by subscribing to farm journals and magazines, such as *Progressive Farmer*. She also corresponded with—and occasionally hired—experts on various matters, seeking advice on livestock diseases, the selection and planting of trees, and control of apple pathogens.[352]

Bertha also called on the Cone brothers for their advice and assistance. Impelled by their own sense of loyalty and ever-present paternalism, they helped "Sister Bertha" on special projects and, when asked, gave their opinions on a wide range of farm matters. True to her independent ways, she did not always do as the brothers suggested. Still, having a sympathetic ear could be reassuring, and it was undeniably true that the Cone men had many contacts and wielded widespread influence that Bertha found useful.[353]

In 1913, Bertha used her Cone connections to have a dairy designed. D.M. Sullivan, who worked for Proximity Manufacturing, prepared the architectural drawings for a 12-stall dairy, complete with milk and feed room. Sullivan also may have supervised the actual construction. Whatever he did, in all likelihood, was free to Bertha. Sullivan was not only a Proximity employee, but a long-time acquaintance of Ceasar's. In 1904, he had built for Ceasar an eight-story, 340-room tenement house, not far from the mill at Proximity.[354]

Flat Top Manor Dairy, Watauga County's first Grade A facility, produced milk that was sold to hotels and elsewhere around Blowing Rock. In the 1910s, a tenant made deliveries in a Model T truck. Bertha also shipped cream to the Catawba Creamery in Hickory, where it was processed into butter and other products. In 1915, the dairy received $527 on milk fat sales of 1,815 pounds. That was more than enough to pay the dairyman, who tended the herd of from 12 to 20 cows. Although revenues from local milk sales are not known, creamery sales and the fact that Bertha continued the dairy operations into the 1940s suggest that the operation turned a profit.[355]

Building the dairy was the most important expression of how Bertha imparted her own personality to Flat Top, but there were others. Harvesting apples from steep and rugged China Orchard was very labor intensive. The crop had to be dragged up the mountainside by wooden sleds. Bertha believed that there was a more efficient way of transporting the crop. In 1913, she wrote to the Broderick and Bascom Rope Company in St. Louis, Missouri, to ask if it might be feasible to install an aerial tramway to carry barrels and boxes of apples. Unfortunately, she was told, that was impractical. Undeterred, she looked for other solutions. The following year her brother-in-law Julius, with the assistance of his Greensboro friend Joe Hardy, superintended the construction of what a local reporter facetiously dubbed a "new railroad to China." This cable and rail system consisted of two narrow gauge tracks built on locust and chestnut crossties. The longer track ran 1,700 feet downslope from an engine house, which was built near the Yonahlossee Turnpike. At harvest, workers loaded boxes of apples into wooden carts that were 12 by 4 feet. The filled carts, which were attached to cables and contained 40 to 50 bushels of apples, were then drawn uphill by a fifteen horsepower engine that was mounted on cement blocks in the engine house.[356]

The new system proved effective, though temperamental. If the engine and cable operator sent empty carts back down at too slow a speed, the carts stalled on a small rise. If he sent them too fast, they jumped the track. One frustrated engine operator, having sent a cart down too slowly, overcompensated and let the next one go so fast that it sailed off the track and slammed into and shattered an apple tree. Despite such hazards, the ground tramway served China Orchard until Bertha's death. It not only improved harvesting operations, but demonstrated Bertha's willingness to try new approaches in the management of the estate.[357]

Bertha also proved to be a careful and competent financial manager. Even when wintering in Baltimore, she reviewed each month's farm expense records, making sure that Underdown's computations were correct. She also kept abreast of market prices and advised her foremen when to sell and at what price. In October 1913, for instance, she directed Underdown to "Keep up your prices." Her number two apples, she said, were as good as most growers' number one grade, and should bring five dollars a barrel.[358]

A good manager, Bertha also looked for ways to control costs. In 1914, to cut apple harvest expenses, she attempted to pay pickers on a production basis of three cents a bushel. However, her foreman had trouble keeping up with the number of bushels picked by each hand,

and she reverted to paying her tenants on an hourly basis. Despite this failure, Bertha encouraged her foreman to "keep down expenses in every way, & be as careful & economical for me as you can." Wages were an on-going source of concern. The year before she experimented with production pay, she noted that Underdown had raised the pay of the lower wage hands to a dollar a day (based on ten hours at ten cents an hour). Although she did not overrule him and cut wages to their previous level, she wanted to be sure that she got a commensurate return. She told her foreman, "So I judge that *all* the men are working hard and *earning* their money!"[359]

While the blacksmith, gardener, dairyman, and other more skilled workers earned slightly more, ten cents an hour remained the norm at Flat Top for more than a decade. Annually, that translated to roughly $250 per tenant. To put that wage scale in perspective, in 1922 a car dealer in Boone sold new Fords for $298, while twenty-five cents would buy a haircut and shave at the local barber shop. During the 1920s, most American families earning less than $1,700 a year, nearly seven times that paid at Flat Top, found it difficult to obtain a nutritious diet. Of course, Cone employees paid no rent and could augment their income with their garden produce. This makes it difficult to compare their income and standard of living with that of urban and other rural American workers. In any case, the local labor market was such that Bertha could pay meager wages without losing her best hands to other employers.[360]

Bertha also retained many of her better employees because, when forced, she accommodated their demands. When two of her more capable and trusted workers threatened to quit because they did not like having to buy their firewood, Bertha suggested that Underdown tell them that "If they are careful they will not have to buy so much wood." If this failed to placate them, she told Underdown, then increase their pay to cover the cost of the firewood. But talk to them first, she insisted, and if they would stay without more pay, then "let it go at that."[361]

While Bertha could make concessions about pay, she showed no such flexibility when it came to off-the-job tenant conduct. Just as Moses had, Bertha kept a close eye on her employees and made sure that they lived up to her moral code. Anyone who sipped moonshine or other alcoholic concoctions knew enough to keep quiet, because if

Mrs. Cone "knowed it. . . she'd object." On occasion, she and her foremen dismissed wayward employees. What infraction Harve Baldwin
committed is not known, but in 1914 she had the sheriff put him off the
place. Sometimes dismissed employees either failed to comprehend the
finer points of their discussions with the boss, or, as a matter of pride,
insisted on having the last word. Farm hand Will Teague was passing
by Bass Lake when other workmen hollered to him to ask where he
was going. Teague replied, "Old man Ed [Underdown] fired me and it
made me so damned mad I quit!"[362]

Managing the estate required Bertha's close attention, but did not
consume all her time. Social life at Flat Top Manor continued,
although on a more subdued scale than when Moses was alive.
Residents included Bertha's unmarried sisters, Sophia (Sophie) and
Clementine (Clem). After Moses' death, the three became inseparable.
They resided at Blowing Rock in summer and fall. In winter and
spring they lived at Sophie's house at 1800 Eutaw Place in Baltimore.
In North Carolina, Bertha assumed the role as head of the house; in
Maryland, Sophie did. At least they pretended that was true. In all
probability, Bertha ruled all the time because she controlled the family
income, which derived from her inheritance and dividends. Bertha was
also the first born in her family and, like Moses, received traditional
deference. Her younger sisters always addressed and spoke of her as
"Sister Bertha." Beyond that, she possessed the strongest personality
and unquestionably was the most assertive. No one—tenant or
stranger, friend or relative—dared to break the rules that she set. Her
requirements for the household and the estate applied to everyone,
including relatives. Even Julius Cone, builder of the China Orchard
tram and frequent advisor, had to request special dispensation to fish in
Bass Lake.[363]

Bertha's authoritative, even intimidating, manner stemmed as
much from the way she carried herself as what she said. She spoke
carefully and stood, walked, and sat ramrod straight. She held her head
erect and usually wore a high bone collar which seemed to accentuate
her uprightness. Though Bertha was small and frailly-built, to her
grandnieces, she seemed a woman of "great dignity." Ellen Hirschland,
the granddaughter of Moses' sister Carrie and an occasional visitor,
remembers Bertha as stiff and forbidding. "She was formal and
seemed rather haughty." A house guest in 1912 similarly described her
hostess as a "royal autocratic-modest person."[364]

Sophie, the second born of the Lindau children and a year-and-half younger than Bertha, possessed the most outgoing personality and was the most energetic of the three. At Flat Top Manor, she was the one who invited friends for Wednesday bridge games and filled in the conversation gaps left by her sisters. Bertha recognized that her sister was "a much better mixer" than she. Although Jewish by upbringing, to extend her social circle, Sophie attended the Episcopal Church of Blowing Rock. Never one to put on airs, she often spoke to passers-by. Even the tenants, who had little direct contact with the sisters, remembered "Miss Sophie" as friendly. Generosity, said one relative, "was almost a disease with her." When she received her semiannual annuity (which Bertha had set up for her and other close relatives in 1911), she bestowed gifts "right and left." Once the money was gone, Sophie felt morose, so much so that she sometimes took to bed.[365]

Sophie's occasional bouts of depression, like Bertha's stress-induced illnesses, were short-term emotional disorders. Clem, on the other hand, was a full-blown eccentric. The youngest of Max and Henrietta's seven children, she struck one acquaintance as positively incomprehensible. Painfully shy, Clem often arrived for dinner after the family and guests had been seated at the table. This, she thought, would make her less conspicuous. In fact, it had the opposite effect, since the men would rise and everyone would greet her. During the meal, she rarely spoke. When she did muster the courage to join the conversation, often as not, she would abruptly stop mid-way through her story and, rapping her knuckles on the table, say, "Second thoughts are always best." With that, she would fall stone silent, leaving her listeners to puzzle over the point she was about to make. Though the social setting changed, Clem's behavior did not. As a bridge partner described her, "She sits around perfectly silent and the other people discuss this and that as if she didn't hear. Then somebody will refer some point—literary, historical, or what not—to her, and she emits information." Having responded to the question at length, often in encyclopedic fashion, Clem would once more retreat into her own private thoughts, saying nothing for hours.[366]

Despite their obvious personality differences, the sisters shared many things in common. They were slightly built and about 5'-2" in height. They were also prim and repressed. None could be called a daring dresser, although Sophie would wear different styles. This was not so with Bertha or Clem. In keeping with her conservative and formal ways, the mistress of Flat Top typically wore a long-sleeve, black or white dress which was cut in two or three tiers. For variety, she donned a similarly styled white dress with black polka dots. The only exceptions were Sundays, when she put on a white chiffon dress and strap shoes, and formal occasions, for which she usually wore a black lace dress. Beneath her outer clothing, Bertha wore a high-necked, colorless, net vest, with a high bone collar that accentuated her chin-line and regal posture. Black laced shoes and black or white hose, to match the dress, complemented and completed her attire.[367]

Clem invariably wore a nearly floor-length navy blue dress or skirt and a white, long-sleeve shirtwaist with a high collar. Her laced, high-top shoes were also navy. The style looked vintage 1890s and it never changed. Indeed, the Baltimore seamstress who made the sisters' dresses usually worked from the same patterns. The sisters were not being overly frugal—they owned many tailor-made, high-quality clothes. Their wardrobe simply showed little variety.[368]

Daily activities at Flat Top Manor followed set routines. The three usually awoke at 6 a.m. and spent the next two hours luxuriating in their baths, replete with lilac-scented French soap, and then dressing. Most of the time, Sophie had a lady's maid who helped her dress and assisted with her daily routine. She required this assistance, as she suffered from painful, but not incapacitating, arthritis. Immaculately groomed, at 8 a.m. the three went downstairs to breakfast. Afterward, Bertha talked with her foreman and cook and took care of estate management, while Sophie and Clem often took a morning stroll. Visitors and residents alike found walking a favorite pastime. Bertha preferred short walks, but the others took extended hikes. "One gets so used to walking up here," a guest reported in 1912, "that a few miles more or less doesn't count for a thing." Etta hiked up to ten miles a day when she stayed at Flat Top. She and Sophie often walked together, stopping along the way to identify birds, flowers, and mushrooms.[369]

Clem liked to cut pansies and sweet peas from her personal flower garden located behind the house near the ten-pin alley. Her flowers, especially the pansies, added a splash of color to the upstairs rooms. Clem was also the official guardian of Laddie, a collie that the family owned in the 1910s. Pampering the dog occupied much of Clem's and her sisters' time and attention. They fed and walked Laddie twice a day, making sure that he did not "budge off the porch" for an hour after eating. They also kept him out of drafts and otherwise discussed with great seriousness "the minutest details in caring for him." Despite their solicitous care, Laddie sometimes fell victim to the hazards of rural living. A skunk's deadly aim exiled him to the office, where the windows were "flung wide." Fortunately, the odor subsided in a couple of days and Laddie once more had free run of the house. The attention lavished on the collie seemed a little much to Gertrude Weil, a visitor who wrote, "If that dog's hardy Scotch ancestors could see the way he is coddled and cushioned they would wiggle a few of the stones about their final resting places."[370]

After the customarily sumptuous dinner, the sisters retired to their bedrooms to write letters to relatives and friends. Even though they could and did send telegrams and make telephone calls, they preferred writing. Letters were a more traditional and formal means of communication. Since good form—always a concern at Flat Top Manor—demanded thoughtfully composed letters, the sisters put a great deal of time into their correspondence.[371]

They also read in the afternoons. Their tastes ran from contemporary and classical literature to biographies, mysteries, and, in Clem's case, lurid crime stories. Bertha read French, which she may have learned in her youth at school or in classes offered at Blowing Rock. The manor library contained such works as Balzac's *Le Père Goriot*, Erckmann-Chartrain's *L'Ami Fritz*, and a handy *Cassell's French-English and English-French Dictionary*. The three women read to each other the books that they especially liked.[372]

The women of Flat Top also spent afternoons planning, talking about, and going on excursions. Besides their frequent forays into the village, they made trips to such nearby places as Linville. Clem, who loved art and music, journeyed to New York each year to attend an opera and visit the Metropolitan Museum of Art and Brooklyn Botanical Gardens. They even talked about taking a world tour reminiscent of the one Bertha and Moses had taken in 1906, but those plans never materialized.[373]

Pursuing individual hobbies, such as fine sewing, also occupied the afternoons. When Claribel asked Sophie for the pattern of a hat she liked, Sophie "did that sweet thoughtful thing of making the whole thing." Clem, who slept in the master bedroom with Bertha, kept her personal effects and arranged her flowers in a back bedroom that was originally designed for a house servant. True to her eccentric ways,

Clem's possessions included trunks of exotic soaps, which she collected, and scores of bottles of medicine.[374]

Callers and Wednesday dinner guests included the Mmes. Hughes, Pettus, and Rutledge of Charleston, Dr. and Mrs. Gibbes of Greensboro, Mrs. Mackay of Washington, D.C., Episcopal Bishop Reese, Mrs. Calfcart, the Freer family, Charles and Ruth Cannon, the Stringfellows of Chetola, the Elliott Daingerfield family, Norman Cordon, and Mr. and Mrs. Ogden Edwards. Many of these people lived in summer homes in Blowing Rock and were affluent and socially prominent. The Charleston women hailed from one of the South's oldest and most aristocratic cities, and were undoubtedly among its social elite. Mrs. Mackay was the wife of a high-ranking officer of Southern Railroad; Cannon was another of North Carolina's textile magnates. Elliott Daingerfield, who summered at his nearby retreat, West Glow, was a New York artist, while Cordon was a member of the Metropolitan Opera Company. The governor of North Carolina also visited on occasion. Taken together, visitors to Flat Top comprised a diverse and distinguished company.[375]

Despite the elevated social rank of many guests, Bertha demanded proper behavior. Those who violated her expectations suffered the consequences. For instance, upon noticing that Bertha used napkin rings at her table, an unwary guest exclaimed, "How quaint. I never before heard of using a napkin more than once." That did not set well with the socially self-conscious Bertha, and she never invited the offending party back. Such breaches of protocol were apparently rare, for Flat Top continued to be the scene of social gatherings that occasionally included more than a dozen guests.[376]

Many neighbors reciprocated the formal dinners and afternoon bridge parties at Flat Top. Mrs. Ogden (Mary) Edwards, a long-time summer resident of Blowing Rock and the wife of a retired New York merchant, was a close friend of the sisters and invited them and their friends to her afternoon dinners and parties. At these gatherings, properly attired village elites sipped tea and coffee, discussed appropriate topics, and impressed one another with their substantial learning. Gertrude Weil, a guest in 1912, was fascinated by what she heard and saw. "Here and there were little snatches of French, Latin quotations, and an Italian and Spanish antiphony." As one woman served guests, Weil wrote, she beamed "as if having attained her highest aim—pouring coffee in the society of the elite."[377]

Bertha and her relatives also visited with the Stringfellows and

Daingerfields. In June 1911, Etta reported that she, Bertha, and the Daingerfields had enjoyed dining with the Stringfellows. The ride down to Chetola surely delighted Etta and Bertha. Their neighbor's place did not rival Flat Top in size or vistas, but still it ranked among the community's most charming. As the observant Weil noted, a profusion of flowers lined the approach road and the house appeared to nestle "in a bower of bloom. The pride of the family is the dahlias, and they might well be—great masses of them, and all the same color and in bloom at once. In another row there is a long row of pink phlox." Suzie Stringfellow took great pride in cultivating the flowers on her place and "distributing bulbs and seeds gratuitously among the mountain people."[378]

Horseback and carriage riding remained a favorite activity, although, as the years passed, it became less so for the sisters. This was not because of the proliferation of automobiles. The sisters owned cars, although Bertha never allowed them to be driven on the carriage roads. The three simply preferred quieter activities. This was especially true of Bertha, who once confessed that when it came to strenuous outdoor pursuits, she "never really enjoyed roughing it." But they all enjoyed sitting on the front porch, which was enclosed sometime after 1905 to create a sun room. Company also liked relaxing on the porch and enjoying the view of the orchards, deer park, and Bass Lake. When Sol, one of the four Lindau brothers, visited in August 1912, Gertrude Weil told her mother, "He spends most of his time resting—that means sitting on the front porch and driving. We did get him as far as the lake the other day, where I rowed him around."[379]

At 6:30 p.m. family and guests ate a light supper. There was never a cocktail hour at supper or dinner. Moses may have imbibed socially, but not Bertha. Few callers came in the evenings; that was not the custom in country living. Instead, after supper the sisters might play another game of bridge or dominos, which Sophie and Clem liked. Nothing entertained them more than bridge, one of the most popular activities among leisured ladies of the time. They played with "great abandon" and when they lacked partners for a full four-hand game, they used dummy hands. Evenings also provided the opportunity for conversing with overnight guests and relatives. Bertha was especially interesting when talking about her travels, although unlike Etta, she seldom spoke about Moses. She had some of Clem's taciturnity and kept those thoughts to herself. Bertha was also "awfully sensitive about having the goings on up here discussed," and confided estate matters only to family. Etta could sympathize with that, as "Most people are only curious and not interested." By 10 p.m., the conversation and games had ended and the gas lights in Flat Top Manor were extinguished.[380]

There is no evidence that any of the three sisters were ever seriously courted. Bertha was only fifty when Moses died, but she was apparently too devoted to his memory to even consider establishing relationships with other men. Clem's introverted and eccentric ways make it doubtful that she would have charmed suitors or made a competent wife. Why Sophie never courted is a greater puzzle. She was an outgoing and not unattractive woman. Perhaps she felt such a close bond with her sisters that she had no desire to marry. The Lindaus may not have been as prosperous as the Cones, but they were, in their own way, just as close-knit and loyal to one another. There were, at any rate, worse ways to spend one's life than at Flat Top Manor and in their comfortable house in Baltimore.

In addition to her private social activities, Bertha took an active role in local public education, once again continuing her husband's work. For several years she served as a trustee of Appalachian Training School and as a Watauga County school committeeman. At Sandy Flat School, she continued to pay teacher salaries to extend the term, and while she never gave formal addresses to the students, she and Etta occasionally helped at the school. Beginning in 1911 and for a number of years thereafter, Etta actually taught for a few weeks in the summers. At first, she hoped it would give "some diversion" and relieve the "melancholy sort of existence" she led at Flat Top. Beyond that, like the well-intentioned church workers and missionaries who had come to Appalachia, Etta felt a need to uplift the tenants and poorer mountaineers. The first summer she spent with Bertha she admitted that she was "trying hard to be interested in" the estate's laboring families. They impressed Etta as "a sensitive reticent lot of humans," and she was gratified that they "seem to take to me more readily than to most strangers."[381]

Soon after she started teaching, Etta reported with delight that the children and their parents appreciated her work. She noted proudly—and with an unintended hint of aloofness—that they were "responding much better than we had hoped." Etta emphasized education in skills and folkways, encouraging her young charges to sew and make jams and preserves. As student Clyde Downs recalled, "She'd talk about. . .gathering berries, and one thing and another. Now to Miss Etta Cone that was the very thing to do." Etta hoped that by stressing practical education she would bring upward social and economic mobility to her students. She told Claribel, "My whole brain runs to what I can do with these boys and girls to be higher class people than they are." They might never hobnob with Matisse, but they could still improve their lot in life, and helping them do so was, for Etta, a high calling.[382]

Bertha supported her with enthusiasm. One Fourth of July, she took ice cream and cake to the students and served them herself. To surprise her sister-in-law, Etta had the students sing "Carolina" and "My Maryland," which had been favorites of Moses. Bertha "was really touched," Etta said, "and we both felt the sadness of the occasion with Brother Moses where he is." At least they had the comfort of knowing that "He [Moses] would be so pleased, could he but see and know the real progress these children are making, in manners and other ways."[383]

Etta's concerns about the tenants went beyond education. "It seems all wrong," she wrote, that parents and children slept in the same rooms in the smaller cottages. She ultimately persuaded Bertha to add another room to those tenant houses that had only two rooms. Delighted though she was by Bertha's decision, Etta worried that her good work might go for naught. "Of course it will take some very tactful skillful talking on my part to induce the people (most of them) to take advantage of this *luxury*. Most of them would normally be inclined to store their cabbages, etc. in it [the room addition] for the winter."[384]

Bertha also tried to uplift the local folk in other ways. True to the memory of her husband, she supported efforts to publicize and improve local agriculture and resolved to keep Flat Top a model farm. In 1912, she served on a committee that planned the first Watauga County Fair. This turned out to be a smashing success, thanks in part to its promotion by the editor of the *Watauga Democrat*. Weeks in advance of the fair he urged readers to bring their big pumpkins and to "Give that hog a few more nubbers and buttermilk, and don't forget to throw him a few roasting ears when they come." For her part, Bertha gave encouragement, expressed interest in the people and county, and chipped in twenty-five dollars.[385]

To improve apple growing and harvesting, Bertha arranged for W.N. Hutt, a state horticulturist and "scientific apple man," to demonstrate the "true method of gathering and packing the 'king of fruits.'" Thanks to Bertha's open invitation, a number of mountain orchardists attended the instructive session at Flat Top Orchards. The *Watauga Democrat* applauded Bertha's effort, commenting that "The people of the county should be very grateful to Mrs. Cone for giving them, free of charge, this lesson. . .by an expert brought here at her own expense."[386]

Although the *Democrat* did not say so, Bertha's motives in putting on the demonstration were not entirely altruistic. The previous summer she had entered an apple exhibit in the North Carolina State Fair but was mortified to learn that scale, coddling moth, and poor packing had ruined what Hutt called "the largest and finest" Virginia Beauties he had seen. With characteristic determination, she had asked Hutt to come to Blowing Rock and show how apples should be packed. Although Bertha evidently never won the prestigious awards that her husband did, estate records indicate that she continued to enter apple shows.[387]

Just how much profit Bertha realized from her estate operations is unknown. The available evidence indicates that by the 1920s she was making at least a small profit. As the apple trees matured and reached their productive peak, harvests increased from roughly 20,000 bushels to 40,000 and, in the best years, 50,000 bushels. This meant that she grossed upwards of $60,000 a year in apple sales. While incomplete, estate records suggest that her payroll and miscellaneous expenses totalled slightly more than $20,000 annually. This excludes shipping costs, major equipment purchases, such as farm trucks, expenses associated with building and repairing barns, and the cost of paying her domestic help and otherwise running her household. On the other hand, it does not include revenue from sale of sheep, cattle, and wool.[388]

While apples constituted the primary source of income, estate livestock also contributed. By 1915, Flat Top farms had 250 sheep, eighty-two head of cattle, thirteen horses and mules, and small flocks of chickens and turkeys. Bertha sold the lambs for meat and sheared the ewes for wool. She probably realized a meager profit on this aspect of her farm operations. "Vagrant sheep-killing dogs," said the *Charlotte Observer*, "sorely hindered" her efforts to "conduct the Cone estate for the utility and enjoyment of the mountain people." This problem existed across North Carolina, and even though many recommendations and control measures were taken, dogs always inflicted heavy casualties on the sheep at Flat Top.[389]

Bertha also kept quality cattle. In 1928, she paid the then sizable sum of $100 for a bull. Although there is no evidence that she ever won prizes or reaped significant profits from her livestock, her cattle stock was good enough that she rented her bulls to breed with neighbors' cows.[390]

However profitable, the farm provided an unending supply of fresh meat, eggs, cream and butter, fruits and vegetables, and honey. In winter, Bertha had her foreman ship farm produce to the residence in Baltimore. She also sent Flat Top products to friends and relatives. Apples from the estate showed up on relative's tables in Greensboro, Baltimore, and Atlantic City, and found their way to Gertrude Stein's apartment in Paris. In January 1927, Stein thanked Etta for the "delicious" apples, which were "better than ever and larger and rosier and even more enjoyed and they got here in perfect condition to wish us a happy New Year." In 1951, an aging Henri Matisse recalled visiting Baltimore twenty years earlier and being served a "special kind of apple" that came from the Cone estate.[391]

During World War I, Bertha sent apples to American soldiers in Europe and was proud enough of that act to send a letter to the editor of the *Watauga Democrat*. She wrote, "I notice a request for apples to be sent to our soldier boys. I have written Mr. Underdown to send fifty bushels so as to let our boys enjoy apples from the home country for Christmas." The people around Watauga County, and the "soldier boys," surely appreciated Bertha's thoughtfulness. They could not have guessed how much it must have meant to Bertha to have given them.[392]

In many ways, the 1920s represented Flat Top's zenith. Time had brought the orchards to their colorful and productive peak, and it had erased the rough-edged appearance of new plantings and construction. Saplings had matured into trees, spindly sprigs had developed into handsome hedgerows, and rhododendron grew more densely and flowered more brilliantly. The house and grounds finally looked as though they were a part of the landscape, not imposed upon it. They had acquired the look of permanence.[393]

B.B. Dougherty pronounced the Cone estate "the finest, except one, in North Carolina." He liked it so well that in 1921 he suggested that it be made a summer residence for the governor of North Carolina. People had been talking about building a governor's mansion in Watauga County. It made sense to Dougherty to put it at Blowing Rock, since, as he understood, North Carolina owned the Cone estate. Of course, Dougherty was in error. The estate belonged to Bertha, while she lived, and to the Cone Hospital after that. Still, his suggestion reveals how highly he thought of the estate. Indeed, he judged the place to be worth $2 million. (Fortunately for Bertha, the county tax collector in 1926 appraised her real and personal property at a more modest $130,948. But even this represented a substantial increase from the $48,000 valuation made fifteen years earlier.)[394]

As her husband had done, Bertha always kept the grounds immaculately groomed. Crews raked and swept the carriage roads and kept them in top repair. The lawn around the house was mowed to perfection, "every blade properly grown and trimmed." To enhance the views of already picturesque Bass Lake, Bertha added a double row of hemlocks and large beds of Japanese hydrangeas around it. Blowing Rock residents enjoyed the view of the lake so much that a "suburb" (Lake View) developed upslope near the Yonahlossee Turnpike.[395]

During the 1920s, new technology generated considerable excitement in Watauga County and brought significant change to the Cone estate. In Boone, the arrival of the town's first "aeroplane" drew considerable attention. So, too, did the advent of radio and ready access to motion pictures. In early October 1926, crowds gathered each evening in front of the Pastime Theater to listen to broadcasts of the World Series between the New York Yankees and the St. Louis Cardinals. Meanwhile, theater audiences watched Tom Mix and Tony the Wonder Horse in *The Best Bad Man* and Lon Chaney, starring in *The Phantom of the Opera*.[396]

The changes occurring at the Cone place, while hardly as titillating, were nevertheless a sign of the times. Bertha bought powered sprayers and tractors, which improved the efficiency of her farm operations. She also added electricity to several residences, including the manor and apple barn. She installed an electric light in her kitchen and put a refrigerator on the back porch. Interestingly, she kept her gaslight system. Bertha easily could have afforded to install more appliances and to wire her entire house for electricity. Irons, sewing machines, and vacuum cleaners were readily available. Although the wages of domestic servants rose sharply between 1900 and 1920, Bertha kept enough servants to carry out the essential domestic chores, apparently preferring to pay them $40 to $60 dollars a month rather than purchase the relatively expensive labor-saving appliances. As far as her choice of lighting, she simply may have preferred, as many people did, the warm glow of gaslight to the glare of an incandescent bulb.[397]

Sandy Flat School became an unwitting casualty of the machine age. In 1925, Watauga County instituted school bus service, which made it feasible to transport students to consolidated schools. Two years later, 170 students from several small local schools, including Sandy Flat, began attending classes in the new class "A" school at Blowing Rock. When Sandy Flat closed, Bertha exercised her deed-reserved option to purchase the 3-acre site that she and Moses had conveyed to the county school board more than twenty years earlier. With Bertha's sanction, the empty school was converted in 1928 into the Sandy Flat Missionary Baptist Church. More than half the new church congregation lived on the Cone estate.[398]

The 1920s also brought another change to Flat Top Manor: for the first time, children lived there. Moses and Bertha had been childless. Some said she did not like or want children. She had little patience with them and, according to her nephew Alfred, regarded them "as a necessary evil, or if not that, as a nuisance which had to be tolerated." However, she made an exception for another nephew, Norman. The son of Bertha's youngest brother Albert, a man of modest means, Norman had developed a tubercular knee in childhood. During the 1890s, at the age of three, he had gone to Baltimore to receive medical treatment and, while there, lived with his aunts. For all practical purposes, they raised him, and eventually Bertha paid for his education at the University of Wisconsin and Johns Hopkins. In a sense, Norman became the child Bertha never had. Not surprisingly, given their close relationship, Norman, his wife, Margaret Kelton Lindau, and their daughters, Judith and Nancy, became regular guests at Flat Top, spending most of the summers of the late 1920s and all of the 1930s there.

By this time Bertha was past seventy years old, and she treated her grandnieces like grandchildren.

For the girls, life with their aging great-aunts was not as dismally dull as one might suspect. Under the watchful eye of Nellie Snow, their nursemaid, who lived on the manor's third floor, they roamed and explored the estate. The two rode horseback and, before they were ten, became proficient riders. Always personally escorted, they journeyed to Flat Top Mountain, where they picnicked and climbed the observation tower. They also walked the carriage roads and trails near the manor and, like true children, discovered their own "surprise path." Narrow, overgrown, and never walked by the aunts, the path served as Judith's and Nancy's private domain. There they conducted make-believe tea parties, serving acorns and stones. They also scratched secret messages on slabs of white tree fungus, which, miraculously to young eyes, turned brown where they were cut. In the house they played records in the billiard room. Clem owned a Victrola and an extensive collection of records, including many classical works performed by pianist Harold Bauer. The girls sometimes read on the third floor and played games in the second floor hall sitting room, which was where most informal family activities took place. As a special treat, on Sundays, Bertha's long-time chauffeur, Ed Bumpass, would take off his coat and, using a hand-cranked churn, make "wonderful" peach ice cream.[399]

A particularly memorable event for the girls was the wedding of their cousin Dene Lindau to Dr. Alan Roos. Wearing matching white dresses and red shoes, Judith and Nancy served as flower girls, dispensing rose petals from glass baskets. The bride made her entrance by descending the main stairs, her long train cascading on the steps. The groom and members of the wedding party, including Bertha in her long black dress, waited and watched from the first floor hall room.[400]

Child life at the manor was not completely carefree. Even little girls were expected to comport themselves in a lady-like way and demonstrate proper manners. While seated at the breakfast table, Judith sometimes looked at her tumbler of grape juice, eyed the fine white table cloth, which looked very large, and thought about the mess it would make if she spilled her juice. Such small anxieties hardly diminished the pleasure that summers at Flat Top gave her and Nancy. They liked visiting and, by all indications, their aunts—Bertha included—liked for them to be there.[401]

The grandnieces were too young to know or think much about the constant challenges that Bertha faced in managing the estate. Aside from day-to-day farm operations, she confronted natural disasters and manmade threats. For example, a small landslide blocked the spillway on the Trout Lake dam during a devastating, two-day storm in July 1916. The rising water burst through a 120-foot section of the dam and rushed down the mountainside, smashing two residences and stripping the topsoil to bedrock. The wall of water reached such velocity that it lifted large trees and carried them upright for some distance before they toppled into the "seathing [sic] billows." In some respects, Bertha was fortunate: the local newspaper reported that the storm killed eighty to one hundred people and destroyed a large but undetermined number of homes, mills, and bridges in a thirty county region of Appalachia. Still, the experience was traumatic enough that she never rebuilt the dam on Trout Lake.[402]

The dam at Bass Lake created another alarm. The gate valve on the dam's lower side broke, and when the lake was drained so that the valve could be repaired, part of the earthen dam slumped. Bertha, who was "terribly upset" and "naturally worried," asked Julius and Herman to investigate. After an on-site inspection, they reported that the dam required extensive and costly repairs. Bertha could accept the loss of Trout Lake, but not this one. It contributed too much to the view from the manor, and she soon had a contractor at work overhauling the dam.[403]

Unlike dam repair, some problems were beyond Bertha's control. The chestnut blight was one. During the 1920s the blight effectively eliminated American Chestnut trees from the estate. Edward Cone recalled that on his visits as a boy he had often gathered chestnuts. But around 1927 he asked his Aunt Bertha when they were going "chest-nutting" and she replied starkly, "There aren't any more chestnuts." Though the durable trunks of many dead trees stood for years, the numerous chestnuts all died. A government pomologist recommended that Bertha plant English Walnut and Oriental Chestnut trees, but there is little evidence that she tried. As many other Americans discovered, native chestnuts could not be replaced.[404]

A few problems had ready solutions. When people tried to drive their cars on the carriage roads, entering by way of Chetola, Bertha built a stone wall. Her other entrances were already gated and closed at night. The new wall effectively eliminated access from Chetola and thus took care of that nuisance.[405]

Still, cars caused other, more indirect, concerns. When the state

announced plans in 1928 to widen the Linville to Blowing Rock highway, Bertha worried that the project would take out the hemlock
hedgerow that bordered the road. That, she said, would "mean ruining
the look of my place." Moreover, as she pointed out often and proudly,
Moses had built the hedge. She asked Herman to intervene with the
North Carolina road commissioner to make sure that the hemlocks
would be left undisturbed, adding indignantly, "My husband did much
to build up Watauga County and now they should remember this."
Whatever Herman said worked; the hedgerow stayed.[406]

Bertha's brothers-in-law helped with other special problems, none
more emotionally traumatic than that which occurred in the autumn of
1924. During the evening of October 18-19, vandals dug into Moses'
grave. Wielding picks and sledgehammers, they smashed the rock covering that had been cemented over his casket, then, ripping a picket
from the iron fence that enclosed the cemetery, pried open the wooden
coffin. Julius came from Greensboro to help investigate and to do what
he could to comfort Bertha. Though no one could prove it, he and others around town assumed that the deed had been carried out by people
looking for valuables. For years, rumors had circulated that Moses,
having died without a will, had been buried with some of his money.
Even though this was incorrect, according to the *Watauga Democrat*, it
was "undoubtedly the incentive for the unspeakable crime." Shocked
and stunned, Bertha took to her bedroom and did not go downstairs for
a week.[407]

In 1929, Bertha found herself grieving again, this time over the
death of Claribel. Though she had never liked Bertha or cared for the
Lindaus, Claribel was the second oldest, most confident, and by far the
most dominant of the Cone sisters. In a sense, she was the feminine
Moses. Perhaps that is why Bertha was so shaken by the "awful news"
of Claribel's death. Bertha remembered how Etta had consoled her
when Moses died and now wanted to return the thoughtfulness. "You
will never know how sorry I am and how deep is my sympathy for
you," she told her grief-stricken sister-in-law. "My dearest Etta you
stood by me faithfully in my awful trouble and that I will never forget." If it was any consolation, she continued, "Nature has no
favorites. We all must go when the time comes. So I tell you that your
loving friends are waiting for you to show you that they love you."[408]

Claribel's death was the harbinger of other reversals. Only weeks after her passing, the stock market crashed. The ensuing Great Depression directly affected rural Watauga County. In 1931, the hard-pressed Bank of Blowing Rock asked depositors, which included Mrs. Moses Cone, not to withdraw more than 10 percent of their January balance. As Bertha told Herman, "We have had a hard time to save our little bank here," and she was willing, if he concurred, to honor the bank's request.[409]

As the Depression deepened, cash-strapped farmers who lived near Flat Top filed for federal loans, which were secured by crop liens. To cut costs, or perhaps because demand for her farm produce fell, Bertha trimmed her workers' hours. In either case, she did not do this out of economic necessity. On the contrary, her income during the Depression era actually rose. While most of her neighbors struggled, Bertha's Cone Company stock yielded record dividends, rising from $169,560 in 1930 to $267,293 in 1934, and more than $379,000 in 1937. Taxes took a hefty percentage of her income. Still, she consistently netted in excess of $100,000 a year, which by anyone's measure, made her rich. She rode in a chauffeur-driven Pierce-Arrow or Lincoln and, within reason, could afford any luxury she desired.[410]

Despite this, Bertha remained insecure. She knew that when she died her heirs would not receive the handsome income that she had. She admitted to Bernard Cone, who handled her financial matters, that she may have been "overpersuaded" and made a mistake when she settled Moses' estate in 1911. Bernard fairly bristled at the suggestion. If anything, he replied, Bertha failed to appreciate the "remarkable stewardship" that her brothers-in-law, especially Ceasar, had exercised in setting up the hospital trust and in handling her affairs. Had she sold her stock at the time of the estate settlement, she would have received roughly $1,650,000. If invested, this would have yielded an estimated $20,000 to $30,000 a year, not the $165,000 a year she had averaged instead.[411]

No one could argue that the indenture had left Bertha anything other than very well-off. But Bernard implied that Bertha had no option other than to sell her stock and invest the income, or to convey it, upon her death, to the hospital trustees. She could have fought to retain full ownership of all, or at least a goodly part, of her husband's stock in the company. But doing so might have forced her to negotiate the ownership of Flat Top with the other heirs. Perhaps she believed that the indenture represented the settlement that Moses would have wanted, and while that might not have been her preference, she could accept it, even if reluctantly.

The Cones' stewardship of Bertha's financial affairs did not end in 1911. They not only prepared her tax returns, but also maintained her balance of funds generated by company dividends. When Bertha needed money, she asked them to transfer the amount she wanted to her account, or to write a check to the party in the amount she specified. Bertha respected the financial judgement of her brothers-in-law and conferred with them on a wide range of matters. When trading cars in 1927, she told Herman what she had been offered for her old car and confessed, "As I know nothing of values I am writing to see whether this is fair."[412]

Never did Bertha need the Cones' influence and help more than when she battled the State of North Carolina and the National Park Service over the routing of the Blue Ridge Parkway through her estate. In early 1935, government survey parties began laying out a route that would take the scenic highway, only recently authorized, between Bass Lake and the manor. Concerned about the devastating impact that the highway might have on her views, carriage roads, trees, and shrubs, Bertha launched an opposition campaign that would last, off and on, for several years. She immediately enlisted the aid of the Cones. Upon examining the surveyor's line in April 1935, Herman told Bertha that he agreed it would be "a very foolish thing for the Government to attempt to put their road through your place." He relayed his concerns to Senator Robert Reynolds, while Ben Cone, who wielded "quite an influence in Raleigh," took up the matter with the North Carolina Highway Commission. The chief of the federal Bureau of Public Roads, which coordinated rights-of-way surveys with the state, assured Senator Reynolds that the survey through the Cone estate was only a preliminary one. No route had been chosen, the bureau chief said, and no building was contemplated any time soon.[413]

In the spring of 1939, the surveyors evidently returned. This time Bertha energetically joined the fray, writing National Park Service Director Arno B. Cammerer that her estate, and especially her "magnificent hemlock hedge," ought to be preserved. "I feel it would be a crime to ruin my place," Bertha said, "Some day many people will enjoy and appreciate the work done by my husband." She sincerely hoped that "some way will be found to build the road elsewhere." She bluntly asked the director to keep his ubiquitous surveyors from coming on her property without permission.[414]

Bertha did not limit her protests to writing letters. She invited Congressman Robert Doughton to her home and, over dinner, convinced him that routing the Parkway through her estate "would be a crime." She also entertained Secretary of the Interior Harold Ickes. After dinner, as they sat on the manor porch admiring the as yet unspoiled view, Bertha asked plaintively, "Now can you understand why I am upset about the possibility of the Parkway coming through?" Apparently he could, for he assured her that no road would be built there during her life.[415]

Bertha reiterated her concerns in a letter to President Franklin Roosevelt, beseeching him to ask Doughton what he thought about Park Service plans for her estate. She also indicated a new willingness to compromise. If the government would delay their road until after her death, then, she suggested, "I will not be able to demur."[416]

She repeated the same sentiment two weeks later in another letter to the Park Service director:

> I hope this lovely estate will be left *intact* during *my* lifetime—a fortune has been spent to make a charming place of what was wild mountain country, and after Mr. Cone's death many years ago, I have continued as well as I could, along the lines he laid out. . .I would never consent to the road going through this place. I am eighty-one years old and feel that I want my home place *not to be disturbed* while I live.[417]

Parkway project officials, who by then had had enough of Bertha's determined opposition, agreed; they would postpone construction on the Cone estate until after Mrs. Cone died.[418]

Bertha's victory was not as hollow as it might seem. She knew that the estate would be turned over to the hospital trustees when she died. They were obligated only to keep the carriage roads and grounds open and accessible as a park, not to maintain it as an operating estate, as Moses and she had. By stalling the Parkway construction, she fulfilled her keenly felt responsibility to carry on her husband's work. After she died, the hospital trustees could do as they wished, and, Bertha reasoned, she would not be accountable for that.

The 1940s presented another, far different set of problems. World War II may have seemed far away from bucolic Flat Top, but it affected the estate directly. The country's demand for soldiers, sailors, and civilian defense workers raised wages substantially. In response, Bertha trimmed the number of employees on her payroll, closed her dairy, and reduced the acreage of her orchards. She also responded to the national trends and raised the pay of her workers. In December 1941, the farm's foreman earned $100 a month, while the average hand made 22-1/2 cents an hour. Two years later, her foreman was receiving $125 a month, while laborers were making thirty cents an hour. Long-time tenant Clyde Downs recalled that during World War II he and his fellow employees kept getting "a little more and little more" pay. Never had the tenants gotten so many raises so quickly. Despite the improved pay, some employees took jobs elsewhere. For example, in 1943, Omer Coffey asked for a release to take a job in a defense plant at Kingsport, Tennessee.[419]

To compensate for the increased cost and difficulty in keeping her employees, Bertha reduced her estate staff. Although the number of people on the payroll varied from season to season and year to year, between June 1941 and June 1945 her work force fell by 21 percent, from twenty-nine to twenty-four employees.[420]

Still, many employees stayed. Besides having grown accustomed to life on the estate, they hoped to receive an inheritance when the estate's mistress died. Even though Bertha remained active and in good health, she was now in her mid-eighties. Long-time employees believed that she would will them a small tract of land or perhaps a small retirement. Downs had gotten the impression that "everyone working on her place. . .when she was done with it. . .wouldn't be sorry of it."[421]

As the tenants could plainly see, by the 1940s, time and age weighed heavily at Flat Top. Bertha's once dark hair, which she always parted in the middle, then braided and coiled on the back of her head, had long ago turned a yellow-tinged white. She wore eyeglasses, and her face bore the typical, though not excessive, lines of age. Beyond the outward physical signs of aging, social life at Flat Top also slowed. During the decade, Norman Lindau and his family spent most summers at their own home, Gideon's Ridge, which they had built at Green Park, while Etta usually stayed with Julius or Herman, who also had acquired homes in Blowing Rock. Bertha and her sisters continued to entertain guests, but there was not much "party business" at the manor.[422]

Time did not soften Bertha's strong opinions. Even though she had called on Franklin Roosevelt and other influential Democrats to help in her skirmish with the Parkway, she flatly opposed the New Deal. During election years, she stayed at Flat Top into November so that she could vote Republican. She also despised the hefty income taxes that ate into her annual stock earnings. Could she have gotten away with it, said one relative, Bertha would have had no compunction about evading the income tax altogether, "particularly during Democratic administrations."[423]

Bertha never hesitated to speak out on controversial issues. She showed that during the late 1930s when she championed the annexation of Blowing Rock by Caldwell County. Many people around town complained that Watauga County shorted them on services, and Bertha, the county's second largest taxpayer, was particularly irritated that Watauga had no full-time fire warden to protect her extensive woodlands. Although the annexation never occurred, no one had to guess what the mistress of Flat Top thought about the issue.[424]

Her opinions on personal matters were equally vigorous. She was incredulous when her nephew, Edward Cone, informed her that he intended to study music in college. To her, that was not a pursuit or profession worthy of a serious man, and she said as much. Even compliments could be delivered in a backhanded way, conveying Bertha's judgmental tendencies. When a once-divorced niece introduced her new husband, Bertha said, "Well, I hear you picked a good one this time."[425]

Bertha retained a nagging fear that her foremen were stealing or otherwise taking advantage of her. Ever since she had assumed the management of the estate, she had complained about this regularly to Julius and others. Some of her accusations may have been motivated by a desire for sympathy, since she rarely seemed to take any advice that was given. Still, for reasons unknown, her long-time foreman Ed Underdown left the estate around the late 1930s, and there is some indication that his successors occasionally took advantage of the boss.[426]

The end of the war did not signal a return to life as usual at Flat Top. Clem died in 1945 and was buried on Flat Top Mountain near Moses. Although guests still called occasionally, Clem's death left Bertha and Sophie as the only residents of an increasingly muted manor.

In early June 1947, Bertha suffered a heart attack, but instead of going to the hospital, she remained at Flat Top. She and her physician, Dr. Mary Warfield, may have underestimated the severity of the attack, or perhaps she was simply ready to die. She had implied as much when Claribel passed away in 1929. She was now eighty-nine and had run the estate alone for nearly thirty-nine years. The countless teas, formal dinners, and games of bridge had provided entertainment and diversion, but worrying about apple harvests, fretting over wool prices and sheep-killing dogs, and dealing with her foremen, had extracted a toll. On Friday, June 6, her lungs began "filling with water" and anxious relatives summoned the doctor. At 7:30 a.m. on Sunday, June 8, with Sophie at her bedside, Bertha died.[427]

Her body was taken to Lenoir, where she was cremated, as she had wanted. Her ashes were returned to Flat Top, and at 2 p.m. on June 12, family and friends gathered in the manor for memorial services. The solemn mourners said very little. Norman was so shocked and saddened that he spoke not at all and seemed oblivious to the somber events that transpired around him. Sophie, Bertha's constant companion since 1908, was just as grief-stricken. Less than a year later, she died and was cremated and buried beside her sisters.[428]

In noting Bertha's death, local newspapers reported that she had left an estate worth an estimated $15 million. As specified by the indenture of 1911, most of that, including all her Cone Company stock and Flat Top Manor and estate, passed to the trustees of the Moses H. Cone Memorial Hospital. The remaining personal property and stocks, valued at more than $866,000, were divided according to the will Bertha had prepared in 1945 and amended in 1946. By its terms, she bequeathed $10,000 to the Blowing Rock Hospital and $15,000 to Jewish and community organizations in Baltimore. She also established trust funds and gave one-time cash payments and miscellaneous personal property to her relatives.[429]

Bertha bequeathed various pieces of furniture and cash to a number of her employees. The largest payments, $2,500, went to her farm foremen, while long-time chauffeur Ed Bumpass received $2,000. Most of the estate's workers were not as generously remembered. They received neither the land they thought they might get—that was impossible given the terms of the 1911 indenture—nor an annuity.[430]

Nevertheless, Bertha was quite generous with her family. Some received bequests valued at more than $100,000. This is not surprising. In small ways and with strangers, Bertha could be parsimonious; with those she knew and loved, she was remarkably generous and loyal. Bertha was once approached to contribute money toward refurbishing the governor's mansion, but refused, commenting that, "I take care of my own house, let the governor take care of his." Indeed, she did.[431]

Bertha bequeathed her furnishings and other personal property to no fewer than fifty-five recipients. Going to such lengths struck Bernard Cone as petty. But this was the only property that she personally controlled, and she insisted on disposing of it as she saw fit. It gave her a measure of power that she did not have in fulfilling her decades-long role as a loyal widow.[432]

Bertha also directed in her will that the manor house be closed, never to be opened again for any purpose. That was her private domain. Aside from the many memories the house contained, no one had ever contested her right to control the domestic realm. Flat Top Manor had been hers, and she wanted it kept that way. As time would tell, this wish would not be honored. Bertha could not control people and events after her death nearly as well as Moses had done after his.[433]

CHAPTER 8

THE NATIONAL PARK SERVICE
AND THE CONE ESTATE

At the time of Bertha's death, the future of Flat Top Manor seemed assured and undisputed. According to the indenture that had settled Moses' estate in 1911, the trustees of the Cone Memorial Hospital would own and operate the estate as a permanent "park and pleasureground for the public" and "an everlasting memorial to Moses H. Cone." As specified by Bertha's will, the manor house would remain closed to the public. Only on paper was Flat Top's fate so unambiguous and predetermined.[434]

Although the carriage roads and grounds became a free public park, the hospital board soon turned over ownership of the estate to Bertha's old foe, the Blue Ridge Parkway. Parkway managers not only opened the manor to the public, but they also installed a craft shop and pioneer museum in the house. Almost overnight, the Cone's once-fancy parlor, library, and dining room became the domain of quilts, wood carvings, and spinning wheels. While the craft shop and museum were clearly out of character with what had been the sumptuous country retreat of a powerful industrialist, they harmonized with popular perceptions of Appalachia as a land of log cabins and poor but resourceful pioneers.

Heavily influenced by these attitudes, National Park Service designers had highlighted and even created pioneer images along much of the Blue Ridge Parkway, putting up split-rail fences, preserving a water-powered grist mill, and erecting log cabins and outbuildings. The Cone estate obviously challenged this carefully constructed vision, but Parkway officials, committed to the myth of the pioneer, tried to make it fit anyway. In the process, they proved that they were no more free from the historical milieu of their times than Moses Cone had been of his. Just as turn-of-the-century social attitudes and values had motivated Cone to build his colonial revival manor and to live in it like a paternalistic feudal lord, so too did mid-century perceptions about the mountain South profoundly influence the way the Park Service would manage and interpret the Cone estate.

The hospital board had good reason for wanting to divest itself of

Flat Top. The indenture of 1911 had given it two very different tasks: managing a public park at Blowing Rock, and building and operating a hospital in Greensboro. Aside from geographical separation, the park and hospital had very different missions. They also competed for the same financial resources. Even though the board had inherited Bertha's company stock and the six-figure annual income that it produced, any money spent at Blowing Rock would necessarily deplete funds for hospital development. The trustees also knew that this situation was unlikely to improve with time. The hospital might some day become self-supporting; the park never would. While the indenture had earmarked $10,000 per year for the maintenance of Cone Park, Bernard Cone, with a businessman's astute eye for cost, sized up the estate at the time of Bertha's death and concluded that it would take double or triple that amount to operate it.[435]

The trustees soon found a way out of their dilemma. In July 1947, they approached Blue Ridge Parkway Superintendent Sam Weems to see if the Park Service would be interested in assuming ownership and management of the estate, subject to the provisions of the existing indenture. Park officials professed complete surprise at the proposal. Despite having surveyed routes for the Parkway through Flat Top, they thought that the state of North Carolina was to inherit the property.[436] Though unexpected, the trustees' proposal received quick consideration. Weems, along with the Parkway's resident landscape architect, Stanley W. Abbott, and other Park Service officials inspected the property in the summer of 1947. They were delighted by the "almost virgin quality" of the estate's woods and its recreational potential. The views were good and the carriage roads furnished a high quality, ready-made trail system. They also appreciated the fact that if they took over the Cone estate, they would not need to develop the recreation areas planned for Tompkins Knob to the north and Grandfather Mountain to the south. Accepting the estate would thus save money and keep Parkway facilities and services "on the edge of our best areas."[437]

The Parkway staff saw no reason to maintain the estate's extensive orchards, concluding that it would be better to reforest them and lease the adjoining pastures to local farmers for livestock grazing. The tenants then could be dismissed, except for the overseer. Abbott suggested retaining the overseer to provide security and maintenance until the property could be formally accepted. Parkway officials thought that the manor house, in a good state of repair, would make a nice restaurant and suggested that it be leased under concession contract. If that proved impractical, they proposed making the house a park ranger office or, failing that, razed. The old manor, they concluded, was "not of material importance for its history or its architecture."[438] In relaying these recommendations to his superiors, Weems offered the optimistic opinion that by careful management, estate maintenance expenses could "be reduced to a conservative figure which would compare favorably with maintenance costs in our other recreational areas."[439]

The Park Service directorate agreed with the field office assessment; the Cone property would make a fitting addition to the Blue Ridge Parkway. In spite of the affirmative response, administrative details and legal obstacles delayed for nearly two years the actual transfer of the property to the National Park Service. Some even questioned whether the estate could be transferred under terms of the 1911 indenture. The North Carolina Supreme Court eventually resolved the issue, ruling in a declaratory judgment that the transfer could be executed.[440]

While negotiations and legal debates dragged on, the estate tenants were in a quandary. As one recalled, "There was [sic] several years—I don't know how many—but we were in a state of not knowing what to do." Then, "they just started dismissing people a few at a time and taking the houses down." The shutting down of the estate "was kind of shock to everybody" and "hard on the people," since most of them had not been able to save much money. Still, the tenant had to admit, "It would have been impossible for anybody to try to keep it as it was."[441]

The trustees were as anxious as the tenants to resolve the issue of the estate's ownership and future management. The burden of taxes, protection, and administration was beginning to mount. Finally, on January 21, 1949, the last legal and administrative hurdles were cleared, and the National Park Service assumed responsibility for the management and protection of the Moses H. Cone Memorial Park.[442]

In keeping with the terms of the agreement and the management plan that had been agreed upon by the Parkway and hospital board, the carriage roads and the grounds remained open for hikers and horseback riders. Park officials repaired the dam at Trout Lake, which had been breached in the devastating storm of 1916, and stocked it with rainbow trout, some up to fifteen inches in length. The Parkway also requested special funding of nearly $46,000 to construct a bathhouse and develop a swimming beach. Even though these funds were never approved and Park managers later dropped the proposal for bathing at Trout Lake, a self-guiding nature trail was soon added to the growing list of recreational resources at the Cone Memorial Park.[443]

As much as the Parkway strived to meet its obligation to provide for recreation, one thorny problem remained: what to do with Flat Top Manor and the more than fifty other support structures. Abbott had to admit that the Cone estate was a fine example of rural retreats built by the wealthy in the mountain South "during the horse and carriage days." Although the manor house struck him as rather "ostentatious in its generally naturalistic setting," he was impressed by its exceptionally good state of repair. He also noted, "Remarkably it has changed little since early in the century and has never been reshaped to fit the motor car."[444]

Despite acknowledging that the Cone property exemplified turn-of-the-century country estates, Abbott, Weems, and other Parkway managers apparently never considered preserving its support buildings and carefully tended orchards and pastures, or using furnishings and exhibits to acquaint visitors with the history of the estate. There were several reasons for this.

First, Parkway managers regarded the estate chiefly as a recreation resource, providing opportunities for hiking, fishing, and horseback riding. Outdoor recreation was the primary intent of both the original indenture and the management plan that had been mutually agreed upon by the hospital board and the Park Service. Long before the Cone Park acquisition, the Parkway staff had planned to develop a large recreation area in the vicinity of Blowing Rock, one that would complement those being built at the Peaks of Otter and Rocky Knob in Virginia, and at the Bluffs, near Sparta, and Crabtree Meadows, near Spruce Pine, North Carolina.

By coincidence, while Parkway and hospital authorities negotiated the transfer of the Cone estate, the heirs of Julian Price approached the Park Service and offered to donate some 3,900 acres of land that lay immediately to the south of the Cone property. Price had been principal owner of the Jefferson Standard Life Insurance Company, headquartered in Greensboro. During the 1930s he had purchased his Watauga County tracts and made plans to create a lake and recreation area for use by his employees. However, Price died in an automobile accident in 1946. The Parkway subsequently accepted the tendered land, designating it the Julian Price Memorial Park. A campground and amphitheater, picnic area, and other facilities were soon added to the new park. Together, the adjoining Cone and Price Parks would comprise the largest and most diverse recreation area along the entire Blue Ridge Parkway.[445]

The development of these and other recreation resources helped the Parkway achieve one of its primary purposes, but it also consumed Parkway funds that in other circumstances might have gone toward preserving and interpreting the historic resources of the Cone estate. At the time the hospital board made its offer, the Parkway and the National Park Service still had not recovered from World War II funding cuts. In 1940, the bureau's appropriations, including those for the Civilian Conservation Corps, totalled nearly $34 million. Five years later the Park Service operating budget had shrunk to less than $5 million. The appropriation for 1950 rebounded to $30 million, still $4 million below that of 1940. During the same ten-year period, the National Park System expanded by twenty-one areas and visitation doubled. Parkway visitation followed the national trend, rising from 895,000 in 1941 to 1,996,000 in 1950.[446]

Modest budget allocations and sharply increased visitation were especially burdensome to Parkway administrators. In the late 1940s, the Blue Ridge Parkway was a long way from completion. Park managers had to devote more attention to road surveys and the selection of alignments than to historic preservation. Construction began in September 1935, but had been halted by war in 1942. At that time, only 171 miles of the Parkway's eventual 469-mile length had been paved. In 1947, the same year that the hospital board proposed its donation, Park Service officials estimated that the Parkway would require $18.5 million to complete.[447]

Designing and building the Parkway was complicated by the cooperative nature of the venture. The Bureau of Public Roads shouldered responsibility for road construction, including allocating funds and administering grading and paving contracts. Park Service managers and professional staff routed and landscaped the road, developed recreation facilities, and planned visitor lodging and other accommodations.

Acquiring the right-of-way also involved the states through which the Parkway passed. In the early decades of the century, public sentiment toward national parks, as expressed through the Congress, tended to be conservative. Many people felt that national parks should be created only on lands that had limited commercial value, and that they should be operated at the lowest possible cost. In the West, most National Parks were set aside from publicly owned lands considered commercially worthless.[448] In the East, where there were few public lands, Congress usually required the states and private donors to furnish lands to be designated as national parks. In the case of the Blue Ridge Parkway, the Commonwealth of Virginia and State of North Carolina purchased and donated the lands that eventually comprised the park. Still, some people considered any Federal money spent on the Parkway a waste. A Republican Congressman from Ohio, Thomas A. Jenkins, fumed, "I said at that time and I say now that it [the Blue Ridge Parkway] was the most gigantic and stupendously extravagant and unreasonable expenditure made by the most extravagantly expensive administration in the history of the world." [449]

There were even doubters within the National Park Service itself. Since its establishment in 1916, the bureau had been committed to monumentalism, the preserving of the spectacular landscapes and wilderness areas of the West. More than a few Park Service veterans had a difficult time understanding how, in Abbott's words, "a little ribbon of land 1,000 feet wide and 500 miles long could contribute to our major objective of conserving the fine landscape of America." Internally, the Blue Ridge Parkway was, to put it bluntly, "a red-headed stepchild."[450]

In time, the Parkway would be lauded for achieving the twin purposes for which it was created: to provide jobs and a measure of economic relief during the Depression, and to link the Shenandoah National Park in Virginia and the Great Smoky Mountains National Park in Tennessee and North Carolina by means of a scenic road. But in the late 1940s, skeptics still abounded. Sam Weems was keenly aware of this, and he knew that controlling operating costs was a major concern, all of which helps to explain why he chose not to preserve the historical integrity of the Cone estate.

There was another less pragmatic, but perhaps more important reason why Parkway managers during the 1950s dismantled tenant houses and removed the laundry house, bowling alley, and all but five of the structures on the Cone estate. A country estate, especially one built by the son of a German-Jewish immigrant, simply did not agree with accepted notions about the history and culture of Appalachia.

As a host of scholars have argued in recent years, popular perceptions of Appalachia and its people have been created, altered, and stereotyped to support the social and economic agendas of people outside the region. In the process, two contrasting images have emerged: one is the gaunt and grizzled, corn-cob pipe-smoking, moonshine-swilling, rifle-toting, feuding buffoon; the other is the isolated, independent, resourceful, freedom-loving, all-American, frontiersman.[451] Parkway designers and managers tried consciously and deliberately to portray the mountaineer in the latter terms, that is, as a heroic pioneer. To support this image, they retained (and in some instances created) log cabins and farmsteads, and built miles of split-rail fences along the scenic road. At the same time, they systematically removed or excluded from view elements that did not fit. For example, not a single clapboard farmhouse was preserved within the boundaries of the Parkway, even though such houses were common in the region by the latter half of the nineteenth century.[452] They also eliminated or screened from view any evidence of industrialization. The ornate Cone country estate, built by a textile magnate, hardly harmonized with the pioneer portrait that the Parkway wished to convey.

Historical accuracy was not the overriding concern of the landscape architects who designed the Parkway. Inspired by artists of the Hudson River School, they strove to create a living example of nineteenth century American landscape painting.[453] To the Parkway's creators, the countryside was "the handmaiden of the road." Like cinematography, the scenic highway was, said Abbott, "the method by which the varied and countless scenes composing the Blue Ridge picture are unfolded or, as it were, projected to the visitor." Overlooks "serve as invitations to stop the projection in order to focus attention to best advantage on a detailed study of the various elements composing the representative 'frames' of the picture."[454] The Parkway was an art gallery that visitors could pass through at forty-five miles-per-hour or, if they chose to, stop and study a particular rendering.

The landscape architects did not consciously and deliberately set out to create a false picture of the region. On the contrary, they were convinced that they were "preserving something of the backwoods feeling that otherwise may disappear from the mountains."[455] In the *Blue Ridge Parkway News*, a newsletter aimed at neighboring landowners, Parkway officials lamented the passing of the old pioneer ways. In 1942 the *News* proclaimed:

> The old dwellings and the barns hewn by hand from the forest

itself are beginning to go. . .The very picture which makes the Blue Ridge seem old and solid and early American and very different to the traveler is changing. Thus, these things are fast becoming a story.[456]

This fading scene, this "lived in quality of the mountains," was an essential element in the total landscape composition, and its preservation became a top priority.

Such pioneer and pastoral images were irresistible to Americans of the 1930s and 1940s. As the country became increasingly urban and complex, more and more tourists took to the highways in search of bucolic, picture-postcard views like those being created on the Blue Ridge Parkway. The architects of the Blue Ridge Parkway were careful to supply the sought-after images of a simpler, pioneer time. It has been suggested that when America lost its western frontier it created a surrogate in Appalachia.[457] The Parkway's landscape architects were not inclined to challenge this invention. They were no more immune than others of their generation to the mythology that had grown up about Appalachia. They were as sincere as they were wrong when they reported that the Blue Ridge region "was touched only by the backwash of history" and remained aloof and unscathed by the Civil War. To them, "The life of these people, both past and present, is free of mystery and does not induce speculation or conjecture. It is as self-revealing as it is straightforward and real."[458]

The truth was that until after the Civil War, the mountain South was an undifferentiated region of America. There was no "Appalachia" as such. However, during the latter decades of the 1800s, magazine writers of the local-colorist school churned out hundreds of stories about the "strange land and peculiar people" of the Southern Highlands. Stories of isolated, unchurched, and ignorant mountaineers motivated Northern protestant churches to establish schools and churches and to undertake "uplift" work. "Picturesque" Appalachia came to be looked upon as a problem that needed remedy.[459]

In the ensuing decades, timber, mining, and railroad companies bought and exploited vast areas of the region, creating dramatic social and economic change. Curiously, the Parkway designers never mentioned Appalachia's long and often unhappy experience with industrialization and modernization. Despite having arrived in the region in the early 1930s, Abbott, a Cornell educated New Yorker, observed that mountaineers "are a distinctly country folk of limited horizons," people who "lead a very simple existence. They eat well, sleep well, work hard." Contemplating the idealized "homestead culture" of the mountain folk, Abbott sighed, "Provincial life, gee!"[460]

Certainly Abbott and his Parkway peers did not create the fiction that Appalachia was and always had been a place where independent and resourceful (if not terribly bright) pioneers lived in log cabin clearings in the woods; the local-colorists, settlement workers, and well-intentioned home missionaries did that. The Parkway's architects only mirrored the myths. In a sense, they had to. They and the designers and managers who followed them could not produce a viable scenic view of the region if their composition clashed with the perceptions and tastes of their patrons, the American public. That the prevailing ideas about Appalachia greatly influenced the design, development, and interpretation of the Blue Ridge Parkway was nowhere more convincingly demonstrated than in the strategy for managing the Cone estate.[461]

The initial recommendation to make Flat Top Manor a restaurant or office was rather quickly reconsidered. Weems had a better idea. In April 1951, he visited the Penland School of Handicraft and asked its director, Lucy Morgan, if the school would be interested in establishing a training and craft sales center in the manor. Located in Mitchell County near Spruce Pine, Penland was certainly the closest of the various handicraft centers that had been established in the region, and Morgan had to admit that she liked the superintendent's idea. Unfortunately, she told Weems, Penland did not have the money to underwrite such a program.[462]

Undeterred, Weems decided to make a direct approach to the Southern Highland Handicraft Guild. He invited the board of directors to a picnic on the lawn at Flat Top Manor. At the appropriate moment, Weems made his pitch. "Well, do you suppose," said one waffling board member, "we could gross as much as $500 a month?" The Superintendent confidently responded, "I will underwrite it right now, on my own." That was apparently good enough for the Guild. The board met soon after the picnic and decided to accept Weems' offer.[463]

Opened in 1951, the Parkway Craft Center seemed the perfect solution to the Cone "problem" because it provided a means of occupying and doing something with Flat Top Manor that complemented the Parkway's pioneer theme. It also agreed with the popular image that mountaineers not only lived in log cabins, but whiled away their time by making quilts, coverlets, and sundry other items.

The park staff considered craft sales an important extension of the story that the Parkway was attempting to tell. As Abbott informed park concessionaires, "We have endeavored in the planning of the Blue Ridge Parkway to emphasize in every way that we can the qualities of local color inherent in the varied countryside." Run-of-the-mill five-and-ten-cent-store souvenirs would not be acceptable in Parkway gift shops. Instead, concessionaires must carry items that "will in themselves be distinctive and so unusual as to be talked about." Besides handcrafted items, sales could include sorghum molasses, preserves, and herbs, "those products which are to the Blue Ridge as the Florida grapefruit is to Florida."[464]

In addition to craft sales, Parkway officials at the start of the 1952 season installed a Pioneer Museum exhibit in the craft center. Dedicated that June, the museum featured a collection of early mountain tools and furniture, quilts, and other items that Frances Goodrich had donated to the Guild many years before. Located in the what had been the Cones' parlor on the first floor, the modest exhibit was described as small but "interesting and attractive." And the public liked it. Rangers and concessionaire employees reinstalled it each spring for a number of years.[465]

Demonstrations augmented the center's interpretive and educational programs. Offerings included spinning and weaving, knotting, fringing, pottery, shuckery, hooking, lapidary, enamels, broomcraft, and woodcarving. These usually featured traditional arts and local craftspeople, although there were exceptions. For example, a special exhibit in 1956 highlighted the tapestries woven by Sirkka Ahlskog, a visiting instructor at Penland. Ahlskog's work was described by Lucy Morgan as "very modern—maybe ultra modern and those artists up there [at Parkway Craft Center] should like it."[466]

As Weems had confidently predicted, the center earned a profit from the start. In 1952, its first full season of operation, gross sales topped $12,000, while net profits totaled $1,700.[467] The center also provided multiple benefits to the Park Service. Under its concessionaire contract, the Guild returned a modest building use fee, agreed to take care of routine housekeeping and interior painting at the manor, and to pay for craft demonstrations. These were important considerations to budget-conscious Parkway administrators.[468]

The craft center proved so popular, profitable, and mutually beneficial that in the mid-1960s Guild and Parkway managers proposed the construction of an entire Early Americana village on the old Cone estate. As proposed, the village would dwarf the Parkway's other pioneer displays, such as the one at Mabry Mill, near Meadows of Dan, Virginia. At Americana, the public would be able to browse an old country store and visit a one-room school and appropriately rustic church. They would see first-hand a working farm, complete with farm house, barn, spring house, root cellar, work shed, storage shed, outhouse, chicken house, meat house, pigpen, gardens, fields of crops, and orchards. And they would get to examine two working, water-powered grist mills.

Plans also called for a visitor center and outdoor amphitheater to be located near the manor house. To accommodate the expected surge in visitation, parking capacity at the Parkway Craft Center would be increased by 315 cars.

In addition to the abundant exhibits, the Guild would dramatically expand crafts production, distribution, and sales. A number of "multiple unit buildings" would be built to provide year-round residences, workshops, and demonstration areas for craftsmen. In summer, demonstrators would give programs on spinning and weaving, yarn dyeing, pottery, and woodcarving; in winter, the craftspeople would train apprentices and produce for summer sales. The old apple barn would be converted into a craft production center and warehouse. Park and Guild officials believed that the new complex might enable the Southern Highland Handicraft Guild to achieve a crafts monopoly. The Guild would have the capability to purchase, store, and distribute all the products made by craftspeople in the region.[469]

Several sources would provide funding. To get the project started, Weems would put up the $100,000 he had accumulated from the hospital board's annual donation for the maintenance of Cone Park. Other backing would be sought from the National Park Foundation Board and, of course, from Park Service appropriations. Supporters believed that through large-scale crafts production and marketing, Americana would become self-supporting.[470]

As a major educational goal, Americana would show how the mountaineers came into the region and why their "centuries-old culture prevailed, little changed, until well into the present century." Accordingly, exhibits would focus on the "handicrafts of our forefathers" and extol the hardy folk who practiced self-reliance in "the land of 'do it yourself, or do without'."[471] For the sake of supposed historical accuracy, craft demonstrations would be limited to techniques and objects that were used in the region prior to 1910. "Even though the original culture existed long after 1910," a Park Service study team concluded, "from that time on modern communications and transportation methods began to reach the mountain people, bringing into these hills increasing influences of the 'modern' civilization."[472]

Americana planners seemed unaware of the ironies in their proposal. They were setting out to tell a story of isolation and "make do" on a country estate that had been built well before 1910 by a wealthy industrialist, in a community that for three-quarters of a century had been the summer retreat and playground for scores of well-to-do families. They seemed equally oblivious to the fact that the economy of the mountain South always had been influenced by national economic developments and, in many instances, had been intimately linked to regional markets. And no one noted that well before 1910 railroads had penetrated the region, and mine and timber companies had been busily hauling away natural resources. It was as if there were two Appalachias: one that existed, and one that was wished for. Americana planners preferred the latter vision because it complemented the image of the region that the Parkway's landscape architects portrayed, and matched the stereotypical perceptions that prevailed among the public at large. To this extent, Americana would depict the region as the public wished.[473]

Predictably, support for Americana was widespread. In 1966, an Advisory Board to the Southern Highland Handicraft Guild was created to provide business expertise to the Guild's creative craftsmen. Members included Weems, former Park Service Director Conrad Wirth, conservationist Michael Frome, and Mrs. Huber Hanes, wife of the textile magnate. Not surprisingly, all endorsed the Americana project. The Advisory Board on National Parks, Historic Sites, Buildings and Monuments, visiting the Parkway in 1971, also applauded the Early Americana proposal.[474]

After all the planning and anxious anticipation, Americana was never built. The limitations of the site were one drawback. There was too little water to power the grist mills, and the topography was unsuited for the type of development proposed. Planners overcame these obstacles in 1967 by shifting the proposed site to neighboring Price Park, a non-historic Parkway recreational area. A greater and more persistent concern was funding, as construction estimates soared to more than $3.2 million. This was a staggering sum for a Parkway that had always lacked funds for interpretive development. Furthermore, the timing could not have been worse. Mission 66, the Park Service's ten-year, $1 billion construction and development program that had been created to compensate for the neglect the National Parks had suffered during World War II, ended just as Americana planning began.[475]

At the same time, the National Park System had entered a period of rapid expansion. Some sixty-nine parks were established during George Hartzog's tenure as bureau director from 1964 to 1973. In 1968, Congress authorized the extension of the Blue Ridge Parkway to near Cartersville, Georgia, a distance of 180 miles. Although public opposition in the 1970s prevented construction of the Parkway extension, the evaluation of potential routes diverted substantial staff time and funding.[476]

In 1968, the Parkway's new superintendent, Granville B. Liles, complained that lack of construction funds prevented even a start on the Americana project. Private support was no more available than federal funds. Roger Soles, president of the Jefferson Standard Life Insurance Company, the benefactor of Price Park, offered little encouragement. He confessed to Liles that he had no idea as to a possible source of funding, but maybe, he added cheerily, the "Washington purse strings will loosen before long."[477]

Little did Soles know that Washington purse strings were about to be more snugly cinched. The rapid expansion of the Park System had created a construction and development backlog of $2.5 billion. Given the average annual Congressional appropriation for development, the Park Service's Washington office estimated that it would take fifty years to complete the projects that had been requested. To reduce this backlog, the bureau director instructed field areas to review and eliminate all non-essential projects.[478]

Blue Ridge Parkway deletions included funding for the development of the Cone Memorial Park. After planners decided in 1967 to move the Americana project and the Parkway Craft Center to Price Park, several proposals for the Cone estate emerged. One was to improve and open a "motor nature trail" on the existing carriage road from Trout Lake to near the summit of Rich Mountain. This generated only lukewarm staff support, while it invoked the ire of many Blowing Rock residents. They let it be known through letters and petitions that they opposed permitting traffic on any of the estate's trails and roads. There were few regrets when the project was dropped in 1973.[479]

As part of the development backlog review, Parkway managers also aborted the development of the bath house and beach for Trout Lake and facilities for group camping and hostel. These, they decided, could better be provided outside the park. In addition, they deleted entirely the proposal to restore and furnish Flat Top Manor. In 1967, with the expectation that the craft center would soon be relocated to Price Park, the old problem of what to do with Flat Top Manor had reemerged. A study team recommended refurbishing the house, furnishing it with period pieces, and otherwise restoring the estate to its turn-of-the-century appearance. By 1973, in light of funding constraints, this no longer seemed such a good idea. In canceling their request for $480,000, Parkway officials did an about-face and concluded, "There appears little interpretive or historic value in refurnishing this house and exhibiting it as a historic building."[480]

Funding was only one factor in the sudden change of position. In August 1971, Guild Director Robert Gray, at a joint meeting of the Asheville Tourist Association and the local Jaycees, had announced plans for a $3 million Appalachian Heritage Center to be built in Asheville. The proposed center included a craft village, with facilities for folk music and dance, and a visitor center. Superintendent Liles worried that the Heritage Center would duplicate Americana, and he was annoyed that Gray had not consulted him about the proposal. Still, Gray was determined to go ahead with the project "with or without the Parkway." The prospects for the construction of Americana, never encouraging, were now bleak indeed.[481]

In 1974, Gray formally proposed that a Folk Art Center, containing all the facilities suggested in 1971, be built on the Parkway in Asheville. Liles replied that the idea had considerable merit, although it would greatly change the proposal for Americana. Gray suggested that there was no need to link the two projects, but Liles and his planners disagreed. Two years later, with the support of a $1.5 million grant from the Appalachian Regional Commission, the Guild and Park Service concluded an agreement that cleared the way for construction of the Folk Art Center. For all practical purposes, Americana was dead. Without it, Parkway administrators saw no compelling reason to remove the craft center or, for that matter, to shift the focus of interpretation at the Cone estate.[482]

Compared to the years of anxious anticipation that surrounded the ill-fated Americana project, the 1970s and 1980s proved relatively tranquil for the Cone estate. In 1970, the Parkway issued a concession contract for carriage rides and horse rentals, but the service never proved popular and did not survive the decade. The park staff removed the Pioneer Museum during the 1960s or early 1970s. In 1980, they installed an information desk and publications sales outlet in the parlor of the manor. This sales center, operated by a non-profit cooperating association, grossed more than $86,000 in 1992.[483]

Recent decades have verified the accuracy of Bernard Cone's 1947 observation that the hospital board's annual donation of $10,000 a year would be inadequate to maintain the estate in perpetuity. In 1973, historical architects estimated that it would take $25,000 to repair roof leaks at Flat Top Manor. This estimate tripled after further investigation revealed rotted rafters, plates, and studding.[484]

These expenditures proved minor in comparison to those of the following decades. The Parkway's maintenance division laid out more than $80,000 in 1986 to rehabilitate stone retaining walls and carriage roads. In 1990, the reproduction and rehabilitation of balustrades and repair of masonry footings and piers at Flat Top Manor consumed an estimated $90,000. This was a paltry sum compared to the reconstruction of the dams at Bass and Trout Lakes. In 1987, park workers breached both dams because of concerns about their soundness and because, at Bass Lake, ice had damaged the outlet gate and control. Contractors repaired all three dams under a single contract that totalled $3.2 million.[485]

During its nearly half-century administration of the Cone Memorial Park, the Blue Ridge Parkway clearly has met its recreation mandate. Over the years, millions of people have hiked, ridden horseback, jogged, and snow-skied on the carriage roads and trails, and they have fished the lakes and enjoyed the many panoramic vistas. In 1991, an estimated 500,000 people used the park for outdoor recreation, while another 200,000 visited Flat Top Manor.[486]

The Parkway also has preserved and kept Flat Top Manor open to the public, but this does not diminish the historical loss that occurred in the early 1950s when park managers sold or demolished most of the fifty-seven other structures on the estate. As Abbott noted when he evaluated the property in 1947, the Park Service inherited a remarkably complete and little-altered example of a turn-of-the-century country estate. Parkway administrators justified some demolition as required for the parking lot built on the northwest side of the house. But according to one Parkway staff member, the prevailing philosophy at the time was "if you don't need it, get rid of it," and no one saw the need to preserve the support buildings.[487]

Neither did anyone seriously consider preserving the historic scene associated with the estate. The Park Service could not afford to tend hundreds of acres of gardens and orchards any more than it could maintain scores of historic buildings. As a result, the formal gardens and deer parks were abandoned, and pastures either became overgrown or were leased for livestock grazing. The extensive orchards, which included rare cultivars, were left untended and, in time, gave way to regenerating native plants. Some of the tenants were heartbroken to see their former homes destroyed and the grounds neglected. More than twenty-five years after moving from the estate, Ruby Walters often returned to visit the site of her former home "to see if there's flowers coming up where I know they should be."[488]

Certainly limited funding, ever-increasing visitation, and other demands have shaped Park Service decisions about the preservation and ongoing management of the estate. Today, workload factors on the Parkway include the maintenance and administration of nine campgrounds, thirteen designated picnic areas, eleven visitor centers, hundreds of miles of trails, a total of 544 miles of roads, twenty-seven tunnels, nearly 14,000 signs, and 326 buildings, of which ninety-nine are historic structures. In recent years, the staff available to do this work has decreased and, after adjustments for inflation, so has the Parkway's annual operating budget. At the same time, visitation has risen sharply. From 1965 to 1993 it more than doubled to almost 23 million. Meanwhile, money devoted to the maintenance of roads, trails, and buildings in the Cone Park has escalated dramatically.[489]

Even so, much could be done to restore the historic scene and to acquaint the public with the Cones and their country estate. Recently completed Park Service studies and reports contain suggestions for various actions, including selectively replanting orchards, developing exhibits for Flat Top Manor, and relocating the parking lot and approach to the estate so that visitors enter from the front, as the original architect and the Cones themselves intended. The investment required to implement these ideas would be significant and would require the involvement of the long-time tenant, the Southern Highland Handicraft Guild. Given the Parkway's history, federal funding for such an undertaking appears unlikely. Acknowledging this, Parkway Superintendent Gary Everhardt has solicited private assistance to help evaluate options and to take on the challenge of improving the preservation and interpretation of the estate. If broad public support can be mobilized, then Flat Top may yet regain a measure of its former luster. In the process, Parkway visitors might learn more about who Moses and Bertha Cone were and how and why they built their estate at Blowing Rock. They might also better understand that Appalachia was more than a land of log cabins and whimmy diddles.

CHAPTER 9

EPILOGUE

I n one sense, Flat Top Manor is the shining symbol of a family's remarkable success. Herman Kahn, the family patriarch, arrived in America a poor peddler; his first-born son became one of North Carolina's most influential textile manufacturers, built one of the region's premier country estates, and gained a reputation as a generous public benefactor. By anyone's measure, these were major accomplishments. Perhaps during his childhood Moses had read Horatio Alger's stories about newsboys and bootblacks who parlayed hard work, self-reliance, and virtue into business success. To say that he achieved the dream of rags-to-riches is only a slight exaggeration. Moses had not been born into poverty, although in the late 1850s the Cone family was by no means well-to-do.

Considering these modest beginnings, Moses must have taken pride in his achievements. Others did. In 1907, Greensboro Mayor L.J. Brandt proclaimed him "the largest single factor in the development of Greensboro from a mere hamlet to the Gate City of the Carolinas." Not only had his giant mills given employment and spurred economic development, but Cone had been a model citizen. "Your hand has touched on every phase of our life," the mayor said, "always to upbuild, never to tear down."[490]

In many ways, Moses had only completed the long social journey his father had begun before him. When Herman Kahn left Altenstadt in 1846, a brother-in-law told him not to shed tears for his relatives in Germany, "because you may have the sweet hope of finding a second home abroad and a new country. . .a real homeland." Although the writer never said so explicitly, he clearly had high hopes for this relative.[491]

There was nothing unusual about the quest for success and status that Herman had initiated and that Moses and his dutiful widow, Bertha, had continued. Countless other immigrants and their children prospered in America. Many dominated their business rivals and employees and allied themselves with conservative causes. Many also built country estates and practiced philanthropy. The Cones were part of a larger cultural process, one that defined how people gained acceptance and respectability in American society. What distinguished them from many of their peers was the remarkable consistency of their actions. Other families with similar backgrounds may have pursued the same goal, but few did so more unswervingly or with more dedication.[492] In 1908, B.B. Dougherty eulogized his friend Moses Cone, commenting that "His like will not be seen in this country again." Given the particularity of Cone's personal history and his times, Dougherty was more correct in that assessment than he may have intended.[493]

In looking back, it is also apparent that the Park Service managers who inherited Flat Top Manor were, no less than the Cones, subject to the views and popular perceptions of their day. Americans of the 1940s and 1950s still regarded Appalachia as a land of isolated and independent hillbillies and log cabins. The Parkway's landscape architects were only responding to those ideas when they selectively preserved scores of log structures, built split-rail fences and, at Flat Top Manor, installed a craft shop and pioneer museum. Even though Parkway managers now realize that Appalachia was more complex than formerly thought, they lack the funds to undertake extensive changes on the estate or elsewhere along the Parkway. Since its creation in 1916, the National Park Service has given priority to the larger natural areas it manages. This has made it difficult for the Blue Ridge Parkway to compete for the Park Service's limited funding with such large and popular national parks as Grand Canyon, Yellowstone, and Yosemite. And it has made it impossible to preserve a working estate that was once among the finest in North Carolina.

Today, Flat Top's showy apple blossoms and tranquil deer parks exist only in the minds of aging former tenants and long-time Blowing Rock residents. Fewer than 650 of the Cones' 32,000 apple trees remain, while more than half of the estate's 500 acres of pastures have reverted to forest.[494] In the manor's entrance hall, hand-carved wooden birds and bowls have replaced the shiny horse-hair sofas and mahogany tables with vases of gladioluses. In the dining room, 1 p.m. now carries little significance. Where well-dressed ladies and gentlemen once sat down to carefully prepared and formally served country fare, a steady stream of vacationers now browses finely crafted quilts and stylish hand-woven sweaters. Although the architecture of the manor and the carriage roads and lakes have been preserved, the recreational park and craft sales center of today are a far cry from the manicured working estate that Moses and Bertha Cone built. There is a certain historical justice in this. Since the estate was conceived a century ago, the needs and goals of its owners, like the larger social and historical contexts, have changed dramatically. Flat Top Manor reflects and documents these changes. It also bears witness, mute but eloquent, to what these changes have cost.

NOTES

1. *Moody's Industrial Manual, 1983*, vol. 1. (New York: Moody's Investor Service, 1983), 2712; Sharon Travitsky Russin, ed., *Wall Street Journal Index, 1983* (New York: Dow Jones, 1984), 196. *Wall Street Journal Index, 1984*, 208.

2. Mildred Gwin Andrews, *The Men and the Mills: A History of the Southern Textile Industry* (Macon, Ga.: Mercer University Press, 1987), 243.

3. Sydney Cone, Jr., ed. "The Cones from Bavaria," typed manuscript, vol. 1: 3, 20, Greensboro, North Carolina, Public Library.

4. Thomas D. Clark, "The Post-Civil War Economy in the South," in *Jews in the South*, ed. Leonard Dinnerstein and Mary Dale Palsson (Baton Rouge: Louisiana State University Press, 1973), 163; Maribeth Crandell, *Moses H. Cone: His Family, His Fortune, and His Life* (Greensboro, N.C.: Cone Printing Services, 1977), 1; *Population Schedules of the Seventh Census of the United States, 1850, Virginia: Lunenburg County* (Washington, D.C.: National Archives, General Services Administration, 1964), 1.

5. Crandell, 1, 13; Samuel Adler, untitled typed manuscript in Washington County-Jonesborough, Tennessee, Library: n.p., 1.

6. Paul Fink, *Jonesborough: The First Century of Tennessee's First Town* (Springfield, Va.: National Technical Information Services, 1972), 16, 81, 139-40; Captain Ross Smith, *Reminiscences of an Old-Timer* (Privately Printed, 1930), 37-39; Adler, 4.

7. Crandell, 1; *Population Schedules of the Eighth Census of the United States, 1860: Tennessee, Washington County* (Washington, D.C.: National Archives, 1965),134-35.

8. Washington County, Tennessee, Deed Book 38, 48.

9. Tennessee Civil War Centennial Commission, *Tennesseans in the Civil War* vol. 1 (Nashville: 1964), 312; Adler, 2

10. Adler, 3. An advance to Susan Watkins for $105.15 was guaranteed with a "piano and piano cover, mahogany sideboard, 2 falling leaf tables, pr. Brass knob fire irons, and 12 windsor parlor chairs." Watkins apparently repaid the loan. Washington County, Tennessee, Deed Book 40, 214.

11. Washington County Deed Book 37, 594, and Book 40, 475; Washington County Chancery Court Minute Books for 1865, 601, and 1866, 218. Other foreclosures included the Addison Wilson farm of 92.5 acres, acquired in 1868 (Book 41, 58), and 84 acres received from J.C.B. Patton in 1872 (Book 43, 203).

Alfred Jackson had a remarkably undistinguished military career. For most of the war, he skirmished with bushwhackers and pursued deserters. Patricia L. Faust, ed., *Historical Times Illustrated Encyclopedia of the Civil War* (New York: Harper & Row, 1986), 389.

12. Washington County Chancery Court Minute Books for 1866-1867, 120, 236, 309-10, 358-60.

13. Washington County Minute Book for Chancery Court, 1866-1867, 133-37, 246-52, 327, 374. Guggenheim may have been related to Helen Cone. She had been a Guggenheimer prior to her marriage, and it was not unusual for immigrant families to alter their names, just as Herman Kahn had.

14. Besides the social upheaval and their courtroom reversals in Jonesborough, the Cones' three-month-old son Albert died there in 1867. Sydney Cone, Jr., "The Herman Cone Family," typed manuscript, Blue Ridge Parkway Archives, 1966.

15. Robert J. Brugger, *Maryland: A Middle Temperament, 1634-1980* (Baltimore: Johns Hopkins University Press, 1988), 314-16, 356-57; Ben Cone and Ceasar Cone, II, interview by E.P. Douglass, Southern Oral History Project, transcript, Southern Historical Collection, University of North Carolina, Chapel Hill.

16. *Charlotte Observer*, 8 September 1963; Adler, 9-10.

17. *Greensboro Patriot*, 16 December 1908.

18. *Knoxville Sentinel*, 22 March 1917; *Knoxville City Directory* (Knoxville,Tenn.: Ogden Bros., 1886), 127.

19. Nancy Lindau Lewis and Judith Lindau McConnell, tape recorded interview by the author, 11 October 1993; Alfred M. Lindau, "History of the Lindau Family," photocopy of manuscript, in possession of Mrs. Judith McConnell; Judith McConnell, "Notes on Genealogy of the Lindau Family," photocopy in possession of the author; *Greensboro Daily News*, 9 June 1947.

20. Moses Cone to Carrie and Moses [Long], 24 May 1884, photocopy from collection of Ellen C.B. Hirschland.

21. Lindau, 3; Marriage Certificate for Moses Cone and Bertha Lindau, in collection of Judith McConnell.

22. Douglas McElrath, archivist, Maryland State Archives, unrecorded interview by author, 11 April 1991. Information was taken from census records and city directories.

23. Crandell, 3; "The Cone Family and the Textile Industry" *Orphan's Friend and Masonic Journal*, 1 July 1941.

24. Cone Export & Commission Company, *Half Century Book: 1891-1941* (Greensboro, N.C.: 1941), 4-5.

25. Broadus Mitchell, *The Rise of Cotton Mills in the South* (Baltimore: Johns Hopkins University Press, 1921), 265.

26. Jack Blicksilver, *Cotton Manufacturing in the Southeast: An Historical Analysis* (Atlanta: Georgia State College of Business Administration, 1959), 25-27; Holland Thompson, *From the Cotton Field to the Cotton Mill: A Study of Industrial Transition in North Carolina* (New York: Macmillan, 1906; reprint Freeport, N.Y.: Books for Libraries, 1971), 101-4; Nancy Frances Kane, *Textiles in Transition: Technology, Wages, and Industry Relocation the U.S. Textile Industry, 1880-1930* (New York: Greenwood Press, 1988), 9-10.

27. *Asheville Citizen*, 25 August 1922; Harry W. Fulenweider, *Asheville City Directory and Business Reflex, 1890* (Charleston, S.C.: Walker, Evans & Cogswell, 1890), 201.

28. McElrath interview. Based on information contained in city directories.

29. *Manufacturer's Review and Industrial Record*, 15 June 1891, 402.

30. Articles of Incorporation, Cone Export and Commission Company, Cone Mills Corporation Archives. Jay Guggenheimer was probably a maternal relative. Anderson Price, listed as a resident of Bergen County, New Jersey, apparently never took an active part in company operations.

31. Mitchell, 256.

32. Balance Sheet, 1891, Cone Export and Commission Company, Cone Mills Archives.

33. Pilot Mills Company Papers, Legal Papers, Perkins Library, Duke University.

34. Cathy McHugh, *Mill Family: The Labor System in the Southern Cotton Textile Industry, 1880-1915* (New York: Oxford University Press, 1988), 7.

35. Various lists of stockholders, Cone Mills Archives.

36. Gary Richard Freeze, "Model Mill Men of the New South: Paternalism and Methodism in the Odell Cotton Mills of North Carolina, 1877-1908" (Ph.D. diss., University of North Carolina, Chapel Hill, 1988), 122; Blicksilver, 21; Diane L.F. Afflick, *Just New from the Mills: Printed Cottons in America, Late Nineteenth and Early Twentieth Centuries* (North Andover, Mass.: Museum of American Textile History, 1987), 21. When Lawrence S. Holt violated his contract with the Cones and sent his goods elsewhere to be finished, the brothers sued. They won a $5,000 judgment and compelled Holt not to do any finishing himself for three years. *Greeensboro Patriot*, 26 June 1895.

37. Mary J. Oats, *The Role of the Cotton Textile Industry in the Economic Development of the American Southeast: 1900-1940* (New York: Arno Press, 1975), 92.

38. Ethel Arnett, *Greensboro, North Carolina* (Chapel Hill: University of North Carolina Press, 1955), 171, 419; Gayle Hicks Fripp, "Greensboro's Early Suburbs," in *Early Twentieth Century Suburbs in North Carolina* (Raleigh: North Carolina Department of Cultural Resources, 1985), 49.

39. *Report on Manufacturing Industries in the United States, Eleventh Census, 1890* Part 3 (Washington, D.C.: U.S. Department of the Interior, Census Office), 206-7.

40. Samuel M. Kipp III, "Urban Growth and Social Change in the South, 1870-1920: Greensboro, North Carolina, as a Case Study" (Ph.D. diss., Princeton University, 1974), 128.

41. Arnett, 170-72.

42. David Schenck Diary, 17 March 1890, Southern Historical Collection, University of North Carolina at Chapel Hill; quoted in Edward L. Ayers, *The Promise of the New South: Life After Reconstruction* (New York: Oxford University Press, 1992), 61.

43. John Henderson to "My Darling Wife," 18 April 1890, Southern Historical Collection, University of North Carolina at Chapel Hill; quoted in Ayers, 61.

44. Guilford County, North Carolina, Deed Book 99, 544.

45. Bernard Cone to Bertha Cone, 12 February 1937, Cone Mills Archives.

46. *Greensboro Patriot*, 4 March 1896.

47. North Carolina Bureau of Labor, *Biennial Report of the Secretary of State* (Raleigh: State Printer, 1897), 35; Kipp, 195; *Half Century Book*, 9; *Greensboro Patriot*, 13 September 1899.

48. Arnett, 172; Certificate of Incorporation, Revolution Cotton Mills, Cone Mills Archives; North Carolina Bureau of Labor, *Biennial Report*, 1901, 200-201; *Greensboro Patriot*, 31 January 1900.

49. Moses [Cone] to Reuben [Lindheim], 19 May 1901, Ceasar Cone Papers, Appalachian Collection, Appalachian State University.

50. *Greensboro Patriot*, 2 March 1902, 23 April 1902 and 9 July 1902.

51. Lucile Mae Smith, "The Looms of Caesar Cone" *Sky-Land Magazine* 1 (August 1914): 575; North Carolina Bureau of Labor, *Biennial Report of the Secretary of State, 1907*: 212-13, 228-29; *Greensboro Patriot*, 15 July 1903 and 11 November 1903.

52. *Watauga Democrat*, 17 December 1908. Although Greensboro always remained the base of the Cone textile empire, over the years, the family gained partial or complete ownership of dozens of other plants and continued its denim dominance. In 1977, Cone Mills Corporation was the largest such manufacturer in the United States, producing 25 percent of the country's denim. *Forbes*, "'Caesarism' at Cone Mills," 15 March 1977, 70.

53. *Greensboro Patriot*, 14 August 1907.

54. Ibid., 6 January 1897 and 22 February 1899. Most turn-of-the-century mill owners built employee villages. Between 1900 and 1910, nearly 90 percent of the South's textile labor force lived in company housing. Oats, 9.

55. Thompson, 140-43.

56. *Greensboro Patriot*, 5 June 1901 and 21 March 1906.

57. McHugh, 63. See also Jacquelyn Dowd Hall and others, *Like a Family*

(Chapel Hill: University of North Carolina Press, 1987). Ministers in the Cone villages and around town had ample sin to worry about. In May 1904, Greensboro police reported 27 bawdyhouses in the city and several others nearby. Perhaps there was no connection, but less than a month after this report was published, a tent revival was underway at White Oak. *Greensboro Patriot*, 25 May 1904 and 8 June 1904.

58. *Greensboro Patriot*, 19 March 1902, 4 November 1903 and 23 July 1902.

59. *Greensboro Patriot*, 10 July 1907, 5 July 1905 and 24 June 1908; *Lenoir News*, 30 June 1908.

60. Brent D. Glass, *The Textile Industry in North Carolina* (Raleigh: North Carolina Department of Cultural Resources, 1992), 46.

61. Kipp, 191.

62. Melton A. McLaurin, *Paternalism and Protest: Southern Cotton Mill Workers and Organized Labor, 1875-1905* (Westport, Conn.: Greenwood Publishing,1971), 140; *Lenoir Topic*, 6 June 1900.

63. *Charlotte Daily Observer*, 9 May 1900 and 15 May 1900; Transcript of meeting between Ceasar Cone, O.P. Dickerson, J.C. Smith and others, Cone Mills Archives; *Greensboro Patriot*, 9 May 1900.

64. *Greensboro Patriot*, 9 May 1900; Andrews, 80.

65. Ibid., 12 April 1899 and 3 July 1907.

66. Ibid., 25 March 1908, 1 April 1908 and 8 April 1908. A penitent Germany later begged forgiveness, volunteering to leave the state or country, or, if preferred, to work under Cone's direct supervision. The author was unable to determine what forgiveness or leniency, if any, the prisoner was shown, but one suspects that Cone was not much interested in supervising him.

67. North Carolina Bureau of Labor, *Biennial Report*, 1899, 241.

68. Ceasar Cone [and others] to "Gentlemen", 21 January 1901, and Minutes of a Meeting of Cotton Mill Owners and Managers in Greensboro, N.C., January 16, 1901, in William Alexander Smith Papers, Perkins Library, Duke University; Marianne D. Watson, "'Do Not Grind the Seed Corn': Reformers, Manufacturers, and the Battle Over Child Labor Legislation in North Carolina, 1901-1913" (M.A. thesis, North Carolina State University, 1984), 69-71. In 1903 the General Assembly passed legislation that contained the provisions promoted by the manufacturers two years earlier.

69. McLaurin, 25.

70. *Greensboro Patriot*, 20 March 1901.

71. Ibid., 17 September 1902, 29 October 1902 and 19 November 1902.

72. Ibid., 30 August 1905, 22 May 1907, and 3 May 1899.

73. Ibid., 3 January 1906; *Greensboro Daily News*, 10 December 1908;

Proceedings of the Grand Lodge of Ancient, Free and Accepted Masons of North Carolina (Raleigh: Oxford Orphan Asylum, 1902), 159; *Greensboro Patriot*, 20 September 1905, 21 October 1908 and 6 January 1904.

74. Even in their community affairs, the Cones often acted assertively. In 1899, Ceasar sent workmen out in the middle of the night to remove an unused street car track that had been judged a nuisance by the city alderman, precipitating a legal battle with B.J. Fisher, who claimed the track as his property. *Greensboro Patriot*, 11 October 1899 and 29 November 1899.

75. Richard L. Zweigenhaft and G. William Domhoff, *Jews in the Protestant Establishment* (New York: Praeger, 1982), 77; Fripp, 51; William Henry Chafe, *Civilities and Civil Rights: Greensboro, North Carolina, and the Black Struggle for Freedom* (New York: Oxford University Press, 1980), 22.

76. *Watauga Democrat*, 23 November 1905. Based on a story carried in the *Charlotte Chronicle*.

77. Peter J. Schmitt, *Back to Nature: The Arcadian Myth in Urban America* (Baltimore: Johns Hopkins University Press,1990), xvii.

78. Schmitt, introduction, passim; Karen M. Genskow, "The Country Estate in Illinois" *Historic Illinois* 10 (February 1988): 3, 12-14; Jan Cohen, *The Palace or the Poorhouse: The American Home as a Cultural Symbol* (East Lansing, Mich.: Michigan University Press, 1979), 202; Brugger, 366.

79. George B. Tatum, "The Emergence of an American School of Landscape Design" *Historic Preservation* (April-June 1973): 38, 41.

80. Catherine W. Bishir, *North Carolina Architecture* (Chapel Hill: University of North Carolina Press, 1990), 344; Thorstein Veblen, *The Theory of the Leisure Class* (New York: Funk & Wagnalls, 1899), 28.

81. Susan M. Ward and Michael K. Smith, *Biltmore Estate* (Asheville, N.C.: Biltmore Company, 1989), 5; Russell Lynes, *The Tastemakers* (New York: Harper & Brothers, 1949), 121.

82. Ward and Smith, 3.

83. Mark Alan Hewitt, *The Architect and the American Country House, 1890-1940* (New Haven, Yale University Press, 1990), 1; Ward and Smith, 8-9; Victoria Loucia Volk, "The Biltmore Estate and Its Creators: Richard Morris Hunt, Frederick Law Olmsted and George Washington Vanderbilt" (Ph.D. diss., Emory University, 1984), 88.

84. John Emerson Todd, *Frederick Law Olmsted* (Boston: Twayne, 1982), 161.

85. Bowling C. Yates, "The Cradle of Forestry in America," typed manuscript, 21, 23-24, North Carolina Collection, Pack Memorial Library, Asheville, North Carolina.

86. *Manufacturers' Record* 29 (27 March 1896), 139; quoted in Volk, 173.

87. Volk, 137; Buncombe County, North Carolina, Register of Deeds, Book 67, 24.

88. Jacqueline Burgin Painter and Jonathan William Horstman, *The German Invasion of Western North Carolina* (Asheville, N.C.: Biltmore Press, 1992), 16-17.

89. Barry M. Buxton, *A Village Tapestry, The History of Blowing Rock* (Boone, N.C.: Appalachian Consortium Press, 1989), 2, 18-19, 90; John Preston Arthur, *A History of Watauga County, North Carolina* (Richmond: Everett Waddey, 1915), 217-18.

90. Buxton, *A Village Tapestry*, 20, 4, 60.

91. James Beeler, "A Sketch of Blowing Rock, North Carolina, 1900" (Student paper, Appalachian State University, 1980), 2; *Watauga Democrat*, 23 November 1905 and 14 February 1895.

92. Buxton, *A Village Tapestry*, 6.

93. Mrs. Moses H. Cone to Harold L. Ickes, 12 March 1938, photocopy, Blue Ridge Parkway Files.

94. Caldwell County Deed Book 24, 511; Watauga County Deed Book R, 131; Lindau, 5.

95. Various Deed Books for Watauga and Caldwell Counties.

96. Clive Aslet, *The American Country House* (New Haven: Yale University Press, 1990), 20.

97. Buxton, *A Village Tapestry*, 18, 55, 42.

98. Various Deed Books for Watauga and Caldwell Counties.

99. U.S. Department of the Interior, National Park Service, "A Cultural Landscape Report of the Moses H. Cone Memorial Park," by Ian Firth (Unpublished draft report in Blue Ridge Parkway Library, 1990), 3.

100. *Greensboro Patriot*, 13 September 1899; *Watauga Democrat*, 11 January 1894.

101. Sydney Cone, Jr., "The Cones from Bavaria," vol. 2, 126; *Greensboro Patriot*, 14 April 1897; Mrs. Moses H. Cone to Harold L. Ickes, 12 March 1938, op.cit.

102. *Watauga Democrat*, 23 September 1897; *Greensboro Patriot*, 29 December 1897, 2 February 1898 and 13 September 1899.

103. North Carolina Board of Agriculture, *Apple Bulletin* (July 1900), 18, 4-5.

104. *Greensboro Patriot*, 13 September 1899.

105. *Asheville News and Hotel Reporter*, 20 February 1897, quoted in Aslet, 14.

106. *Watauga Democrat*, 4 February 1897; *Greensboro Patriot*, 13 September 1899.

107. Lindau, 4.

108. Guilford County Deed Book 82, 791, and Deed Book 110, 31; *Greensboro, N.C., City Directory*, various directories 1896-1899,

(Atlanta: Maloney Directory Company, 1899), 57; Edwin R. Moore, *In Old Oneonta* vol. 4 (Oneonta, N.Y.: Upper Susquehanna Historical Society, 1965), 80

109. Jan Cohen, 209; Hewitt, 70.
110. Hewitt, 77, 83, 84.
111. Genskow, 2.
112. Michael G. Kammen, *Mystic Chords of Memory: The Transformation of Tradition in American Culture* (New York: Knopf, 1991), 232.
113. Roger Daniels, *Coming to America: A History of Immigration and Ethnicity in American Life* (New York: Harper Collins, 1990), 146, 275; Kammen, 245, 248.
114. Kammen, 112, 217, 222.
115. T. Lee Carlton to W.A. Fries, Invoice, 5 October 1898, Blue Ridge Parkway Archives; *Lenoir Semi-Weekly News*, 2 December 1898; *Watauga Democrat*, 12 January 1899.
116. *Greensboro City Directory*, 1896-1897, 59; *Greensboro City Directory*, 1899-1900, 152; *Greensboro Patriot*, 13 March 1901; *Lenoir Semi-Weekly News*, 3 January 1899.
117. *Lenoir Semi-Weekly News*, 3 February 1899; Henry Holly Hudson, *Modern Dwellings in Town and Country, Adapted to American Wants and Climate* (New York: Harper & Brothers, 1878), 33-34.
118. Harry W. Desmond and Herbert Croly, *Stately Homes in America, from Colonial Times to the Present Day* (New York: D. Appleton, 1903), 394; Mrs. Schuyler Van Rensselaer, *Art Out-of-Doors: Hints on Good Taste in Gardening* (New York: Scribner's, 1925), 109.
119. *Watauga Democrat*, 2 March 1899, 1 June 1899 and 15 June 1899; *Greensboro Patriot*, 26 April 1899; *Lenoir Semi-Weekly News*, 26 May 1899.
120. *Lenoir Semi-Weekly News*, 9 January 1900; *Watauga Democrat*, 17 December 1908.
121. *Lenoir Semi-Weekly News*, 9 January 1900.
122. *Watauga Democrat*, 25 January 1900.
123. Building File and Survey of Moses H. Cone Memorial Park, 1952-1953, Blue Ridge Parkway Files; Charles Palliser and George Palliser, *Palliser's American Architecture* (New York: J.S. Ogilvie, 1888), n.p.
124. Receipt Book, Blue Ridge Parkway Archives.
125. Building Files, Blue Ridge Parkway; Moses H. Cone to J.D. Brown, 28 October 1904, Blue Ridge Parkway Archives.
126. *Watauga Democrat*, 15 October 1908 and 22 October 1908; Invoice from Eagle Generator Company, 20 August 1900, Blue Ridge Parkway Archives; Carl Hollers, interview by Kent Cave and Tom Robbins, 2 October 1975, Blue Ridge Parkway Library. Late Victorians loved gaslight because it was cheap, convenient, and gave quality illumina-

tion. One enthusiast called it the most useful triumph of the day and confidently, but incorrectly, predicted that, for years to come, gaslight would "constitute the chief means of artificial illumination." William Paul Gerhard, "Artificial Illumination" *American Architect and Building News* 42 (December 1893): 109-10.

127. Clyde Downs, interview by Tom Robbins and Kent Cave, 21 November 1975, Blue Ridge Parkway Library; Kammen, 138; *Watauga Democrat,* 8 July 1897; F.L. Mulford Diary, Blue Ridge Parkway Archives.

128. Downs interview, 1975; Ted Pease, interview by Tom Robbins and Kent Cave, 7 August 1975, Blue Ridge Parkway Library. The heating system no doubt drew plenty of fresh air. Victorian architects repeatedly stressed the need for proper ventilation of houses. Charles Palliser and George Palliser, *New Cottage Homes and Details* (New York: Palliser & Co., 1887), n.p.

129. Catherine W. Bishir and others, *Architects and Builders in North Carolina* (Chapel Hill: University of North Carolina Press, 1990), 193-94.

130. *Greensboro Patriot,* 22 June 1898.

131. *Greensboro Patriot,* 3 May 1899. As examples of prices, porch balusters, the decorative supports for the porch and balcony rails, cost $1.80 each. Large porch columns with capitals ran $19 apiece. Invoice, Cape Fear Manufacturing Company, 6 March 1900, Blue Ridge Parkway Archives.

132. *Lenoir Semi-Weekly News,* 16 February 1900.

133. Invoice, J.R. Rich and Son, 16 June 1900, Blue Ridge Parkway Archives; Bishir and others, 271, 269.

134. *Watauga Democrat,* 24 January 1901.

135. *Greensboro Patriot,* 13 September 1899; U.S. Bureau of the Census, *Population Schedules,* Watauga County, 1900; Firth, 14.

136. Miscellaneous Journal, Blue Ridge Parkway Archives; J.D. Brown Ledger Book, 172; Downs interview.

137. Monthly Ledger, December 1899, Blue Ridge Parkway Archives; *Watauga Democrat,* 25 May 1899; Volk, 155-57.

138. *Lenoir Semi-Weekly News,* 8 September 1899; *Greensboro Patriot,* 21 December 1898 and 6 May 1903. Commissioners heard misdemeanor cases and exercised other judicial powers similar to those of a modern-day federal magistrate.

139. F.L. Mulford Diary, 6 July 1900; *Lenoir Semi-Weekly News,* 8 September 1899; Firth, 11.

140. Watauga County Deed Book 2, 95.

141. *Greensboro Patriot,* 13 September 1899; Henry Vincent Hubbard and Theodora Kimball, *Introduction to the Study of Landscape Design* (New York: Macmillan, 1917), 71, 93.

142. *Lenoir Semi-Weekly News*, 8 September 1899; Postcard Collection, Perkins Library, Duke University.
143. Firth, 30; *Lenoir News*, 1 May 1908; Hollers interview.
144. Mrs. Ruby Moody Walters, interview by Kent Cave and Tom Robbins, 5 June 1975, Blue Ridge Parkway Library.
145. Arthur, 220.
146. Mulford Diary, 28 November 1899; *Lenoir News*, 13 December 1907 and 19 June 1908.
147. Invoice, 6 September 1900, Blue Ridge Parkway Archives.
148. Charlie Isenhour, interview by Judy Cornett, 29 May 1975, Blue Ridge Parkway Library; Mulford Diary, 1 June 1900; E.P. Powell, *The Country Home* (New York: McClure, Phillips, 1904), 256.
149. Mulford Diary, 1 June 1900; Isenhour interview; Invoice, 12 July 1900, Blue Ridge Parkway Archives; E.P. Powell, 312.
150. Downs interview.
151. James Beeler and others, "An Analysis of the China Orchard in the Moses H. Cone Estate, 1900-1947" (Student paper, Appalachian State University, 1980), 89.
152. North Carolina Board of Agriculture, *Apple Bulletin* (July 1900): 22; Firth, 21; Beeler and others, 97.
153. Firth, 22; *Watauga Democrat*, 21 July 1900.
154. Beeler and others, 94-95.
155. Firth, 20, 55.
156. *Greensboro Patriot*, 13 September 1899; Mulford Diary, 3 January 1900 and 8 January 1900; Pease interview; Payroll Ledger, 15 May 1911 and 31 May 1911, and Account Journal, 15 November 1907, Blue Ridge Parkway Archives.
157. *Greensboro Patriot*, 18 June 1902.
158. Mulford Diary, 9 November 1899, 11 November 1899 and 11 August 1900; Watauga County, Record of Mortgage, Book G, 575, Book H, 371, 539.
159. *Lenoir Semi-Weekly News*, 5 January 1900.
160. Mulford Diary, 30 January, 1 February, 28 April, 10 May, and 18 August 1900; Mulford Diary, 8 December 1899.
161. *Watauga Democrat*, 12 May 1904; *Lenoir News*, 19 July 1907.
162. Moses Cone, Memorandum, 29 October 1904, Blue Ridge Parkway Archives.
163. *Watauga Democrat*, 21 July 1900; Harriet Payne to Gertrude Weil, 17 October 1912, Gertrude Weil Papers, North Carolina State Archives.
164. Walters interview.
165. *Greensboro Patriot*, 13 September 1899; Arthur, 220.
166. There is no detailed inventory of the furnishings and other objects that were in Flat Top Manor in the early 1900s. The descriptions given in

this chapter are based on Bertha's detailed last will and testament, written in 1945, and interviews and sketches provided by Bertha's grandnieces, Judith (Mrs. Isham) Lindau McConnell and Nancy (Mrs. R.W.B.) Lindau Lewis. They lived at Flat Top during the summers of the late 1920s and 1930s, and continued to visit until Bertha's death in 1947. They also inherited a number of objects that were in the house. According to Mrs. McConnell and Mrs. Lewis, the manor's furnishings and decor changed remarkably little during the decades they lived there and visited. Although it cannot be determined with certainty, it seems likely that the house's decor remained essentially unchanged over time.

167. Kenneth L. Ames, "The Battle of the Sideboards," *Winterthur Portfolio* 9 (1974): 1; Katherine C. Grier, *Culture & Comfort: People, Parlors, and Upholstery, 1850-1930* (Rochester, N.Y.: Strong Museum, 1988), 7; Clifford E. Clark, Jr., "The Vision of the Dining Room: Plan Book Dreams and Middle-Class Realities," in *Dining in America, 1850-1900*, ed. Kathryn Grover (Amherst: University of Massachusetts Press, 1987), 158; Kenneth L. Ames, "Material Culture as Non Verbal Communication: A Historical Case Study," *Journal of American Culture* 3 (Winter 1981): 619.

168. Judith McConnell, family photographs; Volk, 124.

169. Lewis and McConnell, 6 October 1990; George D. Carroll, *Diamonds from Brilliant Minds* (New York: Dempsey & Carroll, 1881), 7.

170. Lewis and McConnell, 6 October 1990; Grier, 149, 215.

171. Lewis and McConnell, 6 October 1990

172. Kenneth L. Ames, "Meaning in Artifacts: Hall Furnishings in Victorian America" *Journal of Interdisciplinary History* 9 (1978): 21; Carroll, 3-4, 7-8.

173. McConnell, 6 October 1990.

174. Grier, 103.

175. Lewis and McConnell, 6 October 1990; McConnell, furnishings sketch, January 1994.

176. Lewis and McConnell, 6 October 1990 and 28 July 1993; McConnell, furnishings sketch; Bertha L. Cone, Last and Will and Testament, 27 October 1945.

177. Grier, 94.

178. Robert Shackleton and Elizabeth Shackleton, *The Quest of the Colonial* (New York: Century, 1907; reprint, Detroit: Singing Tree Press, 1970), 82.

179. B.A. May, "Progressivism and the Colonial Revival: The Modern Colonial House, 1900-1920," *Winterthur Portfolio* 26 (Summer/Autumn 1991): 117.

180. Lewis and McConnell, 6 October 1990.

181. Ibid.; McConnell furnishings sketch.

182. Kenneth L. Ames, *Death in the Dining Room, and Other Tales of Victorian Culture* (Philadelphia: Temple University Press, 1992), 9, 13; Grier, 143.

183. Bertha Cone to Gertrude Weil, 8 September 1912, Weil Papers; Lewis and McConnell, 6 October 1990 and 28 July 1993.

184. Lewis and McConnell, 28 July 1993; Susan Williams, *Savory Suppers and Fashionable Feasts: Dining in Victorian America* (New York: Pantheon, 1985), 33; John F. Kasson, "Rituals of Dining: Table Manners in Victorian America," in *Dining in America*, 133.

185. James Robert Moody, unrecorded interview by the author, 15 April 1992; Lewis and McConnell, 6 October 1990.

186. Lewis and McConnell, 28 July 1993

187. Lewis and McConnell, 4 July 1993 and 28 July 1993; Williams, 79.

188. Lewis and McConnell, 6 October 1990; Edward Cone, tape recorded interview by the author, 27 July 1993; Daniel Sutherland, *Americans and Their Servants: Domestic Service in the United States from 1800 to 1920* (Baton Rouge: Louisiana State University Press, 1981), 89; Williams, 152.

189. Lewis and McConnell, 6 October 1990 and 4 July 1993. The usual coffee, tea, and occasional wine did not come from the estate. The latter was probably served on the most formal occasion, since wine was a beverage associated with wealth and, thus, a status symbol. According to Lewis and McConnell, alcoholic beverages were never served during the 1930s and 1940s.

190. Williams, 37, 39; Kasson, 137-38.

191. Williams, 46; Kasson, 140, 137, 125-26.

192. Kasson, 134.

193. Ibid., 125, 132.

194. Lewis and McConnell, 28 July 1993.

195. Lewis and McConnell, various interviews; McConnell, furnishings sketch; Williams, 64-65; Ames, *Death in the Dining Room*, 44, 76; Clark, in *Dining in America*, 161.

196. Lewis and McConnell, 6 October 1990 and 28 July 1993.

197. According to Lewis and McConnell, Bertha kept a staff of about seven during the 1930s and 1940s. Among them were a chauffeur, butler, laundress, one or two chamber and parlor maids, cook, and cook's helper. The staff was probably larger during Moses' lifetime, since the Cones, according to their tenants, entertained more often then.

198. Clifford Edward Clark, Jr., *The American Family Home* (Chapel Hill: University of North Carolina Press, 1986), 155-56.

199. Helen Campbell, "Household Art and the Microbe," *House Beautiful* 6 (October 1895): 221-22.

200. Anna Leach, "Science in the Model Kitchen," *Cosmopolitan* 27 (May

1899): 103. Leach extolled "sunshine, fresh air, cleanliness" as the "priceless things. There is no such disinfectant as the sun."

201. Laura Shapiro, *Perfection Salad: Women and Cooking at the Turn of the Century* (New York: Henry Holt, 1986), 41.

202. Most city dwellers preferred coal-burning stoves because the fuel was easier to obtain than wood. According to Judith McConnell, Bertha later replaced the manor's wood burner with a coal range. Before that, the Cones burned wood gathered from the estate. McConnell, furnishings sketch; Moses Cone to J.D. Brown, 25 October 1904, Blue Ridge Parkway Archives. Originally, these pendulum clocks were promotions given to retailers who sold large numbers of Cone cigars. They are inscribed "H. Cone & Sons, Cigars, Baltimore." The clock in the Flat Top Manor kitchen, now owned by Edward Cone, continues to keep time. Edward Cone interview.

203. Lewis and McConnell, 6 October 1990.

204. Receipt, Odell Hardware to Mrs. Moses H. Cone, 19 May 1911, Blue Ridge Parkway Archives; David W. Miller, "Technology and the Ideal," in *Dining in America*, 72.

205. Laura Shapiro, 69, 86, 88; Eleanor T. Fordyce, "Cookbooks of the 1800s," in *Dining in America*, 108-9, 112. Shapiro has suggested that Victorians emphasized good etiquette and promoted science in the kitchen to compensate for and "regulate the messy sprawl of American society and to filter out the most unsettling aspects of its diversity."

206. Lewis and McConnell, 6 October 1990; McConnell, furnishings sketch.

207. Williams, 52; Ames, *Death in the Dining Room*, 13, 17.

208. Lewis and McConnell, various interviews; McConnell, furnishings sketch.

209. Ibid.; McConnell, furnishings sketch.

210. Lindau, 4-5.

211. Ibid., 4.

212. May, 120; Lewis and McConnell, 4 July 1993; Clifford Clark, *The American Family Home*, 157.

213. The Cones bought many of their fixtures and furnishings from Odell Hardware in Greensboro. Brothers J.M. and J.A. Odell started their store in 1872. By 1899, their business had grown to include 52 employees and enjoyed annual sales of $350,000. The Cones and Odells were also old and close business associates. The Odells owned several textiles mills and sold the products of at least two of them through the Cone Export and Commission Company. In addition, J.A. Odell was an original incorporator of the Proximity Manufacturing Company. Among the items purchased from Odell Hardware for Flat Top Manor were Columbia enameled tubs, 5-1/2 foot ($35.50 each); #8 Perfect Wood Furnaces (two for $220); four-light chandeliers ($30 each); #7 onyx tea

kettle ($0.50), and eight-ring muffin pans (two for $0.30). William S. Powell, *Dictionary of North Carolina Biography*, vol. 4 (Chapel Hill: University of North Carolina Press, 1991), 386; *Greensboro Patriot*, 3 May 1899; Articles of Incorporation, Proximity Manufacturing Company, Cone Mills Archives; various receipts in Blue Ridge Parkway Archives.

214. Lewis and McConnell, various interviews; McConnell, furnishings sketch; Bertha Cone will.

215. Lewis and McConnell, various interviews. Claribel and Etta donated only two of their nine Renoir lithographs to the Baltimore Museum of Art. They apparently gave away the other seven, some of which are rare early proofs. Brenda Richardson, *Dr. Claribel & Miss Etta: The Cone Collection of the Baltimore Museum of Art* (Baltimore: Baltimore Museum of Art, 1985), 169. The author is indebted to Ellen C. B. Hirschland for sharing clippings and information concerning art at Flat Top Manor and the art collecting endeavors of the Cone sisters.

216. Lewis and McConnell, 11 October 1993.

217. Gertrude Weil to Mother, 6 August 1912, Weil Papers. In the winter, when the Cones lived in Baltimore, Bertha would send housekeeping instructions to her foreman. Mrs. Moses H. Cone to Ed Underdown, 5 January 1914, Blue Ridge Parkway Archives.

218. Lewis and McConnell, various interviews; Sutherland, 4,144.

219. Sutherland, 34. The Cone help lived in two cottages that were behind the manor. One cottage was reserved for females, the other for males.

220. After Moses died, Bertha's two unmarried sisters lived at Flat Top in the summers. The younger one slept in the master bedroom with Bertha and used one of the small back bedrooms as her sitting room. The small adjacent bathroom was reserved for her exclusive use. The other back bedroom became a dining room for Bertha's grandnieces.

221. Bertha Cone, will; Lewis and McConnell, 4 July 1993. Manufacturers of household cleaners and soaps were quick to cash in on the crusade against germs and disease. In 1900, Ivory brand was heavily advertised as "the soap that floats." Clifford Clark, 155; Marshall B. Davidson, ed., *The American Heritage History of Antiques, from the Civil War to World War I* (New York: American Heritage, 1969), 329.

222. Tastemaker Edith Wharton, in *The Decoration of Houses*, called colonial antiques travesties, while Charlotte Perkins Gilman, in her novel *The Yellow Wallpaper*, used the image of a colonial house as a symbol of blind conservatism and repression. Celia Betsky, "Inside the Past: The Interior and the Colonial Revival in American Art and Literature, 1860-1914," in *The Colonial Revival in America*, ed. Alan Axelrod (New York: Norton, 1985), 260, 274.

223. Davidson, 216, 237; Grier, 183.

224. *Greensboro Patriot*, 18 June 1902.

225. *Watauga Democrat*, 24 October 1907.

226. *Greensboro Patriot*, 29 May 1907; *Lenoir News*, 26 June 1908; Lewis and McConnell, various interviews.

227. Sydney Cone, Jr., "The Cones from Bavaria" vol. 2, 81; *Charlotte Daily Observer*, 10 December 1908; David Dreyfuss to Reuben Lindheim, 13 August 1907, Ceasar Cone Papers.

228. Hollers interview; *Greensboro Patriot*, 15 June 1908 and 31 July 1907; Francis T. Underhill, *Driving for Pleasure* (New York: D. Appleton, 1897; reprinted as *Driving Horse-Drawn Carriages for Pleasure*, New York: Dover, 1989), 80-81.

229. *Lenoir News*, 8 September 1905.

230. E.P. Powell, 354.

231. Lindau, 3.

232. Bertha Cone to Gertrude Weil, 8 September 1912, Weil Papers.

233. *Lenoir Topic*, 29 August 1900.

234. *Lenoir News*, 19 July 1907.

235. Hollers interview.

236. Judith McConnell, 4 July 1993.

237. *Greensboro Patriot*, 3 May 1899, 27 June 1900 and 22 October 1902.

238. Volk, 148; *Watauga Democrat*, 21 October 1897.

239. *Watauga Democrat*, 26 October 1899 and 21 June 1900; *Greensboro Patriot*, 15 August 1900; *Charlotte Daily Observer*, 31 January 1900; *Century Magazine*, "In the Crowd at the Paris Exposition," November 1900: 155.

240. *Watauga Democrat*, 15 January 1903. Cone's check may have been for $25, instead of the reported $28. The former amount seems more appropriate as a prize. Also, Cone's saying that he would not swap his check for $250 suggests that he was alluding to a sum ten-times greater.

241. *Watauga Democrat*, 17 September 1903.

242. *Watauga Democrat*, 23 November 1905, reprinted from the *Charlotte Chronicle*, n.d.

243. Pease interview; Account Journal, 15 August 1904, 31 March 1906, and 15 February 1907, Blue Ridge Parkway Archives; Glass, 18.

244. Omer Coffey, tape recorded interview by the author, 19 October 1991.

245. Pay Ledgers, 1900 and other years, Blue Ridge Parkway Archives.

246. U.S. Bureau of the Census, *Population Schedules of the Thirteenth Census*, Watauga County. Some people have suggested that, out of benevolence, the Cones hired and made tenants—or caretakers, as they preferred to be called—of the hardscrabble farmers whose land they had bought. In fact, aside from a few families, the Cones bought most of their Flat Top acreage from absentee landowners and middle class residents, such as Blowing Rock merchant J.B. Clark and Lenoir

businessman J.M. Bernhardt. The majority of families who went to work on the estate had not lived there previously.

247. Time Book for 1913 and Wood Ledgers for 1925 and 1926, Blue Ridge Parkway Archives.

248. Omer Coffey interview. To control such orchard pests as aphids, borers, and bark lice, the Cones used a variety of insecticides and fungicides, including whale oil soap, a mixture of tobacco and hot water, kerosene emulsion, and copper carbonate. They also applied dry bordeaux, a mixture of copper sulphate, lime, and water.

249. Beeler and Chandler, 97; Omer Coffey interview; *Watauga Democrat*, 29 April 1915.

250. *Watauga Democrat*, 17 September 1913.

251. Lewis and McConnell, 4 July 1993 and 11 October 1993.

252. Coffey interview.

253. Downs interview.

254. *Watauga Democrat*, 17 December 1908.

255. Daniel J. Whitener, ed., *History of Watauga County, North Carolina, 1849-1949*, n.p., n.d.; Ruby J. Lanier, *Blanford Barnard Dougherty, Mountain Educator* (Durham, N.C.: Duke University Press, 1974), 51-53.

256. *Watauga Democrat*, 16 April 1903 and 9 April 1903.

257. Ibid., 21 May 1903.

258. Ibid., 4 July 1904 and 28 July 1904.

259. Ibid., 17 December 1908. Sandy Flat School was one of four that served the Blowing Rock community. Before bus transportation, counties kept their school districts small, limiting the distance that children had to walk. As a result, there were many schools. In 1900, rural Watauga County had 71 schools. Enrollment totaled less than 4,000, for an average of not quite 60 students per school. Whitener, 66.

260. Watauga County Deed Book 16, 243.

261. *Greensboro Patriot*, 8 November 1905; Account Journal, 15 July 1905 and 31 August 1907, Blue Ridge Parkway Archives. Cone apparently was not heavy-handed in soliciting donations from his employees. Donations from workers tended to be small and infrequent.

262. *Watauga Democrat*, 24 September 1908; Buxton, "Historic Structure Report," 29; *Greensboro Patriot*, 8 November 1905.

263. *Greensboro Patriot*, 8 November 1905; *Lenoir News*, 2 November 1906.

264. *Watauga Democrat*, 4 December 1913 and 29 March 1906.

265. Ibid., 8 October 1908.

266. *Greensboro Patriot*, 11 February 1903 and 15 July 1903.

267. Ibid., 2 May 1906.

268. Cone may have thought that building a church would generate strong social pressures against Colt and his whiskey-making activity. Also,

state laws or local ordinances may have banned the operation of stills in proximity to a church.

269. Monthly Account Ledger, 17 November 1899, and Mulford Diary, 17 November and 22 November 1899, Blue Ridge Parkway Archives.

270. Founded by Emily C. Prudden in 1887, the Institute was located on the southeast side of the village, near the present-day junction of Main Street and U.S. Highway 321 Bypass. The 60 or so girls who attended the Institute were instructed in religion, home economics, and the "three Rs." In the early 1890s, Prudden turned over Skyland to the American Missionary Association. Buxton, *A Village Tapestry*, 111; Arthur, 253.

271. *Lenoir Semi-Weekly News*, 13 June 1900.

272. *Greensboro Patriot*, 8 March 1899, 15 February 1899 and 16 January 1901.

273. E.J. Justice to Moses Cone, 10 February 1906, Cone Mills Archives; *Daily News & Observer*, 4 February 1906, clipping in Cone Mills Archives.

274. *Greensboro Patriot*, 6 September 1905 and 27 December 1905.

275. Edward Cone interview.

276. Claribel Cone to Etta Cone, 7 December 1919, Baltimore Museum of Art, Cone Archives; Sydney Cone, Jr., "The Cones from Bavaria," vol. 1, 11.

277. Sydney Cone, Jr., "The Cones from Bavaria," vol. 1, 74.

278. Edward Cone interview.

279. Theodore P. Greene, *America's Heroes: The Changing Models of Success in American Magazines* (New York: Oxford University Press, 1970), 158.

280. Ibid., 79.

281. *Greensboro Patriot*, 8 November 1905.

282. *Charlotte Daily Observer*, 11 April 1908.

283. *Lenoir Semi-Weekly News*, 14 February 1899.

284. *Charlotte Daily Observer*, 11 April 1908; *Greensboro Patriot*, 15 April 1908.

285. Moses Cone to Thomas Settle, 7 October 1896, Thomas Settle Papers, Southern Historical Collection, University of North Carolina, Chapel Hill.

286. *Greensboro Patriot*, 24 June 1896.

287. Robert H. Wiebe, *The Search for Order, 1877-1920* (New York: Hill and Wang, 1967), 98-99; Naomi Cohen, *Encounter with Emancipation: The German Jews in the United States, 1830-1914* (Philadelphia: Jewish Publication Society of America, 1984), 154.

288. Wiebe, 99; Naomi Cohen, 153.

289. *Watauga Democrat*, 24 October 1907; *Greensboro Patriot*, 12 August 1908.

290. *Lenoir News*, 1 October 1907.

291. *Watauga Democrat*, 7 November 1907.

292. By the late nineteenth century, timber companies had turned to the southern Appalachians to meet the country's increasing demand for wood. These companies purchased and cut huge tracts of timber, with little concern for the long-term welfare of natural resources or local people. In 1899, Dr. Chase P. Ambler, an Asheville physician, organized the Appalachian National Park Association, which urged the establishment of a national park or forest reserve in western North Carolina. However, it was not until March 1911 that the United States Forest Service secured approval to purchase lands for the reserve. By 1940, the federal government had acquired more than 800,000 acres of timber lands in western North Carolina. For a discussion of the impact of industrialization on Appalachia, see Ronald D. Eller, *Miners, Millhands, and Mountaineers: Industrialization of the Appalachian South, 1880-1930* (Knoxville: University of Tennessee Press, 1982), 43, 87, 112, 115-20.

293. *Greensboro Patriot*, 10 August 1904; *Watauga Democrat*, 8 October 1908; *Charlotte Observer*, 8 September 1963; *Greensboro Patriot*, 14 August 1907 and 21 August 1907; A.B. Kimball to David Dreyfuss, 20 December 1905, Cone Mills Archives.

294. Barbara Pollack, *The Collectors: Dr. Claribel and Miss Etta Cone* (Indianapolis: Bobbs-Merrill, 1962), 251; Brenda Richardson, 9.

295. Brenda Richardson, 55; Bertha Cone to Etta Cone, 27 March 1898, Baltimore Museum of Art, Cone Archives.

296. James R. Mellow, *Charmed Circle: Gertrude Stein & Company* (New York: Praeger, 1974), 41; Bruce Kellner, ed. *A Gertrude Stein Companion* (New York: Greenwood Press, 1988), 171; Pollack, 18-19, 23; Brenda Richardson, 52, 296.

297. Brenda Richardson, 52.

298. Kellner, 204; Pollack, 23; Ellen C. B. Hirschland, "The Cone Sisters and the Stein Family," in *Four Americans in Paris* (New York: The Museum of Modern Art, 1970), 78; William Stadiem, *A Class by Themselves* (New York: Crown, 1980), 219.

299. Hirschland, 75.

300. Pollack, 259; Brenda Richardson, 93; Ellen C. B. Hirschland, correspondence with the author, 12 August 1995.

301. Etta Cone to Gertrude Stein, 16 May 1906, Gertrude Stein Collection, Beinecke Rare Book and Manuscript Library, Yale University; Brenda Richardson, 56; Herman Cone Will, City of Baltimore, Register of Wills, Book 78, 71; J.C. Wilmer to Etta Cone, 19 October 1933, Baltimore Museum of Art, Cone Archives; Pollack, 259. The Cone Company stock that the two sisters owned was probably a gift from

Moses and Ceasar. Claribel was a medical doctor, but she did not practice, and there is no indication that Etta was ever employed. Their income apparently was derived entirely from their inheritance and the support of the brothers.

302. Kellner, 272; Brenda Richardson, 62, 85; Edward Cone interview.

303. Pollack, 260.

304. The sisters and Matisse became lasting friends. The three visited socially and, even after Claribel's and Etta's deaths, Matisse continued to speak fondly of them. Edward Cone, "The Miss Etta Cones, the Steins, and M'sieu Matisse: A Memoir," *American Scholar* v. 42, no. 3 (Summer 1973): 459.

305. Brenda Richardson, 56, 94.

306. Claribel Cone to Etta Cone, 20 July 1910, Baltimore Museum of Art, Cone Archives. Etta was also disappointed and hurt by Gertrude's later offer to sell her the original manuscript to *Three Lives*. This was the same manuscript that Etta had typed in 1905-1906 as a favor to Gertrude. Edward Cone interview.

307. Mellow, 42, 346; Sydney Cone, Jr., "The Cones from Bavaria," vol. 2, 135. Claribel's decision to stay in Germany during World War I may have stemmed as much from her affection for Germany and German culture as from the alleged lack of suitable transportation out of the country. While Etta preferred and often stayed in Paris, Claribel spent much of her time in Germany before and after, as well as during, the war.

308. Brenda Richardson, 81-82; Edward Cone, "The Miss Etta Cones," 443-45, 450.

309. Beyond direct monetary support, Moses and the other Cone brothers recommended spending limits and otherwise handled Claribel's and Etta's financial affairs. For example, in 1904 Moses explained to Etta that some company profits for that year had been converted to preferred stock in order to increase the company's capital. That meant, he said, "that you have $1500 more in a 7% dividend paying security than you had last yr. & are richer to that extent." Moses to Etta, 16 December 1904, Sydney Cone, Jr., "The Cones from Bavaria," vol. 2.

310. Lynes, 42, 62.

311. Ward and Smith, 4; *Asheville Citizen-Times*, 25 August 1992.

312. Etta Cone to Gertrude Stein, 6 February 1907, Stein Collection.

313. Ibid.

314. Moses Cone to J.P. Caldwell, 18 October 1907, Ceasar Cone Papers.

315. Etta Cone to Gertrude Stein, n.d., Stein Collection. This letter was probably written in late 1906.

316. Etta Cone to Gertrude Stein, n.d., Stein Collection; Ibid., 27 February 1907.

317. Etta Cone to Gertrude Stein, 30 March 1907, Stein Collection; *Lenoir News*, 12 April 1907.
318. Etta Cone to Gertrude Stein, 6 February 1907, Stein Collection.
319. Ibid.
320. *Greensboro Patriot*, 14 August 1907.
321. Ibid., 31 July 1907 and 12 February 1908.
322. *Watauga Democrat*, 24 October 1907; *Lenoir News*, 4 August 1905.
323. Lanier, 74; *Watauga Democrat*, 5 September 1907, 7 August 1900, 24 September 1908 and 25 June 1908.
324. David Dreyfuss to Reuben Lindheim, 13 August 1907, Ceasar Cone Papers.
325. *Lenoir News*, 7 June 1907, 28 June 1907, 9 August 1907 and 19 July 1907.
326. J.G. Farrell to Moses Cone, n.d., Cone Mills Archives; Minutes of Annual Meeting of Stockholders of Cone Export and Commission Company, 11 November 1908, Cone Mills Archives; Reuben Lindheim to Moses Cone, various letters in Ceasar Cone Papers.
327. Moses Cone to Ceasar Cone, telegram, 9 November 1907; Cone Export and Commission Company By-Laws, 1907, Cone Mills Archives.
328. Ben Cone to Ceasar Cone, 11 November 1908, Cone Mills Archives.
329. Etta Cone to Gertrude Stein, 9 October 1908, Stein Collection.
330. Sydney Cone, Jr., "The Cones from Bavaria," vol. 2, 126. The detail and terminology in this reference suggest that the information comes from a medical record created at the time of Moses Cone's treatment at Johns Hopkins.
331. *Greensboro Patriot*, 14 December 1898.
332. Sydney Cone, Jr., "The Cones from Bavaria," vol. 2, 127.
333. *Charlotte Daily Observer*, 9 December 1908 and 10 December 1908; *Greensboro Daily News*, 10 December 1908.
334. *Charlotte Daily Observer*, 10 December 1908; *Lenoir News*, 11 December 1908.
335. *Lenoir News*, 15 December 1908.
336. *Watauga Democrat*, 17 December 1908.
337. *Charlotte Daily Observer*, 10 December 1908; Statement of assets and liabilities, Cone Export and Commission Company, 1 May 1908, Cone Mills Archives.
338. *Charlotte Daily Observer*, 10 December 1908.
339. Edward Cone interview. This explanation as to why Moses died intestate was relayed to Edward by his father, Julius Cone.
340. Bertha L. Cone and Ceasar Cone, Affidavit and Report of Settlement for the Estate of Moses H. Cone, filed in Superior Court, Watauga County, North Carolina, 4 February 1909 and 5 July 1913, North Carolina State Archives, Estate Records, 1858-1948; Canceled check and advertise-

ment, photocopy, Alston-DeGraffenried Papers, North Carolina State Archives.

341. Indenture of 30 May 1911, photocopy, Blue Ridge Parkway Archives. Women of Bertha's generation were defined as mothers, daughters, sisters, and wives. According to the 'Cult of True Womanhood', the only place for a proper woman was at home. Barbara Welter, *Dimity Convictions: The American Woman in the Nineteenth Century* (Athens: Ohio University Press, 1976), 21, 41.

342. Indenture of 30 May 1911.

343. Ibid.

344. Ward McAllister, *Society as I have Found It* (New York: Cassell, 1890; reprint, New York: Arno Press, 1975), 399-403; Hollers interview. Bertha's stationery had a one-quarter inch black border, signifying deep grief. She continued to use this long after it would have been socially acceptable to change to a more narrow bordered paper, indicative of less profound mourning. This suggests that she viewed herself, and that she wanted others to regard her, as a grieving widow. Examples of her stationery are in the Weil Papers and the Blue Ridge Parkway Archives.

345. Etta Cone to Gertrude Stein, 22 August 1909, Stein Collection; Harriet Payne to Gertrude Weil, 24 August 1912, Weil Papers; Lindau, 2.

346. Etta Cone to Gertrude Stein, 25 July 1909 and 22 August 1909, Stein Collection; Ibid., 16 July 1911 and 11 June 1911, Baltimore Museum of Art, Cone Archives. For the rest of her life, Etta would always tell friends that the reason she never married was because she "never met a man who was the equal of Brother Moses." The comment was not merely a tactful and good-humored way to parry questions about her marital status, but a genuine testimonial to her affection for Moses. Edward Cone, "The Miss Etta Cones," 457.

347. *Greensboro Patriot*, 23 December 1908

348. Etta Cone to Gertrude Stein, 25 July 1909, Stein Collection; Lewis and McConnell, 4 July 1993 and 11 October 1993.

349. Downs interview.

350. Hollers interview; Etta Cone to Claribel Cone, 11 June 1911, Baltimore Museum of Art, Cone Archives.

351. Etta Cone to Gertrude Stein, 26 September 1909, Stein Collection.

352. A number of Bertha's personally owned copies of *Progressive Farmer* and the North Carolina *Health Bulletin* are in Blue Ridge Parkway Archives.

353. Edward Cone interview; various correspondence.

354. D.M. Sullivan, architectural drawing, Blue Ridge Parkway Archives.

355. Isenhour interview; Sales receipts and other dairy records, Blue Ridge Parkway Archives. Making clean, disease-free milk took attention to detail, especially at dairies like Flat Top, which had no pasteurizer to

kill milk-borne bacteria. Cows had to be tested regularly for tuberculosis and sanitation, and processing procedures scrupulously followed. L.H. Bailey, "The Making of Clean Milk," *Country Life in America* 6 (June 1904), 171-72; Downs interview.

356. F.Y.V. Grice, Broderick and Bascom Rope Company, to Mrs. Moses H. Cone, 6 October 1913, Blue Ridge Parkway Museum Collection, Atlanta, Georgia; *Watauga Democrat*, 12 November 1914.

357. Firth, 19; Beeler, 93-94; Coffey interview.

358. Mrs. Moses H. Cone to Mr. Underdown, 7 October 1913, Blue Ridge Parkway Archives.

359. Time Book, 30 September 1914, Blue Ridge Parkway Archives; Beeler, 98; Mrs. Moses H. Cone to Mr. Underdown, 30 October 1913 and 5 November 1913, Blue Ridge Parkway Archives.

360. *Watauga Democrat*, 7 December 1922; Nancy F. Cott, *The Grounding of Modern Feminism* (New Haven: Yale University Press, 1987), 131. There were employment options open to unskilled workers in Watauga County during the 1910s and 1920s. The Boone Fork Lumber Company, for instance, was just a short distance from the estate, but not everyone found the hard, hazardous work of operating saws and other steam-powered equipment appealing. Furthermore, the timber industry offered little job security. The local company, like its competitors elsewhere in Appalachia, routinely opened and shut as the demand for timber rose and fell. *Watauga Democrat*, 30 August 1917, 5 May 1921 and 18 May 1922.

361. Mrs. Moses H. Cone to Mr. Underdown, 5 January 1914, Blue Ridge Parkway Archives.

362. Downs interview; Time Book, 31 March 1914, Blue Ridge Parkway Archives; Omer Coffey interview.

363. Lewis and McConnell, 6 October 1990; Edward Cone interview.

364. Lewis and McConnell, 6 October 1990; Ellen C.B. Hirschland to the author, 4 August 1993; Harriet Payne to Gertrude Weil, 2 October 1912, Weil Papers.

365. Lewis and McConnell, 11 October 1993; Bertha L. Cone to Gertrude Weil, 26 September 1912, Weil Papers; Lindau, 6.

366. Harriet Payne to Gertrude Weil, 17 October 1912, Weil Papers; Lewis and McConnell, 4 July 1993; Gertrude Weil to her Mother, 26 July 1912, Weil Papers.

367. Lewis and McConnell, 6 October 1990.

368. Lindau, 7; Lewis and McConnell, 6 October 1990.

369. Lewis and McConnell, 11 October 1993 and 4 July 1993; Gertrude Weil to her Mother, 26 July 1912, Weil Papers; Etta Cone to Claribel Cone, 9 July 1911 and 16 July 1911, Baltimore Museum of Art, Cone Archives.

370. Gertrude Weil to her Mother, 6 August 1912, 4 August 1912 and 7

August 1912, Weil Papers; Gertrude Weil to Mina, 9 August 1912, Weil Papers.

371. Lewis and McConnell, 11 October 1993.

372. Lewis and McConnell, 6 October 1990 and 4 July 1993; Judith McConnell, notes on books at Flat Top Manor, 1993, photocopy in possession of author.

373. Gertrude Weil to her Mother, 7 August 1912, Weil Papers; Lindau, 7; Harriet Payne to Gertrude Weil, 13 September 1912, Weil Papers.

374. Claribel Cone to Etta Cone, 18 July 1910, Baltimore Museum of Art, Cone Archives; Lindau, 7; Lewis and McConnell, 6 October 1990 and 4 July 1993.

375. Lewis and McConnell, various interviews; Gertrude Weil to her Mother, 7 August 1912 and 15 August 1912, Weil Papers; Edward Cone interview; Excelsior Diary, in possession of Judith McConnell.

376. Lindau, 4.

377. Gertrude Weil to her Mother, 7 August 1912, Weil Papers.

378. Etta Cone to Claribel Cone, 25 June 1911, Baltimore Museum of Art, Cone Archives; Arthur, 211.

379. Aunt Bertha to Herman Cone, 14 May 1932, Cone Mills Archives; Gertrude Weil to her Mother, 18 August 1912, Weil Papers.

380. Lewis and McConnell, 4 July 1993 and 11 October 1993; Gertrude Weil to her Mother, 4 August 1912 and 24 August 1912, Weil Papers; Etta Cone to Claribel Cone, 16 July 1911, Baltimore Museum of Art, Cone Archives.

381. *Watauga Democrat*, 26 May 1913; Flat Top Manor Ledger, Blue Ridge Parkway Archives; Etta Cone to Claribel Cone, 18 June 1911, Baltimore Museum of Art, Cone Archives; Etta Cone to Gertrude Stein, 26 September 1909, Stein Collection.

382. Downs interview; Etta Cone to Claribel Cone, 25 June 1911, Baltimore Museum of Art, Cone Archives.

383. Etta Cone to Claribel Cone, 9 July 1911, Baltimore Museum of Art, Cone Archives. Etta was probably referring to "Maryland, My Maryland," an old and popular song.

384. Etta Cone to Claribel Cone, 16 July 1911, Baltimore Museum of Art, Cone Archives.

385. *Watauga Democrat*, 15 August 1912 and 8 August 1912.

386. Ibid., 29 August 1912, 3 October 1912 and 10 October 1912.

387. W.N. Hutt to Mrs. Moses H. Cone, 24 October 1911; Pay Ledger, 31 October 1920, Blue Ridge Parkway Archives.

388. Coffey interview; *Watauga Democrat*, 13 May 1926; Time Book, 1914, Blue Ridge Parkway Archives.

389. Watauga County Tax List, 1915; Isenhour interview; *Watauga Democrat*, 22 June 1911.

390. Pay Ledger, 31 January 1928, Blue Ridge Parkway Archives; Time Book, 31 October 1913, Blue Ridge Parkway Archives.

391. Lloyd Coffey, unrecorded interview by Kent Cave and Norman Schaich, n.d., typed summary in "Moses Cone Fact Book," vol. II, Blue Ridge Parkway Library; Gertrude Stein to Etta Cone, 1 January 1927, Baltimore Museum of Art, Cone Archives; Edward Cone, "The Miss Etta Cones," 459.

392. *Watauga Democrat*, 20 December 1917.

393. Firth, 7.

394. *Watauga Democrat*, 16 May 1922; B.B. Dougherty to Col. Fred A. Olds, 31 August 1921, Fred A. Olds Papers, North Carolina State Archives; Watauga County Tax List, 1926.

395. Gertrude Weil to her Mother, 26 July 1912, Weil Papers; Firth, 16; *Watauga Democrat*, 14 October 1915.

396. *Watauga Democrat*, 5 July 1923, 14 October 1926 and 21 July 1927.

397. Beeler, 96; Pay Ledger, 31 July 1928, Blue Ridge Parkway Archives; Lewis and McConnell, 4 July 1993; Pease interview; David F. Handlin, *The American Home: Architecture and Society, 1815-1915* (Boston: Little, Brown, 1979), 420; Ruth Schwartz Cowan, "The 'Industrial Revolution' in the Home: Technology and Social Change in the 20th Century," *Technology and Culture* 17:1 (January 1976): 10. The number of paid domestic servants in American homes declined by more than 40 percent between 1900 and 1920.

398. Whitener, 68; *Watauga Democrat*, 24 September 1926 and 15 September 1927; Watauga County Deed Book 38, 177; Buxton, "Historic Resource Study," 29-30.

399. Lindau, 4; Lewis and McConnell, 4 July 1993; Edward Cone interview.

400. Lewis and McConnell, 11 October 1993.

401. Lewis and McConnell, 4 July 1993.

402. Tyler B. Kiener to Regional Engineer, memorandum of 4 May 1948, "Moses Cone Fact Book," vol. 2; *Watauga Democrat*, 19 July 1916.

403. Herman Cone to Aunt Etta, 11 November 1935, Baltimore Museum of Art, Cone Archives; Omer Coffey interview.

404. Edward Cone interview; C.A. Reed to Mrs. Bertha L. Cone, 24 September 1930, Blue Ridge Parkway Archives. The chestnut blight fungus (Endothia parasitica), introduced into the United States around 1900, effectively eliminated this commercially valuable tree from eastern hardwood forests. No cure for this disease has been found.

405. This stone barrier, which still exists, is sometimes referred to as the "Spite Wall." According to some undocumented accounts, Bertha had a falling out with her neighbors at Chetola and built the wall to block their access to the Cone estate. The author was unable to locate a reliable source for this story. However, Bertha was concerned about

people driving on to her estate after dark and fishing in Bass Lake, and she often posted tenants to guard against this activity. Since the other entrances to her estate were gated and closed at night, building a wall to block the access from Chetola would have been an effective control measure.

406. Aunt Bertha to Herman Cone, n.d., Cone Mills Archives; Ibid., 9 May 1928.
407. *Watauga Democrat*, 23 October 1924; Downs interview; Edward Cone interview; Omer Coffey interview.
408. Bertha Cone to Etta Cone, 10 October 1929 and 22 September 1929, photocopies from the collection of Ellen C. B. Hirschland and in possession of author.
409. Aunt Bertha to Herman Cone, 13 January 1931, Cone Mills Archives.
410. Bernard Cone to Sister Bertha Cone, 12 February 1937, Cone Mills Archives; Watauga County Tax List, 1921; Buxton, "Historic Resource Study," 6.
411. Bernard Cone to Sister Bertha Cone, 12 February 1937, Cone Mills Archives.
412. Bertha Cone to Herman Cone, 12 May 1931 and 8 October 1927, Cone Mills Archives.
413. Herman Cone to Bertha Cone, 15 April 1935 and 13 April 1935, Cone Mills Archives; Thomas H. Donald, Bureau of Public Roads, to Senator Robert Reynolds, 23 April 1935, Cone Mills Archives.
414. Mrs. Moses H. Cone to Arno B. Cammerer, 24 April 1939; Arno B. Cammerer to Mrs. Moses H. Cone, 5 April 1939, "Moses Cone Fact Book," vol. 2.
415. Downs interview; Mrs. Moses H. Cone to President Franklin D. Roosevelt, 14 July 1939, Blue Ridge Parkway Files; Edward Cone interview.
416. Mrs. Moses H. Cone to President Franklin D. Roosevelt, 14 July 1939.
417. Mrs. Moses H. Cone to Arthur E. Demaray, 28 July 1939, "Moses Cone Fact Book," vol. 2.
418. Sam P. Weems to Regional Director, 19 September 1946, "Moses Cone Fact Book," vol. 2.
419. Buxton, "Historic Resource Study," 9; Pay Ledgers, Blue Ridge Parkway Archives; Downs interview; Omer Coffey interview.
420. Pay Ledgers, Blue Ridge Parkway Archives.
421. Downs interview; Omer Coffey interview.
422. Lewis and McConnell, 6 October 1990; Edward Cone interview; Downs interview.
423. Lindau, 6-7; Edward Cone interview.
424. *Watauga Democrat*, 21 January 1937 and 28 January 1937.
425. Edward Cone interview

426. Omer Coffey interview; Pease interview. In 1909, Etta told Gertrude Stein, "There is an overseer here who has been stealing & doing all sorts of crooked things & it is taking all of Sister Bertha's wits to get even with this man." Years later, Edward Cone often heard Bertha tell his father, Julius, similar tales of her victimization. While some of these perceptions were grounded in fact, some no doubt grew out of Bertha's own insecurity. Etta Cone to Gertrude Stein, 25 July 1909, Stein Collection; Edward Cone interview.

427. Bernard Cone to Etta Cone, 14 June 1947, Cone Mills Archives; *Greensboro Daily News*, 9 June 1947.

428. *Watauga Democrat*, 12 June 1947; Bernard Cone to Etta Cone, 14 June 1947.

429. *Watauga Democrat*, 26 June 1947; Inheritance Tax Record for Bertha L. Cone, Watauga County, North Carolina, 26 September 1950; Bertha Cone will and codicil.

430. Bertha Cone will.

431. Bertha Cone Inheritance Tax Record; Edward Cone interview.

432. Bertha Cone will; Bernard Cone to Etta Cone, 14 June 1947.

433. Bertha Cone will.

434. Indenture of 30 May 1911.

435. Indenture; Bernard Cone to Etta Cone, 14 June 1947. Turning a profit was not the primary purpose or mission of the Moses H. Cone Memorial Hospital. True to its philanthropic origins, the hospital charter stipulated that "no patient shall be refused admission nor be discharged because of inability to pay."

436. Superintendent's Monthly Narrative Report for July 1947, Blue Ridge Parkway Library.

437. Superintendent, Blue Ridge Parkway, to Regional Director, 1 August 1947, Blue Ridge Parkway Archives.

438. Ibid.; "Statement of Acceptability of the Moses Cone Estate for Purposes of Blue Ridge Parkway," 3 July 1947, photocopy in "Moses Cone Fact Book," vol. II.

439. Ibid.

440. Buxton, "Historic Resource Study," 33. The hospital trustees also considered offering the Blowing Rock property to the State of North Carolina, but at an October 1947 meeting, the state's Department of Conservation and Development passed a resolution that gave the National Park Service "first call" on the estate. Superintendent's Monthly Narrative Report for October 1947.

441. Walters interview.

442. Superintendent's Monthly Narrative Report for December 1949; Watauga County Deed Book 66, 263.

443. Blue Ridge Parkway, Master Plan, 1969, Blue Ridge Parkway Archives;

Superintendent's Monthly Narrative Report for April 1952, August 1954, and April 1955.

444. Stanley W. Abbott to Superintendent, memorandum report, 29 July 1947, Blue Ridge Parkway Archives.

445. Harley E. Jolley, *The Blue Ridge Parkway* (Knoxville: University of Tennessee Press, 1969), 135. Price had been a guest at Flat Top Manor during Moses' day and may have been inspired to buy the adjoining real estate while visiting the Cones.

446. Conrad Wirth, *Parks, Politics, and the People* (Norman: University of Oklahoma Press, 1980), 227, 234; National Park Service Division of Recreation Resource Surveys, "Economic Effects of the Blue Ridge Parkway," January 1962, Blue Ridge Parkway Archives.

447. Hillary A. Tolson to Senator Harry F. Byrd, 18 June 1946, Blue Ridge Parkway Files.

448. Alfred Runte, *National Parks, the American Experience* (Lincoln: University of Nebraska Press, 1987), xii-xiv and passim.

449. *Congressional Record* (19 May 1937), vol. 81, pt. 5, 4807; Jolley, 123-24.

450. Stanley Abbott, interview by S. Herbert Evison, summer 1958, Blue Ridge Parkway Files; William C. Everhart, *The National Park Service* (New York: Praeger Publishers, 1972), 33.

451. Henry D. Shapiro, *Appalachia on Our Mind: The Southern Mountains and Mountaineers in the American Consciousness, 1870-1920* (Chapel Hill: University of North Carolina Press, 1978); David E. Whisnant, *All That is Native and Fine: The Politics of Culture in an American Region* (Chapel Hill: University of North Carolina Press, 1983), and *Modernizing the Mountaineer: People, Power, and Planning in Appalachia* (Boone, N.C.: Appalachian Consortium Press, 1980); Jean Haskell Speer, "'Hillbilly Sold Here,' Appalachian Folk Culture and Parkway Tourism," in *Parkways: Past, Present, and Future* (Boone, N.C.: Appalachian Consortium, 1989): 212-20. These authors address in detail the stereotyping of Appalachia as a land of pioneers.

452. Eller, 26.

453. At the time, students of landscape architecture were instructed to study art and nature so that they could make their designs aesthetically more appealing. Accuracy took a back seat to the total landscape effect. In designing historical compositions, many landscape architects of the period created "ruins" to obtain the effect and ambiance desired. The artists of the Hudson River School turned out painting after painting of magnificent and recognizable landscapes. Considering the popularity and the subject matter of this school, and given the practice of landscape architects to follow artistic models, it seems hardly coincidental that Parkway vistas took on a striking resemblance to Thomas Cole's

and Asher B. Durand's treatments of the "Kaaterskill" mountain region of New York. Likewise, the similarity between the Parkway's pastoral and pioneer farm scenes and Jervis McEntee's 1896 "Autumn, Landscape" appears more than casual. Visually, the Parkway was a living, animated landscape lifted from the easels of the Hudson River School. Metropolitan Museum of Art, *American Paradise: The World of the Hudson River School* (New York: Harry N. Abrams, 1988), 117, 120-21, 278, 328; Hubbard and Kimball, 76.

454. Abbott interview; Blue Ridge Parkway, General Interpretive Statement, Blue Ridge Parkway Archives.

455. Abbott interview.

456. *Blue Ridge Parkway News*, April-July 1942, Blue Ridge Parkway Library.

457. Rodger Cunningham, *Apples on the Flood: The Southern Mountain Experience* (Knoxville: University of Tennessee Press, 1987), 103.

458. Blue Ridge Parkway, General Interpretive Statement, Blue Ridge Parkway Archives. The Civil War deeply divided the mountain South and gave rise to guerrilla raids and countless acts of violence. See Phillip Shaw Paludan, *Victims: A True Story of the Civil War* (Knoxville: University of Tennessee Press, 1981), passim.

459. Henry Shapiro, 3; Speer, 215.

460. Abbott interview.

461. Much period literature supported the stereotypical images of Appalachia. Muriel Earley Sheppard's *Cabins in the Laurel*, published in 1935, the year that construction on the Blue Ridge Parkway began, purported to be a faithful description of the people of western North Carolina's Toe River Valley around Spruce Pine. However, editors at the University of North Carolina Press carefully tailored the text and accompanying photographs to emphasize the folk aspects of the culture. They featured farms, rustic cabins, churches, and older people, while ignoring town life, cars, farm tractors, mica mines and miners that were an established part of the area. Charles Alan Watkins, "Merchandising the Mountaineer," *Appalachian Journal* (Spring 1985): 220, 223 and passim.

462. Superintendent's Monthly Narrative Reports for April and for May 1951, Blue Ridge Parkway Archives.

463. Sam P. Weems, Interview by S. Herbert Evison, 16 July 1971, National Park Service, Harpers Ferry Center Library, Harpers Ferry, W. Va.

464. Stanley Abbott, Instructions to Park Operators Regarding Merchandise Authorized for Sale in Gift Shops, February 1946, Blue Ridge Parkway Files.

465. Superintendent's Monthly Narrative Report for April 1952 and July 1952.

466. Parkway Craft Center, Demonstrations for 1963, Blue Ridge Parkway Archives; Lucy C. Morgan to Sam P. Weems, 15 June 1956, Blue Ridge Parkway Archives.

467. Superintendent's Monthly Narrative Report for October 1952, Blue Ridge Parkway Archives. These revenues continued to grow over the years. By 1986, sales at the Parkway Craft Center exceeded $240,000. Parkway Craft Center, Sales Report 1987, Southern Highland Handicraft Guild Collection.

468. These building use fees ranged from $25 during the 1950's to slightly more than $3,500 in 1991. Sam Weems to Regional Director, 18 May 1954, Blue Ridge Parkway Archives; Richard G. Wyatt, Concessions Specialist, Blue Ridge Parkway, interview by author, 5 December 1991.

469. Sam Weems to Robert Gray, 9 August 1966, Blue Ridge Parkway Archives; Minutes of the Advisory Board of the Southern Highland Handicraft Guild, Meeting of 4 November 1966, Blue Ridge Parkway Archives.

470. Minutes of the Advisory Board of the Southern Highland Handicraft Guild, 4 November 1966; The Craftsmen Production and Training Center, Prospectus, n.d., Blue Ridge Parkway Archives.

471. The Story of Early Americana, n.d., Blue Ridge Parkway Archives.

472. Americana Project, Outline of Findings of the Study Team, March 1967, Blue Ridge Parkway Archives.

473. Park Service officials adopted a similar pioneer interpretation of Appalachian culture at the Great Smoky Mountains National Park, systematically removing the clapboard houses that were at Cades Cove while preserving the log cabins. They also overlooked the fact that people had migrated into and out of the cove for decades and had consistently traded their farm products in regional markets. See Durwood Dunn, *Cades Cove: The Life and Death of a Southern Appalachian Community, 1818-1937* (Knoxville: University of Tennessee Press, 1988).

474. Minutes of the Advisory Board of the Southern Highland Handicraft Guild, 4 November 1966; Advisory Board on National Parks, Historic Sites, Buildings and Monuments, Report to the Secretary of Interior, Inspection of Certain Field Areas of the National Park System, Blue Ridge Parkway Archives.

475. "Road to the Future," Draft Master Plan, 25 October 1967, Blue Ridge Parkway Archives. Between 1956 and the Park Service's Golden Anniversary in 1966, Mission 66 funds built miles of roads, scores of visitor centers, and other facilities, including two ranger residences at the Cone estate. Wirth, 234, 237, 274; Barry Mackintosh, *The National Parks: Shaping the System* (Washington, D.C.: U.S. Department of the Interior, 1991), 62.

476. Granville Liles, "The Art and Craft of Managing a National Parkway," in *Parkways: Past, Present, and Future*, Appalachian Consortium (Boone, N.C.: Appalachian Consortium Press, 1989), 242-44.

477. Granville Liles to Regional Director, 27 August 1968, Blue Ridge Parkway Archives; Roger Soles to Granville Liles, 21 January 1971, Blue Ridge Parkway Archives.

478. Acting Associate Director of Operations to Regional Directors, 13 July 1973, Blue Ridge Parkway Archives.

479. Earl W. Batten, Chief of Maintenance, to Superintendent, memorandum, 12 June 1969, Blue Ridge Parkway Archives; various letters from Blowing Rock residents to Granville Liles, October 1969, Blue Ridge Parkway Archives.

480. Development Backlog Review, n.d., Blue Ridge Parkway Archives; Projects Which Should be Deleted from the Development Program, report, n.d., Blue Ridge Parkway Archives.

481. *Asheville Citizen*, "Heritage Center Plans Are Outlined," clipping dated 31 August 1971, Blue Ridge Parkway Archives; Robert Gray to Granville Liles, 3 September and 7 September 1971, Blue Ridge Parkway Archives; Robert A. Hope, Resident Landscape Architect, to Sam Weems, 13 October 1981, Blue Ridge Parkway Archives.

482. Robert Gray, Proposal for the Development of the Southern Highland Folk Art Center, 17 June 1974, Blue Ridge Parkway Archives; Granville Liles to Robert Gray, 25 June 1974, and Robert Gray to Granville Liles, 3 July 1974, Blue Ridge Parkway Archives.

483. Granville Liles to George Bryson, Jr., 3 June 1970, Blue Ridge Parkway Archives; Malcolm Fogleman, Issues and Directions in Concessions Management, 27 September 1979, Blue Ridge Parkway Archives; Phillip Williams, Business Manager, Eastern National Park & Monument Association, unrecorded interview by author, 3 December 1992. Profits made by the Association, which operates all Parkway visitor center book sales outlets, support interpretive operations and research.

484. James S. Askins, Exhibits Specialist, to Supervisory Historical Architect, memorandum, 13 July 1973, "Moses H. Cone Fact Book."

485. Major Accomplishments, Moses H. Cone Estate, report of 26 November 1991, Blue Ridge Parkway Files. Initial plans recommended that Trout Lake Dam be removed and its embankment material used as fill at Bass Lake. Parkway managers scrapped this idea after they secured funds to repair all three dams. Gary Everhardt, Superintendent, to Regional Director, memorandum, 12 June 1987, also, Director to Regional

Director, memorandum, 12 May 1988, Blue Ridge Parkway Files.

486. Gene Redmon, District Ranger, Blue Ridge Parkway, unrecorded interview by author, 18 December 1991.

487. Pease interview.

488. Walters interview.

489. Statement for Management, Blue Ridge Parkway, 1987, 16, 23-27; Annual Budget Comparison in 1976 Dollars, 1991, Blue Ridge Parkway Files.

490. *Greensboro Patriot*, 14 August 1907.

491. Joseph Rosengart to Herman Kahn, 16 April 1846, in "A Letter," pamphlet published by Cone Mills Corporation, n.d.

492. People continue today to define themselves through their material possessions. Colonial architecture still sends a message, as does owning a house in the country. Commodities help establish one's standing in the larger social order by "making a statement" and lending "pride of ownership." Leisure activities are also important in establishing identity. People proclaim class and group membership by vacationing in Europe, attending polo matches, and watching stock car races.

493. *Watauga Democrat*, 17 December 1908.

494. Firth, 40-41.

SELECTED BIBLIOGRAPHY

Unpublished and Private Papers

Adler, Samuel. Untitled typed manuscript [photocopy]. Vertical files, Washington County-Jonesborough Library, Jonesborough, Tennessee.

Alston-DeGraffenried Papers. North Carolina State Archives.

Blue Ridge Parkway Archives and Library, Asheville, North Carolina.

J.D. Brown Ledger. Owned by Wade Brown, Boone, North Carolina.

Cone Archives. The Baltimore Museum of Art, Baltimore, Maryland.

Ceasar Cone Papers. Appalachian Collection, Appalachian State University.

Cone Mills Corporation Archives. Greensboro, North Carolina.

Cone Papers, Files and Photographic Collection. Greensboro Historical Museum, Greensboro, North Carolina.

Cone, Sydney, Jr., ed. "The Cones from Bavaria." Typed manuscript in 4 vols., Greensboro Public Library, Greensboro, North Carolina.

_____. "The Herman Cone Family." Typed manuscript [photocopy] in Blue Ridge Parkway Archives.

Paul Fink Papers. McClung Historical Collection, Knox County Public Library, Knoxville, Tennessee.

Ellen C.B. Hirschland Collection. Great Neck, New York.

Lindau, Alfred M. "History of the Lindau Family." Typed manuscript [photocopy] in possession of Mrs. Judith Lindau McConnell, Bedford, Massachusetts.

McConnell, Judith Lindau. Notes on the Genealogy of the Lindau Family. Photocopy in possession of the author.

Fred A. Olds Papers. North Carolina State Archives.

Pilot Mills Company Papers. Perkins Library, Duke University.

Postcard Collection. University of North Carolina, Chapel Hill.

Postcard Collection. Perkins Library, Duke University.

Thomas Settle Papers. Southern Historical Collection, University of North Carolina, Chapel Hill.

William Alexander Smith Papers. Perkins Library, Duke University.

Southern Highland Handicraft Guild Collection. Folk Art Center Library, Blue Ridge Parkway.

Gertrude Stein Collection. Beinecke Rare Book and Manuscript Library, Yale University.

Gertrude Weil Papers. North Carolina State Archives.

Yates, Bowling C. "The Cradle of Forestry in America." Typed manuscript prepared for the U.S. Forest Service. North Carolina Collection, Pack Memorial Library, Asheville, North Carolina.

Interviews

Abbott, Stanley. Interview by S. Herbert Evison, Summer, 1958. Transcript, Blue Ridge Parkway, Division of Resource Management and Visitor Services, Asheville, North Carolina.

Coffey, Lloyd. Unrecorded interview by Kent Cave and Norman Schaich, n.d. Typed summary in "Moses Cone Fact Book, Vol. II" Blue Ridge Parkway Library.

Coffey, Omer. Tape recorded interview by the author, 19 October 1991.

Cone, Ben and Ceasar Cone. Interview by E.P. Douglass, 28 July 1981. Southern Oral History Program, transcript, Southern Historical Collection, University of North Carolina, Chapel Hill.

Cone, Edward. Tape recorded interview by the author, 27 July 1993.

Downs, Clyde. Interview by Tom Robbins and Kent Cave, 21 November 1975. Transcript in "Moses Cone Fact Book," Vol. II, Blue Ridge Parkway Library.

Hollers, Carl. Interview by Kent Cave and Tom Robbins, 2 October 1975. Transcript, Blue Ridge Parkway Library.

Isenhour, Charlie. Interview by Judy Cornett, 29 May 1975. Transcript, Blue Ridge Parkway Library.

Koontz, Dorothy Teague. Unrecorded interview by the author, 4 November 1992. Typed summary in possession of author.

Lewis, Nancy Lindau, and Judith Lindau McConnell. Tape recorded interview by the author 6 October 1990.

_____. Tape recorded interview by the author 4 July 1993.

_____. Tape recorded interview by the author 28 July 1993.

_____. Tape recorded interview by the author 11 October 1993.

Pease, Ted. Interview by Tom Robbins and Kent Cave, 7 August 1975. Transcript, Blue Ridge Parkway Library.

Walters, Mrs. Ruby Moody. Interview by Kent Cave and Tom Robbins, 5 June 1975. Transcript, Blue Ridge Parkway Library.

Weems, Samuel P. Interview by S. Herbert Evison, 16 July 1971. Transcript, National Park Service, Harpers Ferry Center Library, Harpers Ferry, West Virginia.

Directories, Indexes, and Trade Publications

Directory of the City of Greensboro, N.C., for 1896 and 1897. Charlotte: Chase Brenizer, 1896.

Fulenweider, Harry W. *Asheville City Directory and Business Reflex, 1890.* Charleston, S.C.: Walker, Evans and Cogswell, 1890.

Greensboro, N.C., City Directory, 1892-1900. Atlanta: Maloney Directory Company, 1899.

Knoxville City Directory, 1886. Knoxville: Ogden Brothers, 1886.

_____. Atlanta: R.L. Polk, 1888.

Manufacturer's Review and Industrial Record. 15 June 1891.

Moody's Investor Service. *Moody's Industrial Manual, 1983*, Vol. 1. New York: 1983.

Russin, Sharon Travitsky, ed. *Wall Street Journal Index*, 1983. New York: Dow Jones, 1984.

Dissertations, Theses, and Student Papers

Beeler, James. "A Sketch of Blowing Rock, North Carolina, 1900." Student paper, Appalachian Collection, Appalachian State University, 1980.

_____, Steve Candler and others. "An Analysis of the China Orchard in the Moses H. Cone Estate, 1900-1947." Student paper, Appalachian Collection, Appalachian State University, 1980.

Freeze, Gary Richard. "Model Mill Men of the New South: Paternalism and Methodism in the Odell Cotton Mills of North Carolina, 1877-1908." Ph.D. diss. University of North Carolina, 1988.

Kipp, Samuel M. III. "Urban Growth and Social Change in the South, 1870-1920: Greensboro, North Carolina, as a Case Study." Ph.D. diss. Princeton University, 1974.

Volk, Victoria Loucia. "The Biltmore Estate and Its Creators: Richard Morris Hunt, Frederick Law Olmsted and George Washington Vanderbilt." Ph.D. diss. Emory University, 1984.

Watson, Marianne D. "'Do Not Grind the Seed Corn': Reformers, Manufacturers, and the Battle Over Child Labor Legislation in North Carolina, 1901-1913." M.A. thesis. North Carolina State University, 1984.

Newspapers

Asheville Citizen. 1922, 1971.

Asheville Citizen-Times. 1992.

Blowing Rocket. 1979.

Charlotte Daily Observer. 1895-1908.

Charlotte Observer. 1963.

East Tennessee Union Flag. 1866.

Greensboro Daily News. 1906, 1908, 1947.

Greensboro Patriot. 1895-1908.

Knoxville Sentinel. 1917.

Lenoir News and *Lenoir Semi-Weekly News.* 1899-1908.

Lenoir Topic. 1899-1901.

Lenoir News-Topic. 1902-1908.

Watauga Democrat. 1895-1948.

Government Publications and Records

Baltimore City, Maryland. Records of Deeds. Circuit Court Records Office.

_____. Wills. Office of the Register of Wills.

Buncombe County, North Carolina. Records of Deeds.

Caldwell County, North Carolina. Records of Deeds.

Guilford County, North Carolina. Records of Deeds.

_____. Records of Mortgages.

North Carolina Board of Agriculture. *Apple Bulletin*. July 1900.

North Carolina Bureau of Labor, *Biennial Reports of the Secretary of State* (1891-1907). Raleigh: State Printer, 1891, 1895, 1897, 1899, 1901, 1903, 1905,1907.

U.S. Bureau of the Census. *Population Schedules of the Seventh Census of the United States, 1850, Virginia: Lunenburg County*. Washington, D.C.: National Archives, General Services Administration, 1964.

_____. *Population Schedules of the Eighth Census of the United States, 1860, Tennessee, Washington County*. Washington, D.C.: National Archives, 1965.

_____. *Population Schedules of the Twelfth (1900) and Thirteenth (1910) Census of the United States*. Washington, D.C.: National Archives.

U.S. Department of the Interior, Census Office. *Report on Manufacturing Industries in the United States at the Eleventh Census: 1890*. Part III. Washington, D.C.: Government Printing Office, 1895.

U.S. Department of the Interior, National Park Service. "A Cultural Landscape Report of the Moses H. Cone Memorial Park," by Ian Firth. Unpublished draft report in the Blue Ridge Parkway Library, 1990.

_____. "Historic Resource Study, Moses H. Cone Estate, Blue Ridge Parkway," by Barry M. Buxton. Photocopy in the Blue Ridge Parkway Library, 1987.

_____. "Historic Structure Report, Moses H. Cone Estate, Blowing Rock, North Carolina," by Barbara J. Gilbert. Photocopy in Blue Ridge Parkway Library, 1987.

_____. "Mabry Mill Historic Resource Study," by Barry M. Buxton. Photocopy in the Blue Ridge Parkway Library, 1989.

_____. "Moses H. Cone Manor House, Historic Structure Report" (Draft). Blue Ridge Parkway Files, 1995.

_____. "Statement for Management," by Division of Resource Planning and Professional Services. Photocopy in Blue Ridge Parkway, Division of Resource Management and Visitor Services.

_____. Blue Ridge Parkway Files, Photographic Collection, and Archives, Asheville, North Carolina.

Washington County, Tennessee. Deed Books.

_____. County Court and Quarterly Court Minutes.

_____. Clerk and Master Minute Books for Chancery Court.

Watauga County, North Carolina. Deed Books.
_____. Record of Mortgages.
_____. Superior Court Judgment Docket Books.
_____. Tax List for 1918 and 1921.
_____. Tax Scroll, 1896-1926.

Books and Articles

Affleck, Diane L.F. *Just New from the Mills: Printed Cottons in America, Late Nineteenth and Early Twentieth Centuries, from the Collections of the Museum of American Textile History*. North Andover, Mass.: Museum of American Textile History, 1987.

Ames, Kenneth L. "American Decorative Arts/Household Furnishings." *American Quarterly* 35 (1983): 280-303.

_____. "The Battle of the Sideboards." *Winterthur Portfolio* 9 (1974): 1-27.

_____ *Death in the Dining Room, and Other Tales of Victorian Culture*. Philadelphia: Temple University Press, 1992.

_____. "Material Culture as Non Verbal Communication: A Historical Case Study." *Journal of American Culture* 3 (Winter 1981): 619-41.

_____. "Meaning in Artifacts: Hall Furnishings in Victorian America." *Journal of Interdisciplinary History* 9 (1978): 19-46.

Andrews, Mildred Gwin. *The Men and the Mills: A History of the Southern Textile Industry*. Macon, Ga.: Mercer University Press, 1987.

Appalachian Consortium. *Parkways: Past, Present, and Future*. Boone, N.C.: Appalachian Consortium Press, 1989.

Arnett, Ethel. *Greensboro, North Carolina*. Chapel Hill: University of North Carolina Press, 1965.

Arthur, John Preston. *A History of Watauga County, North Carolina*. Richmond: Everett Waddey, 1915.

Aslet, Clive. *The American Country House*. New Haven: Yale University Press, 1990.

Axelrod, Alan, ed. *The Colonial Revival in America*. New York: Norton, 1985.

Ayers, Edward L. *The Promise of the New South: Life After Reconstruction*. New York, Oxford University Press, 1992.

Bailey, L. H. "The Making of Clean Milk." *Country Life in America* 6 (June 1904): 170-72.

Balliett, Carl J. *World Leadership in Denims Through Thirty Years of Progress*. Greensboro, N.C.: Proximity Manufacturing Company, 1925.

Bishir, Catherine W., and others. *Architects and Builders in North Carolina*. Chapel Hill: University of North Carolina Press, 1990.

_____, and Lawrence S. Earley, eds. *Early Twentieth Century Suburbs in North Carolina*. Raleigh: North Carolina Department of Cultural Resources, 1985.

_____. *North Carolina Architecture.* Chapel Hill: University of North Carolina Press, 1990.

Blicksilver, Jack. *Cotton Manufacturing in the Southeast: An Historical Analysis.* Atlanta: Bureau of Business and Economic Research, Georgia State College of Business Administration, Bulletin No. 5, July 1959.

Bowers, William L. *The Country Life Movement in America, 1900-1920.* Port Washington, N.Y.: Kennikat Press, 1974.

Brooklyn Museum. *The American Renaissance, 1876-1917.* New York: The Brooklyn Museum, 1979.

Brugger, Robert J. *Maryland: A Middle Temperament, 1634-1980.* Baltimore: Johns Hopkins University Press, 1988.

Buxton, Barry M. *A Village Tapestry, The History of Blowing Rock.* Boone, N.C.: Appalachian Consortium Press, 1989.

_____, and Steven M. Beatty, eds. *Blue Ridge Parkway: Agent of Transition.* Boone, N.C.: Appalachian Consortium Press, 1986.

Campbell, Helen. "Household Art and the Microbe." *House Beautiful* 6 (October 1895): 18-21.

Carroll, George D. *Diamonds from Brilliant Minds.* New York: Dempsey & Carroll, 1881.

Century Magazine. "In the Crowd at the Paris Exposition." 61 (November 1900): 155-60.

Chafe, William Henry. *Civilities and Civil Rights: Greensboro, North Carolina, and the Black Struggle for Freedom.* New York: Oxford University Press, 1980.

Clark, Clifford Edward, Jr. *The American Family Home, 1800-1960.* Chapel Hill: University of North Carolina Press, 1986.

Clark, Thomas D. "The Post-Civil War Economy in the South." In *Jews in the South,* ed. Leonard Dinnerstein and Mary Dale Palsson. Baton Rouge: Louisiana State University Press, 1973.

Cohen, Jan. *The Palace or the Poorhouse: The American Home as a Cultural Symbol.* East Lansing: Michigan State University Press, 1979.

Cohen, Naomi. *Encounter with Emancipation: The German Jews in the United States, 1830-1914.* Philadelphia: Jewish Publication Society of America, 1984.

Condit, Elizabeth C. "The Service Equipment of the Country House." *Architectural Forum* 49 (September 1928): 453-58.

Cone, Edward. "The Miss Etta Cones, the Steins, and M'sieu Matisse: A Memoir." *American Scholar* 42 (Summer 1973): 441-60.

Cone Export & Commission Company. *Half Century Book: 1891-1941.* Greensboro, N.C.: The Company, 1941.

Copeland, Melvin Thomas. *The Cotton Manufacturing Industry of the United States.* Cambridge: Harvard University Press, 1923.

Cott, Nancy F. *The Grounding of Modern Feminism.* New Haven: Yale University Press, 1987.

Cowan, Ruth Schwartz. "The 'Industrial Revolution' in the Home: Technology and Social Change in the 20th Century." *Technology and Culture* 17 (January 1976): 1-23.

Crandell, Maribeth. *Moses H. Cone, His Family, His Fortune, and His Life.* Greensboro, N.C.: Cone Printing Services, 1977.

Cunningham, Rodger. *Apples on the Flood: The Southern Mountain Experience.* Knoxville: University of Tennessee Press, 1987.

Daniels, Roger. *Coming to America: A History of Immigration and Ethnicity in American Life.* New York: Harper Collins, 1990.

Davidson, Marshall B., ed. *The American Heritage History of Antiques, from the Civil War to World War I.* New York: American Heritage, 1969.

Desmond, Harry W., and Herbert Croly. *Stately Homes in America, from Colonial Times to the Present Day.* New York: D. Appleton, 1903.

Eaton, Allen H. *Handicrafts of the Southern Highlands.* Russell Sage Foundation, 1937; reprint, New York: Dover Publications, 1973.

Eller, Ronald D. *Miners, Millhands, and Mountaineers: Industrialization of the Appalachian South, 1880-1930.* Knoxville: University of Tennessee Press, 1982.

Everhart, William C. *The National Park Service.* New York: Praeger Publishers, 1972.

Fink, Paul. *Jonesborough: The First Century of Tennessee's First Town.* Springfield, Va.: National Technical Information Services, 1972.

Forbes. "'Caesarism' at Cone Mills." 15 March 1977: 70.

Genskow, Karen M. "The Country Estate in Illinois." *Historic Illinois* 10 (February 1988): 1-15.

Gerhard, William Paul. "Artificial Illumination." *American Architect and Building News* 42 (December 1893): 109-10.

Glass, Brent D. *The Textile Industry in North Carolina.* Raleigh: North Carolina Department of Cultural Resources, 1992.

Greene, Theodore P. *America's Heroes: The Changing Models of Success in American Magazines.* New York: Oxford University Press, 1970.

Grier, Katherine C. *Culture & Comfort: People, Parlors, and Upholstery, 1850-1930.* Rochester, N.Y.: Strong Museum, 1988.

Grover, Kathryn, ed. *Dining in America, 1850-1900.* Amherst: University of Massachusetts Press, 1987.

Hall, Jacquelyn Dowd, and others. *Like a Family: The Making of a Southern Cotton Mill World.* Chapel Hill: University of North Carolina Press, 1987.

Handlin, David F. *The American Home: Architecture and Society, 1815-1915.* Boston: Little, Brown, 1979.

Hawley, Sherwin. "Good Taste in Country Houses." *Country Life in America* 10 (October 1906): 610-24.

Hays, Samuel P. *The Response to Industrialism, 1885-1914.* Chicago: University of Chicago Press, 1957.

Heinze, Andrew R. *Adapting to Abundance: Jewish Immigrants, Mass Consumption, and the Search for American Identity.* New York: Columbia University Press, 1990.

Hewitt, Mark Alan. *The Architect and the American Country House, 1890-1940.* New Haven: Yale University Press, 1990.

Higham, John. *Strangers in the Land: Patterns of American Nativism, 1860-1925.* 2d ed., New Brunswick: Rutgers University Press, 1988.

Hirschland, Ellen B. "The Cone Sisters and the Stein Family." In *Four Americans in Paris.* New York: The Museum of Modern Art, 1970.

Hubbard, Henry Vincent, and Theodora Kimball. *Introduction to the Study of Landscape Design.* New York: Macmillan, 1917.

Hudson, Henry Holly. *Modern Dwellings in Town and Country, Adapted to American Wants and Climate.* New York: Harper & Brothers, 1878.

Johnson, Katherine B. "Lighting the Home." *Good Housekeeping* 30 (February 1900): 58-60.

Jolley, Harley E. *The Blue Ridge Parkway.* Knoxville: University of Tennessee Press, 1969.

Kammen, Michael G. *Mystic Chords of Memory: The Transformation of Tradition in American Culture.* New York: Knopf, 1991.

Kaplan, Wendy. "R.T.H. Halsey: An Ideology of Collecting American Decorative Arts." *Winterthur Portfolio* 17 (Spring 1982): 43-53.

Kane, Nancy Frances. *Textiles in Transition: Technology, Wages, and Industry Relocation in the U.S. Textile Industry, 1880-1930.* New York: Greenwood Press, 1988.

Keith, Katharine A. "The Modern Pantry." *Good Housekeeping* 31 (December 1900): 358-59.

Kellner, Bruce, ed. *A Gertrude Stein Companion.* New York: Greenwood Press, 1988.

Lanier, Ruby J. *Blanford Barnard Dougherty, Mountain Educator.* Durham, N.C.: Duke University Press, 1974.

Leach, Anna. "Science in the Model Kitchen." *Cosmopolitan* 27 (May 1899): 104.

Lewis, R.W.B. *Edith Wharton: A Biography.* New York: Harper & Row, 1975.

Lynes, Russell. *The Tastemakers.* New York: Harper & Brothers, 1949.

Mackintosh, Barry. *The National Parks: Shaping the System.* Washington, D.C.: U.S. Department of the Interior, 1991.

May, B.A. "Progressivism and the Colonial Revival: The Modern Colonial House, 1900-1920." *Winterthur Portfolio.* 26 (Summer/Autumn 1991): 107-22.

Mayo, Edith, ed. *American Material Culture: The Shape of Things Around Us.* Bowling Green, Oh.: Bowling Green State University Popular Press, 1984.

McAllister, Ward. *Society as I Have Found It*. New York: Cassell, 1890; reprint, New York: Arno Press, 1975.

McHugh, Cathy L. *Mill Family: The Labor System in the Southern Cotton Textile Industry, 1880-1915*. New York: Oxford University Press, 1988.

McLaurin, Melton A. *Paternalism and Protest: Southern Cotton Mill Workers and Organized Labor, 1875-1915*. Westport, Conn.: Greenwood Publishing, 1971.

Mellow, James R. *Charmed Circle: Gertrude Stein & Company*. New York: Praeger, 1974.

Metropolitan Museum of Art. *American Paradise: The World of the Hudson River School*. New York: Harry N. Abrams, 1988.

Mitchell, Broadus. *The Rise of Cotton Mills in the South*. Baltimore: Johns Hopkins University Press, 1921.

Moore, Edwin R. *In Old Oneonta*. Vol. 4. Oneonta, N.Y.: Upper Susquehanna Historical Society, 1965.

Noblitt, Phil. "The Blue Ridge Parkway and Myths of the Pioneer." *Appalachian Journal* 21 (Summer 1994): 394-409.

Novak, Barbara. *American Painting of the Nineteenth Century: Realism, Idealism, and the American Experience*. New York: Harper & Row, 1979.

Oats, Mary J. *The Role of the Cotton Textile Industry in the Economic Development of the American Southeast: 1900-1940*. New York: Arno Press, 1975.

Orphan's Friend and Masonic Journal. "The Cone Family and the Textile Industry." 1 July 1941.

Oxford Orphan Asylum. *Proceedings of the Grand Lodge of Ancient, Free and Accepted Masons of North Carolina*. Raleigh, 1902.

Painter, Jacqueline Burgin, and Jonathan William Horstman. *The German Invasion of Western North Carolina*. Asheville, N.C.: Biltmore Press, 1992.

Palliser, Charles, and George Palliser. *Palliser's American Architecture*. New York: J.S. Ogilvie, 1888.

_____. *Palliser's New Cottage Homes and Details*. New York: Palliser & Co., 1887.

Paludan, Phillip Shaw. *Victims: A True Story of the Civil War*. Knoxville: University of Tennessee Press, 1981.

Pawley, Frederic Arden. "The Country House Room by Room: A Checklist with Suggestions." *Architectural Forum* 58 (March 1933): 194-204.

Pike, Martha V. "In Memory of: Artifacts Relating to Mourning in Nineteenth Century America." In *American Material Culture: The Shape of Things Around Us*, ed. Edith Mayo.

Pollack, Barbara. *The Collectors: Dr. Claribel and Miss Etta Cone*. Indianapolis: Bobbs-Merrill, 1962.

Powell, Edwin C. "Shelburne Farms: An Ideal Country Place."*Country Life in America* 3 (February 1903): 152-56.

Powell, E. P. *The Country Home*. New York: McClure, Phillips, 1904.

Powell, William S., ed. *Dictionary of North Carolina Biography*. Vols. 2 and 4. Chapel Hill: University of North Carolina Press, 1986 and 1991.

Reese, Jennifer. "America's Most Admired Corporations." *Fortune* 127 (8 February 1993): 44-72.

Rhoads, William B. "The Colonial Revival and American Nationalism." *Journal of the Society of Architectural Historians* 35 (December 1976): 239-54.

Richardson, Brenda. *Dr. Claribel & Miss Etta: The Cone Collection of the Baltimore Museum of Art*. Baltimore: Baltimore Museum of Art, 1985.

Richardson, Dr. B. W. "Health at Home." *Appleton's Journal* 8 (1880): 311-12.

Roundtree, Moses. *Strangers in the Land: The Story of Jacob Weil's Tribe*. Philadelphia: Dorrance, 1969.

Runte, Alfred. *National Parks, the American Experience*. Lincoln: University of Nebraska Press, 1987.

Schmitt, Peter J. *Back to Nature: The Arcadian Myth in Urban America*. Baltimore: Johns Hopkins University Press, 1990.

Seale, William. *The Tasteful Interlude: American Interiors Through the Camera's Eye, 1860-1917*. Nashville: American Association for State and Local History, 1982.

Selden, Catherine. "The Woman of To-day, II. The Tyranny of the Kitchen." *North American Review* 157 (October 1893): 431-40.

Shackleton, Robert, and Elizabeth Shackleton. *The Quest of the Colonial*. New York: Century, 1907; reprint, Detroit, Singing Tree Press, 1970.

Shapiro, Henry D. *Appalachia on Our Mind: The Southern Mountains and Mountaineers in the American Consciousness, 1870-1920*. Chapel Hill: University of North Carolina Press, 1978.

Shapiro, Laura. *Perfection Salad: Women and Cooking at the Turn of the Century*. New York: Henry Holt, 1986.

Smith, Captain Ross. *Reminiscences of an Old-Timer*. Privately Printed, 1930.

Smith, Mae Lucile. "The Looms of Ceasar Cone." *Sky-Land Magazine* 1 (August 1914): 573-83.

Speer, Jean Haskell. "'Hillbilly Sold Here'" Appalachian Folk Culture and Parkway Tourism." In Appalachian Consortium, *Parkways: Past, Present, and Future*: 212-20.

Stadiem, William. *A Class by Themselves*. New York: Crown, 1980.

Strasser, Susan. *Never Done: A History of American Housework*. New York: Pantheon, 1982.

Sutherland, Daniel. *Americans and Their Servants: Domestic Service in the United States from 1800 to 1920*. Baton Rouge: Louisiana State

University Press, 1981.

Swaim, Doug, ed. *Carolina Dwelling: Towards Preservation of Place, In Celebration of the North Carolina Vernacular Landscape*. Raleigh: North Carolina State University, 1978.

Tatum, George B. "The Emergence of an American School of Landscape Design." *Historic Preservation* (April-June 1973): 34-41.

Thompson, Holland. *From the Cotton Field to the Cotton Mill: A Study of Industrial Transition in North Carolina*. New York: Macmillan, 1906; reprint, Freeport, N.Y.: Books for Libraries, 1971.

Time. "Carolina Caesar." 17 April 1933: 48-49.

Todd, John Emerson. *Frederick Law Olmsted*. Boston: Twayne, 1982.

Underhill, Francis T. *Driving for Pleasure*. New York: D. Appleton, 1897; reprinted as *Driving Horse-Drawn Carriages for Pleasure*, New York: Dover, 1989.

Van Rensselaer, Mrs. Schuyler. *Art Out-of-Doors: Hints on Good Taste in Gardening*. New York: Scribner's, 1925.

Veblen, Thorstein. *The Theory of the Leisure Class*. New York: Funk & Wagnalls, 1899.

Ward, Susan M., and Michael K. Smith, eds. *Biltmore Estate*. Asheville, N.C.: Biltmore Company, 1989.

Watkins, Charles Alan. "Merchandising the Mountaineer." *Appalachian Journal* (Spring 1985): 215-37.

Welter, Barbara. *Dimity Convictions: The American Woman in the Nineteenth Century*. Athens: Ohio University Press, 1976.

Whisnant, David E. *All that is Native and Fine: The Politics of Culture in an American Region*. Chapel Hill: University of North Carolina Press, 1983.

_____. *Modernizing the Mountaineer: People, Power, and Planning in Appalachia*. Boone, N.C.: Appalachian Consortium Press, 1980.

Whitener, Daniel J., ed. *History of Watauga County, North Carolina, 1849-1949*. n.p., n.d.

Wiebe, Robert H. *The Search for Order, 1877-1920*. New York: Hill and Wang, 1967.

Williams, Susan. *Savory Suppers and Fashionable Feasts: Dining in Victorian America*. New York: Pantheon, 1985.

Wirth, Conrad. *Parks, Politics, and the People*. Norman: University of Oklahoma Press, 1980.

Zweigenhaft, Richard L. and G. William Domhoff. *Jews in the Protestant Establishment*. New York: Praeger, 1982.

INDEX

CPSIA information can be obtained at www.ICGtesting.com
Printed in the USA
BVOW030201030613

322238BV00001B/7/P